ARTHUR E. STILWELL

Stilwell in the early 1900s.
Courtesy of the Kansas City Public Library.

ARTHUR E. STILWELL

Promoter with a Hunch

KEITH L. BRYANT Jr.

Vanderbilt University Press · Nashville 1971

Library of Congress Cataloguing in Publication Data

Bryant, Keith L
  Arthur E. Stilwell.
  Includes bibliographical references.
  1. Stilwell, Arthur Edward, 1861–1928.
I. Title.
HE2754.S8B76   385'.0924 [B]   78–170282
ISBN 0–8265–1173–2

Printed in the United States of America
by Heritage Printers, Inc.
Bound by Nicholstone Book Bindery
Nashville, Tennessee

Title Page Photograph, Locomotive Number One, Courtesy of the Port
Arthur Historical Society. Number One was not the first acquired by the
Kansas City, Pittsburg and Gulf, but was one of the line's most attractive
engines; built by Baldwin in 1895.

For Lewis Atherton

PREFACE

A new man has come out of the West into the railroad world,
a star of the first magnitude, increasing in its brilliancy every day.

He is the Collis P. Huntington and the Edward H. Harriman of the
present day. . . . To the middle Southwest he is what James J. Hill is
to the great Northwest.

It is said of him that one secret of his success in securing financial
support at times when other men fail is in his enthusiasm and his
power of putting dry details in a novel and original form.

He is now regarded as a Napoleon of Finance.

He has instituted more projects for the commercial good of
Kansas City than any other one man.

ALWAYS a favorite subject of newspaper and magazine feature writers, Arthur Edward Stilwell built 2,300 miles of railway, founded several dozen hamlets and villages, and created a city, Port Arthur, Texas, named for himself. Between 1886 and 1912, Stilwell made sizable contributions to the economic growth and the urbanization of the south central states of Oklahoma, Arkansas, Louisiana, and Texas and helped to make Kansas City a major railroad and industrial center. He built a railroad, "straight as the crow flies," from Kansas City to the Gulf of Mexico, projected another railway from Kansas City to the Gulf of California in Mexico, and built most of it before financial reversals terminated construction. Gifted with the ability to sell stocks and bonds in the most speculative ventures, even in the midst of national and international depressions, Stilwell radiated optimism, charm, and a personal magnetism. Confident in himself and the future, determined to create monuments to glorify his family name, and a firm believer in the myth of the self-made man and the gospel of wealth, he dreamed of creating an economic empire in the hinterland of Kansas City and twice almost succeeded. After retiring from an active business career in 1912, he wrote books about Wall Street, financing World War I, and inspirational literature, as well as novels, poetry, plays, and songs. At that time he alleged that his projects were inspired by "spirits" and "brownies" who came to him in his sleep, and once again he became a national figure and the subject of journalistic attention. His memoirs reduced the role of the "brownies" to "hunches," but Stilwell is more often remembered for his psychic experiences than for the economic contributions he made.

Although economic historians are in agreement that by 1890 the American railroad network was practically completed, Stilwell's projects were initiated and constructed during the next two decades. His railways were built through underdeveloped frontier areas. The process of economic change and urbanization in the south central states has been generally neglected by historians, and this study proposes, not only to relate the life story of this complex individual, but also to be concerned with the economic changes that can be imputed to Stilwell. In developing this portrait, an attempt will be made to place Stilwell in his milieu and to show the significant role played by the promoter. As the United States has a private economy, private decision-makers shape the development of the nation and its regions. They decide on the allocation, or misallocation, of resources, and some, such as Stilwell, make entrepreneurial errors of enormous magnitude. But in many cases the decisions produce economic contributions of importance despite the original errors.

No claim will be made that Arthur Edward Stilwell was a typical promoter of his era; indeed, one could almost make the argument that he was *sui generis*. But if we are to understand the processes of economic development and urbanization it is necessary to know what motivated the entrepreneurs and promoters whose decisions shaped the process. The individual is the basic unit around which economic and social systems revolve. Yet, the promoter or entrepreneur must be placed within the context of his times, for the values and goals of the society determine whether the promoter will be judged successful. The history of economic development is then the history of individuals and the decisions they made, for better or worse.

Establishing motivations for any individual is difficult to very nearly impossible, but the dilemma is compounded in this instance because no major collection of Stilwell manuscripts exists. This is true of most entrepreneurs who left few large collections of letters and diaries that might reveal the mental processes leading to their economic decisions. This study therefore rests on Stilwell's published statements, newspaper accounts, corporate records, railway and financial journals, and scattered manuscript sources. Even if a massive array of Stilwell manuscripts existed, there is no assurance that he would have elaborated upon his motivations. A builder, urban developer, author, pacifist, mystic, imperialist, and Christian Scientist, he remained, above all, a promoter with a hunch.

Without the aid of numerous individuals and institutions this project could never have reached fruition. It has been the good fortune of the author to have found librarians and archivists who consistently exhibited interest in the project and a willingness to share their knowledge of the holdings of their repositories. Among those who generously extended personal help were Miss Katherine Goldsmith, historian of the Kansas City Public Library's Missouri Valley Room; Miss Lucy Stiefel, Librarian of the Gates Memorial Library, Port Arthur, Texas; Harry L. Eddy, Librarian of the Bureau of Railway Economics, Association of American Railroads, Washington, D.C.; and Miss Louise Tompkins, Special Librarian of the Pliny Fisk Library, Princeton, New Jersey. The author also wishes to thank the staffs of the Rochester Historical Society, Baker Library of the Harvard Graduate School of Business Administration, Newberry Library, San Jacinto Museum of History, Duke University Library, Louisiana State University Library, Missouri Historical Society, Engineering Societies Library, and the Inter-Library Loan Office of the University of Wisconsin—Milwaukee Library.

Business records make up much of the documentation of this book, and several corporations opened their archives to the author without restriction and with hospitality. L. O. Frith, Executive Vice-President of the Kansas City Southern Railway Company, made available the records of Stilwell's early railroad companies, and to him the author wishes to extend his thanks. R. A. Weingartner, Assistant Treasurer of the Burlington Northern, and George Malcolm-Smith, Manager of the Public Information and Advertising Department of the Travelers Insurance Company, were both helpful in providing access to archives and information about Stilwell's career. Dun & Bradstreet, Inc., gave permission for the use of their archives deposited in the Baker Library.

In Port Arthur, Texas, a number of individuals aided the author, including Mrs. W. F. Fredeman, Mrs. James W. Ellender, Mrs. Francis Leverett and Mrs. James T. Carr. To Dow Wynn, General Manager of the Port of Port Arthur, the author is indebted in many ways. Wynn had gathered a sizable collection of Stilwell materials, preparing to write a biography; he not only gave the author access to this collection, he also abandoned his own project in deference to this one. His efforts to honor Stilwell's memory in Port Arthur have produced the Memorial Docks at the Port of Port Arthur and several artistic monuments of his own design. He has demonstrated the greatest desire to see Stilwell's accomplishments recognized through the publication of this book, and his enthusiasm has been sincerely appreciated. Also, a special word of thanks is due to John R. Rochelle who generously shared his knowledge of the history of the port of Port Arthur.

It has been the author's privilege to have had as colleagues and friends two historians of Kansas City, A. T. Brown and Charles N. Glaab, and he wishes to thank them for the use of their published and unpublished studies of the city and for sharing their insights into the urbanization of Kansas City and their conceptualizations of the role of the promoter.

Thanks are also extended to the editors of the *Southwestern Historical Quarterly* and the Kent State University Press, publishers of *Explorations in Entrepreneurial History*, for permission to reprint materials from those journals.

The Penrose Fund of the American Philosophical Society provided a grant in support of the project, and the College of Letters and Science of the University of Wisconsin—Milwaukee gave the author a reduced teaching assignment to provide time for research and writing. Once again, a special debt is owed my wife, Margaret, who accepted my numerous irritabilities with patience and who labored to improve the prose with a mixture of good humor and stubbornness. To all of the above the author is grateful, but for the errors of fact and infelicities of style which remain, he is solely responsible.

CONTENTS

Kansas City, Mexico and Orient locomotive No. 5, a wood burner used in Mexico; it was built by the Rhode Island works.

Stilwell, Indian Territory, in 1897.

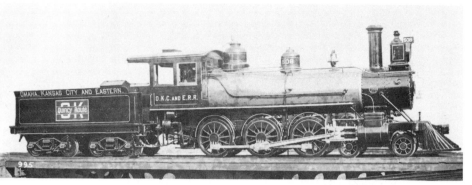

Omaha, Kansas City and Eastern 4–4–0 Number 508.

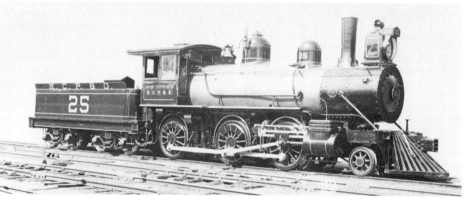

Kansas City, Pittsburg and Gulf 2–6–0 Number 25, built by Baldwin in 1895.

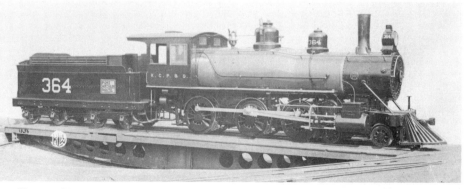

Kansas City, Pittsburg and Gulf Number 364, a 4–6–0 built by Baldwin in 1898.

The main street of Port Arthur in 1897.

Spanish-style station of the Kansas City, Pittsburg and Gulf at Port Arthur.

The interior of Stilwell's private car showing the organ and other furnishings. Inset: the promoter as a young man with side whiskers.

I

THE STILWELLS OF ROCHESTER

ONE of the most enduring myths in American History is the story of the "rags-to-riches" rise of the businessman. From the aphorisms of Benjamin Franklin, to the stories of Horatio Alger and the sermons of Norman Vincent Peale, young Americans have been told that to be a successful businessman one needed only to work hard, be virtuous, and persevere. If the Alger stories are to be believed, it also helped to marry the boss's daughter.[1] Numerous studies have demonstrated that the cult of the self-made man is based upon romantic nostalgia rather than fact. The career of Arthur Edward Stilwell, however, offers a variation on this theme. He recalled in his memoirs that he was born with a "silver spoon" in his mouth; since his father was a jeweler, this could have been more fact than fancy.[2] It was not his father who provided the wealth responsible for this variation, but rather his paternal grandfather, Hamblin Stilwell. Hamblin, the family patriarch, played a significant role in the molding of

1. Two excellent studies of the cult of the self-made man are John G. Cawelti, *Apostles of the Self-Made Man* (Chicago: University of Chicago Press, 1965), and Irvin G. Wyllie, *The Self-Made Man in America* (New York: The Free Press, 1966).

2. Stilwell's memoirs were published serially in *The Saturday Evening Post* and have served as the basis for much that has been written about him. Arthur E. Stilwell and James R. Crowell, "I Had a Hunch," *The Saturday Evening Post* Vol. CC (December 3, 17, and 31, 1927, and January 14 and 28, and February 4, 1928). His childhood is recalled in the December 3, issue. Reprinted with permission from *The Saturday Evening Post* © 1927–28 the Curtis Publishing Company; renewals 1955–56.

young Arthur, as did the experiences of the Stilwell family. When the family lost its wealth and descended to an economic level just short of poverty, young Arthur began the upward climb to regain the financial and social position he remembered so fondly. The environment of his early years shaped the personality of this "self-made man" and is, therefore, most significant.

The Stilwells became residents of Rochester, New York, in the 1820s when that city was only a sizable village surrounding the falls of the Genessee River.[3] Born in 1805 in Saratoga County, New York, of English and Dutch extraction, Hamblin Stilwell emigrated westward joining thousands of other settlers moving in advance of the opening of the Erie Canal. The commercial boom in Rochester attracted families from eastern New York and New England. The village became a large town with carts, stages, rigs, cattle, and people filling the streets. The influx of travelers, businessmen, and canal workers made the town a paradise for young maidens. Among them was fourteen-year-old Lydia Byington who arrived with her parents from Reading, Connecticut, in the spring of 1824.[4] Ambitious Hamblin Stilwell noted the presence of the Byington's daughter, wooed her, and on January 6, 1829, they were married.[5]

During the next forty years Hamblin Stilwell's ambitions led him into two careers: one in business, the other in politics. He often entered and left a field of business, but he remained a faithful worker and office holder for the Democratic party. In 1832 he formed the firm of H. Stilwell and Company to sell lottery tickets, an unquestionably respectable device for charity fund raising. During the same year he served as a delegate to the Democratic party county convention.[6] The Stilwells were acceptable members of Rochester society as indicated by their membership in the First Presbyterian church, the dominant religious institution in the town.[7]

3. The author is indebted to Blake McKelvey's excellent multivolume history of Rochester for the background material in this chapter. See McKelvey, *Rochester the Water Power City 1812–1854* (Cambridge: Harvard University Press, 1945), 71–143.

4. Rochester *Daily Union and Advertiser*, August 11, 1883.

5. Rochester *Daily Advertiser and Telegraph*, January 7, 1829.

6. Rochester *Daily Advertiser*, December 12, 1832; Rochester *Republican*, October 23, 1832. The party of Andrew Jackson, the Democratic party, was still known by its Jeffersonian name, "Republican," in Rochester in 1832.

7. Rochester *Daily Union and Advertiser*, August 11, 1883.

With traffic on the Erie Canal reaching a flood tide, Hamblin became first an agent, and then a proprietor of packet boats on the waterway.[8] The expanding canal operations, the influx of New England Yankees, and improvements in the streets and sewers began to alter the town, but primitive conditions remained, and the infant mortality rate was high. On November 4, 1838, seven-year-old Harriet, then the only daughter of Hamblin and Lydia, died.[9] The Stilwells soon had another daughter, Adele, who joined two older brothers in the family, Edward, and Charles Herbert.

Rochester continued to grow in the 1830s and became a milling center using power generated by the beautiful falls of the Genesee. The nursery business for which the city would become famous also began to attract attention. Even the panic and depression of 1837 failed to harm seriously the economy of the city. An expanding community needed a more complex government, and Rochester adopted an aldermanic system with yearly elections. The Whigs and Democrats vied with each other for control, and the young government suffered from a lack of consistent civic leadership.

Hamblin Stilwell led the Democratic party in Rochester's First Ward in the 1840s and 1850s. He presided over ward meetings, attended county conventions, and in 1842 was elected alderman.[10] Renominated, but defeated in 1844 by a Whig, he campaigned for James K. Polk for president and was one of the citizens of Rochester favorably disposed toward the annexation of Texas.[11] The Whigs, however, dominated city politics in the era, and repeated defeats discouraged Jacksonian Democrats. In the latter party there were no significant leaders from the city at the state or national levels, and men of lesser ability such as Stilwell controlled the local organization.[12]

Hamblin Stilwell prospered in the 1830s and 1840s and was known

---

8. *Directory of the City of Rochester* (Rochester: Canfield and Warren, 1845).

9. Rochester *Republican*, November 13, 1838.

10. Rochester *Daily Advertiser*, October 8, 1840, and March 2, 1842.

11. Rochester *Daily Democrat*, February 28 and April 12, 1844; Rochester *Daily Advertiser*, March 5, February 29, and October 16, 1844.

12. Rochester *Daily Democrat*, June 19, 1845; Rochester *Republican*, September 29 and October 20, 1846 and October 26, 1847; Rochester *Daily Advertiser*, October 25, 1847.

as a man "who is worth considerable."[13] He operated his packet boats and sustained his nephew Mortimer F. Stilwell in a jewelry store. Hamblin's primary business remained canal boats, and as a community leader he promoted the Erie Canal and attended regional meetings encouraging traffic on the waterway. He also worked to improve the community, and he was appointed a director of the Water Works Company by the state legislature.[14]

As a reward for his community service and efforts for the party he was nominated by the Democrats for mayor of the city in 1852. Elected over his Whig opponent by a majority of 129 votes, Stilwell in his inaugural address pledged to reduce taxes and improve public health. Public health remained a serious problem in Rochester as the city had suffered several epidemics. Cholera struck in the summer of 1852, and the city suffered greviously. Mayor Stilwell exerted himself ably, but his own health gave way and he had to retire temporarily from his duties. Divided authority and a weak mayor's office gave little opportunity for strong executive action.[15] Following an undistinguished year of service, Stilwell retired from office in April of 1853.

Despite his lackluster term as mayor, Hamblin Stilwell's business interests proved quite profitable. The family lived at 40 North Sophia in a house described by one reporter as a "mansion." A local newspaper reported that the Stilwells entertained the Rochester common council and that a number of guests came from New York City and abroad. The banquet, "substantial and abundant," was served by Mrs. Stilwell, who retired with the ladies to "contingent apartments" at the conclusion of the meal.[16] Further evidence of the affluence of the family is apparent in several instances including the sending of two sons to Columbia University. Charles Herbert Stilwell was enrolled in the Columbia University College of Physicians and Surgeons and received the M.D. in 1847. If

13. Dun and Bradstreet Collection, Volume 162, Item 142, New York (Manuscript Division, Baker Library, Harvard University, Graduate School of Business Administration, Boston, Massachusetts).

14. Rochester *Daily Democrat*, February 25, 1847; *The Daily Union* (Rochester), October 9, 1852.

15. Rochester *Daily Advertiser*, February 27, March 4, and April 9, 1852; Rochester *Daily Democrat*, March 4, and April 6, 1852; and William F. Peck, *Semi-Centennial History of the City of Rochester* (Syracuse: n.p., 1884), 143.

16. Rochester *Daily Advertiser*, December 16, 1852.

Charles Stilwell practiced medicine, he did not practice long, for by 1858 he had joined Mortimer Stilwell in a jewelry firm financed by Hamblin.[17]

As the seventeenth largest city in the nation, Rochester enjoyed rapid growth and prosperity in the decade before the Civil War. Several large corporations were organized in the city, an example being the Western Union, and the community also became a major junction on the New York Central Railroad.[18] New civic leaders were emerging as the city grew, but the Stilwells continued to play minor roles in the life of the "Flower City."

Charles Stilwell operated his jewelry business through the period, and in January of 1859 he married twenty-year-old Mary Augusta Pierson. The wedding took place in Chicago at the bride's home.[19] The only daughter of Stephen H. Pierson, Mary Augusta came from a family of ministers and missionaries. On October 21, 1859, she gave birth to a son who was named Arthur Edward. The Charles Stilwell family lived near the home of baby Arthur's paternal grandparents and not far from the jewelry store, which stood at the fashionable corner of Buffalo and Exchange.

The jewelry store did not succeed. Business was, at best, "dull," and the store would never have been operative at all without Hamblin's financial backing. While Charles and Mortimer Stilwell were men of "good character" and integrity, they were also of limited ability and means. In 1861 Mortimer left to join the "volunteer force," and Charles became the sole operator of the store. As Arthur Stilwell would recall, his father and uncle were "exceedingly poor business men," and in 1862 the firm failed.[20] Charles Stilwell made a career of failure, and young Arthur neither forgot nor forgave his father. He may also have wondered later why his father had not served in the war, especially with his medical training.

But in 1862 baby Arthur would not have had such doubts. A chubby-

17. Charles Seymour, Assistant Registrar, Columbia University, to the author, May 8, 1969; Dun and Bradstreet Collection, Volume 162, Item 142, New York.

18. Blake McKelvey, *Rochester: The Flower City 1855–1890* (Cambridge: Harvard University Press, 1949), v–vii, 1–61.

19. Rochester *Union and Advertiser*, January 12, 1859.

20. Stilwell, "I Had a Hunch," December 3, 1927, 4; Dun and Bradstreet Collection, Volume 162, Item 316E, New York.

faced boy with long blond hair, he was doted upon by his grandfather. One picture of Arthur shows him in a long dress, tights, button shoes, and seated upon a hassock.[21] As he grew, Hamblin Stilwell took him on trips; he undoubtedly provided his educational and other expenses. Arthur would recall that "in childhood I was extremely delicate and had to be carried around on pillows until I was about seven years of age. . . . My grandfather was very fond of me; I was his first grandchild and his pet."[22] A craggy-faced old man with a high forehead, a scraggly beard, and deep-set eyes, Hamblin was forboding in appearance, but he apparently was a warm and generous person. Arthur decided at an early age that his grandfather symbolized success and his father failure.

Hamblin continued his political career, and Charles attempted to follow in his father's footsteps. Hamblin served as a supervisor from the First Ward, being re-elected several times, and in 1863 won a major victory against a radical Republican. He was made a commissioner of Mount Hope Cemetery, one of the showplaces of the city, and was named by the Governor as a manager of the Western House of Refuge, a farm for wayward boys located near Rochester. Despite his business debacle, Charles Stilwell played minor roles in civic affairs and in 1868 succeeded his father as supervisor of the First Ward.[23]

Charles continued to use his father's name in politics and his money in business. Hamblin took over the jewelry store himself, and it proved more successful. Hamblin Stilwell was a man of means in the 1860s, worth between $40,000 and $50,000. His house was valued at $15,000, he owned other houses and lots, and he also served as a trustee of the Rochester Savings Bank. In 1868 he owned one hundred shares of stock in the New York Central Railroad which were worth nearly $10,000.[24] Hamblin traveled often to New York City on business, and, if Arthur's memories are correct, took his grandson with him. They stayed at the Astor House on lower Broadway and once paid a call on Commodore Vanderbilt, president of the New York Central. According to Arthur,

21. Kansas City *Post*, July 20, 1907.

22. Stilwell, "I Had a Hunch," December 3, 1927, 4.

23. Rochester *Daily Union and Advertiser*, March 3 and April 8, 1862, February 12 and March 4, 1863, December 6, 1864, and March 4 and July 25, 1868.

24. Dun and Bradstreet Collection, Volume 162, Entry 32, New York; Rochester *Daily Union and Advertiser*, September 6, 1870.

after one of these visits Hamblin asked his grandson what he wanted to do when he grew up. "I'm going West and build a railroad," he replied.[25] When Hamblin repeated the story to his friends in a jocular way, the boy was impressed, and the incident assumed even greater significance. Many years later, Arthur Stilwell maintained that his grandfather had been a director of the New York Central and a founder of the Western Union, but this was not the case. These were golden years for young Arthur, and as an adult his remembrances were enhanced by the distance of time.[26]

Because of poor health, Arthur did not attend elementary school beyond the fourth grade. A tall boy with long curly hair, he probably appeared to his playmates as a sissy. If one photograph is an indication, he was well attired—a fashionable coat with large lapels and a bow tie.[27] That he was a spoiled child is suggested in several passages of his memoirs. Sibling rivalry undoubtedly affected Arthur, and most intriguing is his failure to mention in his memoirs the existence of his brother Charles Herbert Junior, who was born in 1863, another brother who died when quite young, or his sisters Annie Pierson and Florence May.[28] Even allowing for Arthur Stilwell's enormous ego, it is apparent that the omission was calculated. Arthur also made little mention of his mother in the memoirs, but in an earlier publication he recalled that from her came his love for noncombative and peaceful methods and his belief that gentleness as a trait would benefit a businessman, who need not have the ferocious and devouring traits of the lion or wolf.[29]

While his mother may have influenced Stilwell, he always identified with his grandfather. "His father was Charles Stilwell," a feature writer once commented. "But it was from his grandfather that he inherited his peculiar tact, energy, and ability in the management of large affairs."[30]

25. Stilwell, "I Had a Hunch," December 3, 1927, 4.

26. Ann Kuss, New York Central System, to Dow Wynn, October 27, 1967, and Edward F. Sanger, Western Union Company, to Wynn, October 30, 1967 (Arthur E. Stilwell Collection, Port of Port Arthur, Port Arthur, Texas).

27. Stillwell, "I Had a Hunch," December 3, 1927, 4; Kansas City *Post*, July 20, 1907.

28. Rochester *Daily Union and Advertiser*, December 7, 1882; the *Union and Advertiser* (Rochester), February 15, 1894.

29. Arthur E. Stilwell, *Cannibals of Finance* (Chicago: Farnum Publishing Company, 1912), 189.

30. New York *Herald*, September 27, 1908.

Hamblin's affairs had grown in size, and Charles Stilwell took over the operation of the jewelry store once again. This arrangement lasted only a year, for on August 28, 1870, Hamblin died.

The death of his grandfather marked not only Arthur Stilwell's first encounter with significant anguish but also with the beginning of a less-than-financially-prosperous adolescence. The funeral was attended by a large body of former mayors, dignitaries, and older citizens, enhancing the boy's estimate of his grandfather's importance. With Hamblin's death, the store continued to be operated by Charles under the direction of the estate. Although Hamblin left an estate valued at more than $40,000, Charles's share was only $3,000.[31] Arthur also received a small legacy, but this was little consolation for the loss of his grandfather. He was going through adolescence—a dreamy, imaginative child, removed because of ill health from the rough-and-tumble activities indulged in by most children. He often sought solitude in order to conjure up visions of financial success and economic creativity such as his grandfather had experienced.[32]

A rash of speculation hit Rochester after 1865. Many people in the city earned sizable incomes as the community grew. Large, imposing buildings on the main streets and the mills along the Genesee suggested financial solidity. Yet, Rochester fell behind the growth rate of other cities, and even before the panic of 1873 several leading Rochester businessmen went bankrupt.[33]

One of the businessmen was Charles Stilwell. In 1872 the store closed, and Charles moved into smaller quarters above the old business site. A confidential financial report stated that he had expensive habits and, although honest, was not considered a good manager. A debt of $5,000 to Hamblin's estate was relieved, but the next year it was reported that Charles's habits were now "intemperate." By 1875 Charles Stilwell's business was permanently closed, and he was reduced to clerking in the city treasurer's office.[34]

---

31. Rochester *Daily Union and Advertiser*, August 29, 1870; Dun and Bradstreet Collection, Volume 162, Entry 32, New York.
32. Stilwell, "I Had a Hunch," December 3, 1927, 4 and 161.
33. McKelvey, *Rochester: The Flower City*, 98–199.
34. Dun and Bradstreet Collection, Volume 162, Entry 32, New York; *The Rochester Directory* (Rochester: Drew, Allis & Co., 1877).

Young Arthur now found his family living on a subsistence level. School did not attract him, and with many factories closed and unemployment rampant the possibility of finding a decent position was slight. That school was unattractive is not surprising. As Rochester's historian has noted, "If the school of hard knocks was still the most potent source of knowledge in Rochester, the city's hesitant and frugal educational program was at least partly at fault."[35] Arthur decided to try the school of hard knocks and ran away from home.

Only fourteen or fifteen years old, and with only seventy dollars in his pocket, he traveled westward to Saint Louis. A former neighbor in Rochester ran a hotel in that city, and Arthur found employment as cashier in the hotel's billiard room. The young boy with no experience or ability at billiards became an easy mark for the men who came in to play. The cashier was expected to play in the interest of the hotel, and his loss of a game meant the contest was on the house. With losses mounting, Arthur quit. He remembered that his motive for quitting was the cost to his employer; one suspects his ego may have been the cause, or perhaps he was fired. Subsequent employment as a mailing clerk exposed him to a group of young men pilfering postage. Refusing to join them and looked upon as a "queer duck," he left that position and Saint Louis. He traveled to New York City but remained there only briefly. His mother asked him to return home; his father had lost more money.[36]

Returning to Rochester, Arthur became aware of the plight of his family:

As the son of a wealthy man, I had always worn made-to-order clothes and had come to look with contempt upon the ready-made kind, which we called hand-me-downs. After my return, father wanted to buy me some of this cheap apparel, but I protested against joining the hand-me-down army. Then he told me that his losses, which I had supposed were not serious, were really terrific and that his income had been reduced to $150 a month. This explained to me for the first time why the family had moved from one of the finest houses in town to one that rented for thirty-five dollars a month.[37]

Determining to pay his own way, Arthur withdrew $400 from the bank —money which his grandfather had given him—and opened a small print

35. McKelvey, *Rochester: The Flower City*, 149.
36. Stilwell, "I Had a Hunch," December 3, 1927, 161.
37. *Ibid.*

shop. Business from family friends earned him from fifteen to seventy dollars a week. He also apparently sold a patent medicine called "Stilwell's Specific." The label on the bottle had pictures of a bear and a lion and an inscription saying "If you can't *bear* the pain after taking Stilwell's, you're *lion*."[38] Neither the print shop nor the medicine proved profitable, and when a local stationer offered Arthur a job as a commercial traveler, he left Rochester. After 1878, Stilwell severed all direct ties with his home town and his family.

The failures of his father, the death of his grandfather, and the declining reputation of the family plagued this sensitive young man. He determined to make his own way, to re-establish the family name, and to follow the path of his grandfather. When his brother Charles Junior died in 1882 and his grandmother and mother passed away in 1883 and 1893, there is no evidence Arthur was present. His father became the health officer of a suburb of Rochester, and his sisters apparently married well, but young Arthur took no further part in family affairs.[39]

Selling stationery did not prove lucrative, so Arthur Stilwell accepted a position as soliciter for the New York Advertising Company and began selling space in railroad timetables printed by that company. As rail lines were being opened throughout the country, the companies sought to use advertisements to offset the costs of printing timetables. Nineteen-year-old Arthur, a Rochester newspaper reminded its readers when announcing his new position, "is well known to the business public as being thoroughly reliable."[40] His company sent him to Virginia to contact railroads and potential advertisers. He obtained free passes from the railroads and free lodging and meals from the hotels that took space in his timetables; travel and living expenses were therefore slight, and he prospered. He took advantage of this experience to learn all he could about railroad operations. Stilwell would later recall that he also desired to be outside more, rather than in a print shop, as traveling helped improve his health. Writing copy also turned him into a "word hound," augmenting his meager education.

38. The Kansas City *Journal*, January 4, 1907.

39. Rochester *Daily Union and Advertiser*, December 7, 1882, April 23, 1883 and August 11, 1883; the *Union and Advertiser* (Rochester), May 27, 1893 and February 15, 1894.

40. Rochester *Daily Union and Advertiser*, January 8, 1878.

While traveling through Virginia selling advertisements for the Atlantic, Mississippi and Ohio and the Virginia Midland railroads, Arthur found time to court his childhood sweetheart, Jennie A. Wood. When he was fifteen he had told his parents that in four years he intended to marry Jennie, a girl he had seen at school; he could only describe her as having "brown eyes." The Stilwells had approved his choice, but soon the Wood family moved from Rochester to Virginia, and the young couple were separated for several years. Arthur's income had reached more than $2,000 a year from the timetables and other items he sold on the road, and when Jennie's father gave his consent, the couple made arrangements for a wedding. Arthur at nineteen was not of age, and when they went to the Five Forks Courthouse in Dinwiddie County, the clerk challenged him by asking his age. Quick witted, the young man responded, "Guess my age." The clerk drawled, "I guess twenty-two," to which Arthur rejoined "You're a bird," and the license was issued.[41]

On June 10, 1879, Arthur Edward Stilwell and Jennie A. Wood were married at the home of the bride's parents in Ionia, Virginia. Arthur's place of residence was given as Washington and his occupation as publisher. Using his rail passes and hotel due bills, he took his bride on a honeymoon.[42] That the couple were completely devoted to each other there can be no doubt. Inseparable for the next forty-nine years, their marriage could almost be described as perfect. Stilwell wrote in his memoirs,

What I had been longing for more than anything else these past few years I now had—the adorable girl who was the complete and sole mistress of my heart, a sympathetic and loving companion to whom my ambitions and my successes were the most important things in the world. If I made little mistakes which others might use to their own aggrandizement or possibly laugh at, I knew there was some refuge where I could always find tenderness and understanding. My wife and my home became in those days the source of all inspiration, and they have never changed their character.[43]

Jennie Stilwell must have had patience as well as love, for shortly after their marriage Arthur embarked on another venture.

41. Stilwell, "I Had a Hunch," December 3, 1927, 161–162, 165.
42. *Ibid.*; Marriage Certificate of Arthur E. and Jennie A. Stilwell, June 6, 1879, copy in the Stilwell Collection; Rochester *Daily Union and Advertiser*, July 7, 1879.
43. Stilwell, "I Had a Hunch," December 3, 1927, 165.

A friend in New York City wrote Arthur that a position had opened in a printing house there. The newlyweds left Virginia and Arthur took the job. Less than three months later, however, this same friend went to Kansas City, Missouri, where he found a printing shop available at a low rental. Elaborately equipped, the shop had been sold at a sheriff's sale and was available for only sixty-five dollars a month. In 1879 the Stilwell's moved to Kansas City, and Arthur worked in the shop located on Union Avenue in the West Bottoms. A flat area near the Missouri River, the Bottoms often flooded, and the Stilwell concern, located in a basement, become inundated in one of these periodic disasters. The working conditions in the damp basement proved harmful to Arthur's health, and he contracted a severe case of typhoid fever. During his convalescence he decided that his health required that he not work inside a shop. He contacted several engraving and lithographic firms and was offered a position as their representative in Chicago. Once again the Stilwells moved.[44]

Demonstrating his penchant for extravagance, Arthur moved his young bride into the Southern Hotel on Wabash Avenue, despite her objections to the cost. He entered the photo-engraving business, selling illustrations to book publishers. An objection to the business was the necessity of traveling and leaving Jennie alone for long periods of time. One reason for living in the Southern Hotel was to meet prosperous people, and one of their acquaintances was C. H. Hammons, the Illinois agent of the Travelers Insurance Company. Hammons offered Arthur $1,200 a year and expenses to become his assistant. Further, traveling would be restricted so that he could be with Jennie more. Arthur accepted.[45]

Stilwell's salesmanship ability developed rapidly in the early 1880s. His salary tripled in two years as his insurance clients increased in number. Arthur studied various kinds of policies and concluded that straight life insurance did not provide the purchaser with adequate protection. In 1884 he introduced two new concepts of life insurance. *The Travelers*

44. *Ibid.*; New York *Herald*, September 27, 1908; Howard L. Conard, *Encyclopedia of the History of Missouri* (New York: The Southern History Co., 1901), VI, 86.
45. The Chicago *Tribune*, November 27, 1898; Stilwell, "I Had a Hunch," December 3, 1927, 165.

Record of May 1884 announced the "coupon-annuity endowment" to the agents of the company. The coupon-annuity endowment was a policy payable to the insured in stallments during a term of years to provide a regular income. The coupon annuity introduced the idea of giving the policyholder a monthly income after the purchaser reached a certain age. Travelers was the first company to offer this form of insurance, which has become known as a "retirement-income policy."

The second policy Stilwell introduced was less successful. It was an accident insurance policy that combined life and accident contracts. The contract paid a certain sum for accidental death, total disability, dismemberment, or loss of sight, but did not pay medical bills or a weekly indemnity. In the event of the insured's death from any cause after the policy was in effect for three years, it paid the beneficiaries the amount of regular premiums paid, or if the insured were still alive after a specified number of years he was paid the amount of the annual premiums. The contract had merit under some circumstances but left much to be desired. It was discontinued some years ago.[46]

Stilwell traveled to Hartford and presented his policies to the president of the Travelers, who was not impressed. On his way to Hartford, Arthur had stopped in New York City, where the New York Life Insurance Company offered him a position doubling his salary. With this as a lever, he badgered the Travelers into investigating and adopting his proposed policies. Arrangements were made whereby Stilwell received a royalty of fifty cents on each thousand dollars of insurance sold under his policies as long as he stayed with the firm. Both policies sold well, especially the coupon-annuity endowment, and Stilwell earned, by one account, more than $25,000. He became, briefly, the state agent for The Travelers in Rhode Island and Connecticut, but his insatiable ambition was not satisfied.[47]

Driving himself to exhaustion, Stilwell accepted the advice of the president of The Travelers and took a trip to Europe for four weeks. Arthur and Jennie toured England and the continent. They sailed both directions on the *Amsterdam*, where they met a young Dutch coffee mer-

46. Information furnished by George Malcolm-Smith, Manager, Public Information and Advertising Department, the Travelers Insurance Company, February 5, 1969.

47. Stilwell, "I Had a Hunch," December 3, 1927, 166, 168.

chant who would later play a major role in Stilwell's railroad and urban promotions.[48]

Returning to the United States, Stilwell decided to take the profits from the policies and to go back to Kansas City. The Travelers offered him a salary of $8,000 a year to stay with the firm, so he recalled, but he refused. Although selling insurance had been very rewarding for Stilwell, "he was too much of a radical for the old-line ideas about marketing," as one writer has said, "but the life insurance game taught him how to sell things, and that experience was the basis of his success in floating millions of dollars worth of railroad stock in England, Holland, and this country."[49] His associates in Chicago had noted that, "he was crammed full of schemes." Those who knew Stilwell in Chicago in the early 1880s would not embrace his schemes, "for his friends here, with one or two exceptions, said he was nothing but an enthusiast who needed a balance."[50] Undaunted by the lack of confidence in his ideas, the Stilwells moved west.

When Arthur Stilwell moved to Kansas City in 1886 he was twenty-six years old. His personality and character traits were substantially developed and his life style rather firmly established. The forces that motivated him as a businessman and promoter and his ambitions and drives reflected his experiences as a child, youth, and young man. Because of Stilwell's inner complexities, it seems appropriate to pause at this stage of his life and attempt an analysis of the man and his motives.

Numerous accounts of Stilwell by reporters and associates refer to his "commanding presence," or his fashionable dress, or his handsome countenance. Despite the illnesses of his youth, Stilwell developed into a man of considerable stature. He was at least six feet tall, weighing between 180 and 200 pounds, and his physique was described as "athletic." His hair remained light brown or blond and wavy as it had been when he was a child. A rather handsome man with a fair complexion, he had striking blue eyes, a pronounced nose, and in his youth wore a thick mustache waxed and turned up at the ends. His voice was "musical and powerful," but his friends did not feel him an intruder in conver-

---

48. *Ibid.*, December 31, 1927, 26.
49. Edwin Markham, "Where the Railroad Presidents Come From," *System, The Magazine of Business*, XXX (August 1916), 182.
50. The Chicago *Tribune*, November 27, 1898.

sation, loud, or boisterous. In Kansas City he became known as a "figure of elegance" and "impeccability." Always exceptionally well groomed and fashionably attired, he strode the streets of Kansas City with grace and confidence. His clothing, while not flamboyant, reflected expensive tastes. He carried a gold-headed cane, inscribed with his name, and some felt he "affected the mannerisms of an English duke." A model of decorum and irreproachable manners, he rarely drank, although he was a generous dispenser of good wines, and did not smoke. His appearance commanded respect and provided a physical basis for his infectious enthusiasm for every aspect of his life, including his religious beliefs.[51]

Stilwell's religious views were shaped as a consequence of a serious illness. He claimed in his memoirs that he had a history of good health, but he had developed typhoid in Kansas City in 1880 and suffered from a spinal ailment while living in Chicago. When medical doctors proved unable to relieve the spinal difficulty, Stilwell sought the aid of a Christian Science practitioner. Despite Stilwell's initial absence of faith, within four days the practitioner cured the ailment. As with many others cured by Christian Science, Arthur became a convert to that faith. Although his grandparents were faithful Presbyterians and his mother a life-long Baptist, there is no indication that he was interested in institutional religion until the healing experience. It may be surmised that his previous religious affiliation, if any, was within traditional Protestantism, but after conversion to Christian Science, "nothing being ever half done with him, his religion became part of his everyday life." He rose early each day to read the Bible, becoming an admirer of the language of the scriptures and the inspirational message of the Psalms. Christian Science emphasized the positive and accented victory over evil. While its founder, Mary Baker Eddy did not use the term "optimism" and said that Christian Science was more than a "cheerful, healthy-mindedness," this theology supported Stilwell's general sense of optimism and hope. He believed that he "made a success not in spite of taking religion into his business, but because of it." He repeated often that Christian Science controlled

51. Kansas City *Journal-Post*, March 22, 1937; *The Orient Magazine*, IV (October 1928), 5; "Little Stories about Big Men," *Transportation*, V (July 1929), 29; *The Wednesday Magazine*, II (October 15, 1947); W. R. Draper, "Promoting the Orient," *Railroad Magazine*, (November 1949), 106; Port Arthur *News*, March 4, 1961; Kansas City *Star*, April 4, 1937.

his life and that the religion of Mrs. Eddy was "the key to whatever success there has been in his life."[52]

Christian Science was squarely in the tradition of American idealism with antecedents in Transcendentalism and Shaker mysticism. "It was," as Stow Persons has shown, "strikingly successful in persuading comfortably situated urban dwellers in a materialistic and humanistic civilization that everything except God, Goodness, Love, and Intelligence was the false imagery of mortal mind."[53] Raised in an environment of religious fundamentalism, healed of an illness by Christian Science, and perpetually the optimist, Arthur Stilwell embraced this religion with enthusiasm. A lover of music, he later wrote several religious hymns which reveal the fundamentalism of his beliefs. One song, "The Prince of Galilee," shows that he accepted the Virgin Birth and the Resurrection. Another, "The Bethlehem Babe," indicates that he believed in the healing miracles of Jesus.[54]

As did many railroad executives, Stilwell encouraged his employees to attend church services. He brought his religious beliefs into his business activities, and it was often stated that when he ran short of funds for his promotions he prayed and the money became available. There is no indication that his religious views harmed his business career. While promoting one railroad, a Wichita, Kansas, booster wrote of Stilwell, "it matters little to this city whether his religious tenets are Christian or Moslem as long as he succeeds in this great enterprise."[55] The musical talent reflected in his religious compositions is minimal at best, but as in most endeavors Stilwell was self-taught, and what he lacked in ability he made up for in enthusiasm.

This unbounded faith in his own ability often led Stilwell to pro-

---

52. New York *Herald*, September 27, 1908; Stilwell, "I Had a Hunch," December 17, 1927, 102; the Chicago *Record-Herald*, March 23, 1906; and Robert Peel, *Christian Science, Its Encounter With American Culture* (Garden City: Anchor Books, 1965), 95.

53. Stow Persons, *American Minds: A History of Ideas* (New York: Henry Holt and Company, 1958), 428.

54. Kansas City *Star*, May 5, 1906; New York *Herald*, September 27, 1908; Arthur E. Stilwell, "The Prince of Galilee," Song with Piano Accompaniment (New York: G. Schirmer, n.d.).

55. O. H. Bentley, *History of Wichita and Sedgwick County, Kansas* (Chicago: C. F. Cooper & Co., 1910), 579.

nouncements which reveal an enormous ego. According to his own accounts, he never failed in his endeavors except when his opponents used unfair tactics; his accomplishments were never fully recognized; all his promotions were far more successful than he, or any one else, ever envisioned; and much more could have been achieved had not people interferred in his life's work.[56] To Stilwell, however, these views did not smack of conceit, but rather illustrated his most "outstanding and most prolific of all traits," confidence in himself. He sharply differentiated between self-reliance and conceit; obviously, he was blessed with the former. Hope in the future, he said, gave him an enormous capacity for work, and his desire to achieve justice and to fight for principle provided the strength to overcome adversity.[57]

Stilwell's confidence and optimism made him disdain the quitter and the complainer. He told a newspaper reporter,

The world doesn't like a complainer. Things are done in certain ways because they have always been done that way, and certain forms, methods and powers are bowed down to because business men are not courageous enough to strike out from the shoulder and do the natural thing, whatever it is.[58]

In the midst of apparent disaster, and later in the twilight of his years, Stilwell never admitted to failure. When he had lost control of one railroad and his position in another was threatened, he claimed only the greatest of successes. When faced with a serious change of fortune, he rebounded with renewed vigor and exhuberant faith in the future.[59]

A constant source of faith was his wife, Jennie. In the dedication of one of his books, *Cannibals of Finance*, Stilwell wrote, "This book is dedicated to my good wife, who was my constant companion in all my travels during most of these years of persecution, and whose encouragement and unselfish devotion sustained me in the darkest hours." Jennie Stilwell accompanied her husband in his travels but never appeared in his public life. Though no children were born to them, their marriage appears to have been happy. One wonders that no photographs of Jennie are to be found, especially since Arthur's picture frequently appeared in

56. Stilwell, *Cannibals of Finance*, introduction, n.p.
57. *Ibid.*, 53; Stilwell, "I Had a Hunch," December 31, 1927, 24.
58. New York *Herald*, September 27, 1908.
59. Stilwell, *Cannibals of Finance*, 28, 41–42, and "I Had a Hunch," January 14, 1928, 78.

newspapers and magazines. When Arthur entertained—and he did so lavishly—it was in a hotel dining room or his private railway car. His extreme protectiveness suggests that Jennie may have been weak physically, perhaps even an invalid. Although she traveled with him to some desolate villages and endured much discomfort as he promoted his rail lines, when they retired to New York in the 1920s he refused invitations for visits entailing long journeys because of her. After he suffered an accident in an elevator in 1913, they were together every day until his death fifteen years later.[60] Jennie Stilwell must have possessed not only faith in her husband but also a capacity to accept constant alterations in his business activities, living in hotel rooms and moving about the country with frequent trips to Europe. She served her husband as a constant source of comfort.

Significant as was the role played by Jennie in Arthur's life, however, it never equaled the inspiration, motivation, and ambition that the memory of Hamblin Stilwell provided. Again and again, Arthur entered businesses, promoted schemes, and made career decisions based upon what he thought or remembered that his grandfather had done.[61] Even his decision to go west to Kansas City in 1886 came as a result of Hamblin's influence. In one of his most revealing letters, Arthur wrote to George M. Pullman in 1896, describing the impact of his grandfather on his life. Thanking Pullman for an interview and hoping for the Palace Car manufacturer's financial aid, Stilwell wrote,

During all my boyhood, when other children were being fed upon Robinson Crusoe and Mother Goose Melodies, I was listening at the knees of my Grandfather to the story of the struggles of the pioneers in Rochester and heard day after day of the difficulties encountered in building the Erie Canal, starting the Western Union and constructing the New York Central. All of these things interested me beyond measure and I became possessed with a desire to follow in the steps of my Grandfather, moving into the West, as he had done, and aiding in building up some great enterprise. This desire followed

60. Arthur E. Stilwell, *Live and Grow Young* (New York: Youth Publishing Company, 1921), 52; Stilwell, *Cannibals of Finance*, 100; Stilwell to E. H. Shaufler, March 13, 1927, quoted in Francis Leverett, "Arthur E. Stilwell, 1859–1928" (unpublished masters thesis, University of Texas, 1955), 109–110.

61. The Chicago *Record-Herald*, March 23, 1906; Stilwell, *Cannibals of Finance*, 188–189.

me every day of my life and has been a cloud by day and a pillar of fire by night to guide me in my business career.[62]

The memory of his grandfather loomed large in Stilwell's decisions to enter business as a career, to move to Kansas City and become a nationally known promoter of railroads and cities. The influence of the vicissitudes of the Stilwell family and the environment of Rochester had molded this young man as he entered the most significant period of his life.

62. Stilwell to George M. Pullman, December 16, 1896, copy in the Stilwell Collection.

II

THE PROMOTER AND HIS METHODS

DURING his business career, Arthur E. Stilwell built two major and two minor rail lines, founded many hamlets and towns, and organized two trust companies and numerous other marginal enterprises. Marshalling his considerable talents, he sold stocks and bonds to investors who were overwhelmed by his infectious enthusiasm. Many of the projects he embarked upon had been talked about, or even started, by others, but he alone obtained the financial support to see them brought to, or close to, fruition. Stilwell was neither a manager of business nor a manipulator of securities. Rather, his contribution was the creation of enterprises and their subsequent promotion. Unlike Jay Gould, he did not make money trading stocks, and unlike John D. Rockefeller he was a poor business manager. Yet Stilwell received accolades often meted out to American business tycoons:

He is the Collis P. Huntington and the Edward H. Harriman of the present day, and it may well be of the future, say the financial prognosticators. To the middle Southwest he is what James J. Hill is to the great Northwest. . . . [He] has had two railroad termini named after him and possesses the imagination of a writer of epic poetry combined with the genius and ability of a great financier.[1]

This enthusiastic report of Stilwell's economic contribution is typical of the coverage and comment he received in the daily press and in business magazines. He was, however, not a great financier; his skill was the

1. Saint Louis *Globe-Democrat*, December 18, 1910.

ability to raise capital. He did not prove to be an able manager and depended upon his associates for the day-to-day operation of his enterprises. Where then does Arthur Stilwell fall in defining the role of the entrepreneur, and what were the techniques he used to win the acclaim of the press?

Historians and economists have long sought to define terms such as *businessman* and *entrepreneur*. Social scientists generally agree that these individuals played a vital role in the economic development of the United States in the nineteenth century, but there is no agreement as to who these persons were or as to what role they fulfilled. Within the vibrant, capitalistic economy of the Gilded Age, numerous men engaged in a wide variety of enterprises, yet each performed a slightly different function and many made unique contributions. Stilwell's contribution was that of the promoter. Since the term assumes great significance in his life, an attempt will be made to define it.

The economist Joseph Schumpeter devoted great energy and considerable talent to defining the terms *entrepreneur* and *promoter*, seeking definitions with a universal applicability. Distinguishing between the promoter and the enterpreneur, Schumpeter wrote,

Modern industry furnishes many instances of entrepreneurship vested in a company promoter. . . . In a sense, the promoter who does nothing but "set up" new business concerns might be considered as the purest type entrepreneur. Actually, he is mostly not more than a financial agent who had little, if any, title to entrepreneurship—no more than the lawyer who does legal work involved. But there are important exceptions to this.[2]

Stilwell would be an exception to this definition; he did far more than "set up" new businesses. He originated concepts or, more typically, enlarged upon the ideas of others, infused the concept with vigor and enthusiasm, raised the capital to begin operations, and guided the destiny of the enterprise, if only in its initial stages.

Schumpeter also emphasized the role of innovation in entrepreneurship. To him, the doing of new things or the doing of things already being done, but in a new way, provided the distinctive characteristics of the entrepreneur. He clearly differentiated between the management-administrative function and entrepreneurship. Despite his general den-

2. Joseph A. Schumpeter, "The Creative Responses in Economic History," *Journal of Economic History* VII (November 1947), 154.

igration of the promoter, Schumpeter did recognize the importance of creativity and promotion: "the essence of entrepreneurship lies in the perception and exploitation of new opportunities in the realm of business. . . ."[3]

In a critique of the Schumpeter definition of the "creative entrepreneur," Fritz Redlich notes that "a highly creative entrepreneur is not of necessity a good entrepreneur (builder and shaper of enterprises)."[4] Some creative entrepreneurs were tragic failures, Redlich argues, because they were poor entrepreneurs in the traditional sense—this is, as business managers or administrators—and they prove unable to direct an enterprise. Redlich does emphasize the characteristic of Schumpeter's creative entrepreneur that generally applies to the career of Arthur Stilwell, the characteristic of intuition—the capacity for grasping essential facts, discarding the unessential, and foreseeing things in a way which subsequently proves to be true. Prescience, then, is of monumental importance to a promoter of business, and certainly Stilwell's career shows at least initial foresight in the development of his enterprises.

Redlich also emphasizes the need for the creative entrepreneur to pick up ideas and shape them in such a way as to achieve reality. "His main task, however, is the execution of ideas, nobody being a creative entrepreneur who does not possess this ability: to make ideas come true."[5] Arthur Stilwell had such a talent; others had dreamed of constructing railroads from Kansas City to the Gulf of Mexico and across the prairies of Oklahoma and Texas and the mountains of Mexico, but only he would build the shining iron rails along these routes.

More than achieving a level of creativity, or even personal satisfaction, the promoter or creative entrepreneur fulfills a function within the economic life of the nation. Redlich concludes that the entrepreneur has a function in the enterprise, and furthermore, his is the basic function. He is the creator of the enterprise viewed as a social structure, as a "going

3. Schumpeter, "Der Unternehmer" in Ludwig Elster *et al.* (eds.) *Handworterbuch der Staatswissen-schaften* (Jena 1928), 483, cited by Heinz Hartmann, "Mergers and Enterpreneurs: A Useful Definition," *Administrative Science Quarterly* III (March 1959), 430.
4. Fritz L. Redlich, *History of American Business Leaders* (Ann Arbor: Edwards Brothers, Inc., 1940) 12.
5. *Ibid.*, 13.

concern" and the enterprise exists through him alone. Often he has created and shaped the enterprise, he has continually to reshape it; otherwise, it would cease to exist. . . . He directs the enterprise. He is its leading spirit around whom the spirit and morale of the enterprise are built. He decides upon the character and upon the program of his enterprise.[6]

Certainly the guiding spirit, if not the only spirit, of Stilwell's enterprises was the promoter himself.

Schumpeter and Redlich reject, then, the traditional concept of the entrepreneur as manager. Classical economists such as Jean Baptiste Say had conceived of the role of the entrepreneur as synonomous with a business manager. Redlich argues that the concept of the entrepreneur embraces neither the risk-bearer nor the manager, but the leading figure in the enterprise; a concept which Arthur Stilwell fits remarkably well.[7] As Arthur Cole has noted, Say and the traditionalists failed to incorporate into their analysis the spirit of adventure and innovation, elements without which entrepreneurship is impossible. Cole has also dealt with the promoter as a concept and has written that, "The promoter would . . . fall outside the fold [of entrepreneurship] unless he participated actively in the launching of new enterprises."[8] Infused with an enormous capacity for the spirit of adventure, Stilwell would leave the stale task of management to others, it was in the conceptual and promotional aspects of entrepreneurship that he found satisfaction, and would thus come very close to Cole's definition.

Numerous examples of similar men abound in studies of business leaders. R. Richard Wohl in his study of Henry Noble Day, an entrepreneur of Hudson, Ohio, offers a description of Day in one passage which could readily be used to depict Arthur Stilwell. Wohl wrote of Day,

Over all of them [his businesses] he exercised leadership not from any technical competence, nor from any special business acumen. His authority stemmed from his control over the basic conception of the plan for development which he had devised for the town and the area; and this authority was con-

6. *Ibid.*, 10.
7. *Ibid.*, 8.
8. Arthur H. Cole, "An Approach to the Study of Entrepreneurship: A Tribute to Edwin F. Gay," *Journal of Economic History* VI (Supplement, 1946), 4; *Ibid.*, "Entrepreneurship and Entrepreneurial History," in *Change and the Entrepreneur* (Cambridge: Harvard University Press, 1949), 91.

tinuously implemented by his further control over its most strategic element: he had access to capital.[9]

Stilwell exercised the same initiative in devising his enterprises and their goals, and sought and found capital for these enterprises. As in the case of Day, however, when the sources of capital dried up, the enterprises collapsed or fell into other hands.

Arthur Stilwell possessed many of the traits of the creative entrepreneur, but he comes closest to being the purest type of entrepreneur —the promoter. The conceiver, the enthusiast, the seeker and locator of capital, the adventurer, the guiding spirit—all of these things were embodied in Stilwell. Why? What motivated him? Were his motivations those of the "Robber Baron" or the "Captain of Industry"?

Matthew Josephson's study of the predatory capitalists of the Gilded Age emphasized acquisition of wealth as the primary motivation of the "Robber Baron."[10] This study became the basis for a general sense of indignation among scholars who attacked the entrepreneur because of his alleged pecuniary interest. Historians and economists assumed that the primary motivation of business leaders was individual financial gain. More recently this view has been challenged by those who argue, by way of social science methodology largely, that motivations are far more complex. These scholars have used the term "Captains of Industry" to describe some of the business leaders to whom Josephson referred. For example, Redlich states that, "Indisputably, pecuniary motives are not the final motives of the Captain of Industry."[11] Arthur Cole has taken the same position, contending there were few "public-be-damned" types, and that inadequate attention had been given to the mixed motivations of entrepreneurs.[12] Cole further contends that economists and historians have assumed or believed that the business leader seeks only to maximize profits, but that this is only a belief.[13]

---

9. R. Richard Wohl, "Henry Noble Day, a Study in Good Works 1808–1890," in William Miller (ed.), *Men in Business* (New York: Harper and Row, Publishers, 1962), 182.

10. Matthew Josephson, *The Robber Barons* (New York: Harcourt, Brace and World, Inc., 1962).

11. Redlich, *History of American Business Leaders*, 4.

12. Cole, "An Approach to the Study of Entrepreneurship," 8–9.

13. Arthur H. Cole, *Business Enterprise in its Social Setting* (Cambridge: Harvard University Press, 1959), 30–32.

Arthur Stilwell too deplored the idea that business leaders were predators of the jungle engaged in a fight for profits and survival. Entrepreneurs had various codes of conduct and goals, but he and others fought for more than personal gain.[14] Stilwell's motivations for entering the business world as a promoter encompass more than a simple desire for personal profits. The memories of his grandfather's successes, real or imaginary, the failure of his father, the declining prestige of the family, the absence of successful experiences as an adolescent; all these factors actively drove the young man. He sought success for the sake of success; he dreamed of creating an economic empire in the south central states; he gloried in promoting new enterprises; and like most pragmatic Americans he took great pleasure in "getting things done." The foregoing is not to suggest Stilwell refused to accept the material fruits of his labors. A man with expensive tastes and a man who knew how to enjoy the pleasures of life did not reject profits.

Stilwell had to make profits, as did most creative entrepreneurs; otherwise he would pass out of existence. Only profits would allow him to achieve his ultimate goals. Inspired by his own creative ability and possessed by ambition and vanity, he brought or attempted to bring a handsome return to his investors. Stilwell personally profited, but usually from subsidiary enterprises rather than from the principal development. There is strong evidence that this was a general pattern among railroad promoters. In the south, financier-managers derived few returns from their rail promotions, receiving instead income from such sources as real estate and land sales.[15] From the meager evidence available, and from Stilwell's own statements, it appears that his personal financial gain was small and that the profits received came principally from land speculation.[16] If personal gain was not Stilwell's primary motivation but a combination of other factors, how then did he make the decisions leading to the creation and development of his enterprises?

14. Arthur E. Stilwell and James R. Crowell, "I Had a Hunch," *The Saturday Evening Post* CC (December 3, 1927), 3.
15. Thomas C. Cochran, *Railroad Leaders; The Business Mind in Action* (New York: Russell and Russell, 1965), 203–206; Maury Klein, "The Strategy of Southern Railroads," *The American Historical Review* LXXIII (April 1968), 1065.
16. Arthur E. Stilwell, *Cannibals of Finance* (Chicago: Farnum Publishing Company, 1912), 41; W. R. Draper, "Promoting the Orient", *Railroad Magazine*, L (November 1949), 117.

Arthur Stilwell received enormous publicity in the last ten years of his life because of the revelations which appeared in his books, speeches, and interviews. Writing or speaking many years after he made the decisions, after a serious accident had forced his retirement from a business career, and while living outside the attention of the general public, Stilwell proclaimed that his decisions were based upon "hunches," "spirits," or the appearances of "brownies" in his dreams. The locations of his railroads, the decisions to develop particular townsites, and even the books he wrote were products of these spiritual encounters, he revealed.[17] Newspapers of the time and sensation-seeking journalists since have repeated, distorted, and added to his revelations.[18] Even some historians have accepted Stilwell's statements without noting the separation of time and distance and the declining public interest in him when he described his psychic experiences.[19]

It is interesting that when Stilwell was making crucial business decisions, he never spoke of "mystical" sources, and when explaining his selection of goals or methods, he usually indicated an economic reason for his decision. At the time the decision was reached, or perhaps in retrospect, it was quite possible to raise the question of the rationality of his choice. But, as Leland Jenks has written, entrepreneurs are not rational automatons but dynamic personalities. Personalities grow, they are not static, and the decisions may reflect a variety of roles played by the business leader.[20] Even if the aspect of mysticism is eliminated, some of his decisions were not rational if profit maximization was the ultimate goal. As Redlich has said, however, "it would, undoubtedly, be a mistake to believe that the decisions of the entrepreneur were always rational de-

17. In his memoirs, Stilwell wrote of "hunches," or of the influence of dreams, but in other books, such as *Live and Grow Young* (New York: Youth Publishing Co., 1921), 3–5, he spoke of "messages from the Spirit World." See also the New York *World*, April 6, 1924.

18. See for examples Stuart Palmer, "Arthur Stilwell . . . Psychic Empire Builder," *Fate Magazine* VI (March 1953), 40–46 and Brad Steiger, "Men Who Made Millions by Listening to Ghosts," *Saga the Magazine for Men* XXXVII (February 1969), 23–25, 81–82, 84.

19. J. Fred Rippy, *Latin America and the Industrial Age* (New York: G. P. Putnam's Sons, 1944), 163.

20. Leland H. Jenks, "Approaches to Entrepreneurial Personality," *Explorations in Entrepreneural History* II (January 15, 1950), 91–99.

cisions; they are just as irrational as are his motives."[21] Businessmen were not immune from resorting to bizzare sources of information in their efforts to diminish chance and uncertainty. Even a "Robber Baron" such as Commodore Vanderbilt sought out a seeress for advice.[22] It could well have been knowledge of Vanderbilt's reliance on the practical side of spiritualism that Stilwell recalled in the years of his retirement.

In any attempt to create a model for decision-making, the factor of irrationality looms large. A consideration in terms of irrationality is the penchant among promoters for persistent overoptimism. Certainly Stilwell exemplifies this trait. The creative entrepreneur has to deal with what he perceives to be the market place. False images are, nevertheless, images and alter the decision-making process. Interpretation, blended with optimism and intuition, introduces irrational variables. Factors other than marginal cost are significant to entrepreneurs often guided by misconception. The development of theories to explain the acts of businesses which depend on consistent or rational decision-making will nearly always fail to fit real situations.[23] Arthur Cole has suggested that the decision-making process, even when errors are made, can lead to successful ventures despite the element of irrationality. He concludes,

Anyway, it seems that cold, rational calculation of risks and chances of success has never controlled the launching of business enterprise, especially in economies that have been undergoing rapid or reasonably rapid growth under conditions of free enterprise. To be sure, there undoubtedly have been numerous businesses begun under unsound economic conditions which have survived and prospered by dint of supernormal exertions and ingenuities of their entrepreneurs.[24]

In his pioneering study of corporations, Arthur Dewing suggested that entrepreneurs made decisions based on psychological rather than economic factors; their motives reflected a desire for conquest and achievement. He contended that the four main factors were ambition, a creative impulse, profits, and speculation. Arthur Stilwell's career strong-

21. Redlich, *History of American Business Leaders*, 10.
22. Edward Chase Kirkland, *Dream and Thought in the Business Community 1860–1900* (Chicago: Quadrangle Books, 1964), 10.
23. Thomas C. Cochran, "Economic History, Old and New," *The American Historical Review*, LXXIV (June 1969), 1567.
24. Cole, *Business Enterprise in its Social Setting*, 164.

ly suggests the importance of the first two characteristics. His ambitions were unbounded, and he had an overwhelming desire to create new business enterprises. He determined to turn vague adolescent dreams into reality. Stilwell used profits as a superficial justification for expansion and as part of an appeal for capital. He did not engage in speculation; indeed, he issued numerous denunciations of men who engaged in stock manipulations.[25] Stilwell's decisions reflected his desire to achieve overwhelming personal ambitions and to fulfill a creative impulse.

Decisions are not made in historical or economic vacuums. The entrepreneur must be placed within his community and the national economic structure. Arthur Stilwell's career spans the period of American history from the 1870s and the rampant, unregulated growth of enormous enterprises and trusts, to the less-than-halcyon days of the decade before the First World War. His business decisions and personal motivations were affected by national factors, and he, in turn, had a limited effect on the economy of the south central states. Stilwell reached the apex of his influence at a time when businessmen were still unshackled by bureaucratic restraints and independence of action was still possible. Economic turbulence and depression as well as the competitive tactics of his opponents meant that the entrepreneur needed a body of associates to support him and aid in carrying through the enterprise. Stilwell acquired associates who contributed mightily to the successes he could claim.

In the pursuit of creative entrepreneurship and in founding and operating many enterprises, the dream and passion were Stilwell's, but other men contributed their talents also. One of Stilwell's strongest attributes was his ability to select associates and imbue them with his drive and enthusiasm. In the construction of his railroads he consistently found talented engineers to select the final routes and direct the laying of track and the building of bridges. The office forces in his companies were devoted to him and to his plans. In Kansas City he found faithful allies in the local business community who not only served as officers and board members of his firms but also contributed capital. His primary sources of funds were eastern or European, and from New Haven, Boston, and particularly Philadelphia, came the financial resources he needed. Stilwell never finan-

    25. Arthur Stone Dewing, *The Financial Policy of Corporations* (New York: The Ronald Press Co., 1941), II, 854–858.

cially controlled his creations himself but had a following among the investors who generally provided him with the votes he needed at meetings of stockholders or directors, a situation not unlike that found in other railroads.[26] Stilwell recognized the importance of the group of associates he acquired, and, despite his enormous ego, he described himself as their "emissary" and "work horse."[27] Of particular importance were the investors and financial advisors he had obtained for his enterprises.

Arthur Stilwell became a promoter of railroads after the railway boom of the 1870s and 1880s had ended. While the local lines around Kansas City were built before 1893, the main promotion, the line to the Gulf, came during and after the depression of that year. His second line was built after 1903, not an auspicious time for promoting an entirely new railroad of considerable length. Railroad construction declined rapidly between 1893 and 1897 so that Stilwell bucked a national trend.[28] Nevertheless, he fervently promoted his schemes to link Kansas City to the Gulf of Mexico and the Gulf of California.

In deciding where to construct his railroads, Stilwell apparently failed to raise the usual questions about such ventures. When a railroad was projected, and before construction commenced, the most significant question was, Should this line be built at all? The rational answer depended upon whether the rate of return from the investment would prove profitable and whether capital for construction was available. Stilwell and many other promoters tended, however, to answer the question with less exact or visionary estimates of the capital available, the gross and net receipts, and the direct and indirect profits of the projected line.[29] One student of the question of railway location during the 1890s wrote,

The profit in a railway property depends, *first*, on the judgment shown in selecting the region through which it is to be built; and, *secondly*, on the skill with which the line laid down is adapted to be of the greatest use to the greatest number of people (giving large gross revenue) at the smallest cost for the service rendered (giving small operating expenses). The first is dis-

26. Cochran, *Railroad Leaders*, 11.
27. Stilwell, "I Had a Hunch", December 31, 1927, 24.
28. Alfred D. Chandler Jr., (comp. and ed.) *The Railroads* (New York: Harcourt, Brace and World, Inc., 1965), 14.
29. Arthur M. Wellington, *The Economic Theory of the Location of Railways* (New York: John Wiley and Sons, 1900), 13.

tinctively the province of the projectors; the last is distinctively the province of the engineer.[30]

In selecting a competent engineer, Stilwell proved highly successful; it was the choice of routes through generally unprofitable regions that proved his downfall.

The financing of railroad ventures was highly speculative in the period in which Stilwell operated. With visions of vast profits from railways and their subsidiaries as a lure, promoters eagerly sought to seize the opportunities for high rates of return offered by a rapidly expanding economy. Without exercising caution to determine whether adequate financing was available, they plunged into construction and extension of rail lines.

Railways are not undertaken unless they are expected to be profitable, not to the general public, nor to other parties in the near or distant future, nor to those who lent money on them, *but to those who at first control the enterprise.* If the means in hand be not sufficient for the projectors to complete the road for operation and to control its operation afterwards, the result is usually complete loss.[31]

Too often, not only was capital insufficient, but bonds were issued to pay interest on those previously sold. Stilwell, however, did not engage in this practice, he simply underestimated the financial needs of his ventures and, consequently, had to increase constantly the authorized capitalization. In the virgin territories through which he built his main lines, local traffic was insufficient to provide the cash earnings the railroads had to have, and through business failed to develop. Even deferred payment of fixed charges proved inadequate to prevent a financial debacle as did the elaborate and interlocking system of borrowing. Stocks, bonds, car-trust certificates, and other devices stretched borrowing far beyond the ability of the enterprises to pay. The result was a large floating debt, no reserve capital, and low earnings.[32]

Despite the manifold hazards involved in investment in western railroads, local boomers, eastern capitalists, and foreigners purchased stocks and bonds in the railways and their related enterprises. Professors Arthur Johnson and Barry Supple in their excellent study of the investment prac-

---

30. *Ibid.,* 16–17.
31. *Ibid.,* 15.
32. Simon Sterne, *Recent Railroad Failures and Their Lessons* (New York [Reprinted from *The Forum,* March, 1894], 1894), 8–10.

tices of some Bostonians suggest why these risks were incurred. They believe that investors placed their capital in western railroads for two reasons:

Some investors committed their capital to land transportation in the expectation that this sector might both encourage and benefit from long-run economic development.

and,

Others placed their capital in railroads with an eye to existing traffic, or to current levels of potential demand, or to tactical pressure vis-à-vis competition, or to stock manipulation.

The former are characterized as "developmental" investors, and the latter as "opportunistic" investors. Different expectations on the part of the investors led to a variety of policies and procedures.[33] Arthur Stilwell expected to see long-range development lead to the prosperity of his promotions. When he had orchards planted in Arkansas to provide future freight traffic, he was viewing his scheme in a "developmental" fashion. To attract investors who were often quite "opportunistic" in their goals, however, he provided investments with immediate high rates of return. Townsite promotions, construction company stocks, and subsidiary operations attracted the capital he needed for construction. His personal goals were "developmental," though he provided his investors with potentially "opportunistic" profits. He too would earn some money from opportunistic situations, but his long-range goal of personal accomplishment remained paramount.

The original sources of Stilwell's capital were his business allies in Kansas City, friends among his insurance contacts, and a group of Philadelphia investors affiliated with Drexel and Company and Drexel, Morgan and Company. The latter group furnished the bulk of the funds for the trust company Stilwell formed and for his railroad operations before 1893. Drexel and Company was not playing an unaccustomed role in providing capital for western railroad promotions. As investment bankers, the firm had allocated capital, arranged for sales of securities, and often presided over financial reorganizations of railways.[34] Within the Drexel firm there were several men who specialized in railroad securities, and they became

33. Arthur M. Johnson and Barry E. Supple, *Boston Capitalists and Western Railroads* (Cambridge: Harvard University Press, 1967), 9.
34. Chandler, *The Railroads*, 45.

Stilwell's contacts in eastern financial circles.[35] These men, representing an ally of one of the major financial operations on Wall Street, would act as a restraining influence on Stilwell and his ambitions.

When Stilwell's railroad to the Gulf collapsed in 1899 and a receivership ensued, he became very bitter, and, in financing his line to Mexico, tried to obtain capital outside of "Wall Street." In his anger he wrote, "there are two ways to build a railway. One is to go to Wall Street and tell the financiers about it. If they like it they'll build it and let you be a secretary. Another way is to build it without Wall Street aid."[36] Other railroad promoters had sought to finance their operations outside of the eastern United States money market, but few were successful. Some, like James J. Hill and Stilwell after 1893, went to Europe for funds; Hill and Stilwell both obtained Dutch capital. In financing the railroad to Mexico, Stilwell received substantial support from English investors. But, by his own admission, it was impossible to avoid dealing with the investment bankers. Stilwell railed against the "Money Trust" and the "Cannibals of Wall Street," but he, like David Moffat and others, failed when the investment houses denied them capital.[37]

The main device Stilwell used to induce investors was the collateral-trust mortgage. A collateral-trust bond was a mortgage secured, not by real property or franchises, but by the deposit of stocks or bonds of other companies with a designated trustee. The bonds depended for interest upon revenues from deposited stocks and bonds and other guarantees the issuing company made. The collateral-trust mortgage was in widespread use in the 1890s and was easier to sell than common stock because the investor was given some security for which an established company was responsible. These bonds were used for expansion, to take over other roads, and to finance construction. Stilwell made good use of this form of finance by creating railroad subsidiaries, issuing stocks to a construction company, which then issued collateral-trust bonds secured by a mortgage

35. Edward G. Campbell, *The Reorganization of the American Railroad System, 1893–1900* (New York: Columbia University Press, 1938), 170, 172, 187–188, 195, 275.

36. New York *Herald*, September 27, 1908.

37. See Stilwell's *Cannibals of Finance, passim*; Frederick A. Cleveland and Fred Wilbur Powell, *Railroad Promotion and Capitalization in the United States* (New York: Longmans, Green, and Co., 1909), 293.

on the stocks and bonds of the railroad.[38] They also allowed Stilwell to let his penchant for creating subsidiaries run rampant and, at the same time, gain the capital he sought.

Stilwell's railroad companies issued bonds to construction companies he formed, and the latter sold collateral-trust bonds in the name of the construction company. His trust company sold the securities of the various enterprises. The use of a construction company as a method of finance was typical in the expansion of American railroads. The construction company used the securities of the railroad as collateral to raise funds to build the line. The construction company often received excessively high prices for work done, and the profits went to "insiders." The construction company device, however, permitted the growth of railways when other methods of raising capital failed. The construction operation offered higher profits than railway earnings, and as securities of newly created railroads were of dubious value, the construction company received sizable bonuses for accepting them.[39] The absence of records makes it impossible to ascertain whether Stilwell's construction companies attained a high rate of profit for their investors; one would assume that such was the case.

Not only did the promoter use the construction company to attract investors of an "opportunistic" nature; he also created a multitude of related subsidiaries. This too was the normal practice. "The hope of quick returns from construction companies, townsite planning, and other subsidiary ventures undoubtedly bulked large in the considerations of these promoters."[40] Stilwell created a myriad of land companies, lumber and coal subsidiaries, terminal corporations, and related enterprises to attract investors and used the stocks of these companies as bonuses for investment in the railroad and construction operations. Flamboyant "puff pieces" praised these ventures as absolutely sound and described in the most romantic language their potential profits. Again, this was a standard railroad promotion effort, and puff pieces, pamphlets, broadsides, and

---

38. William Z. Ripley, *Railroads Finance and Organization* (New York: Longmans, Green and Company, 1915), 143–156; Frederick A. Cleveland and Fred Wilbur Powell, *Railroad Finance* (New York: D. Appleton and Company, 1912), 73–74; Thomas Warner Mitchell, "The Collateral Trust Mortgage in Railway Finance," *Quarterly Journal of Economics* XX (May 1906), 443–466.
39. Cochran, *Railroad Leaders*, 99–100, 111; Chandler, *The Railroads*, 45–46.
40. Cochran, *Railroad Leaders*, 94.

brochures were vital instruments of the promoter. Professional writers and public relations men were hired to produce the literature, and the "unsolicited" testimonials which were features of this genre.[41]

In the process of promotion, the opportunities for corruption appeared with great frequency. "From promotion to exploitation is little more than a step. If there was profit in projecting and building a well constructed railroad by those who controlled its operations afterwards, how much greater appeared the prospect of profit to those who could build as cheaply as possible and sell out their interest at speculation prices!"[42] A recent study of the Kansas Pacific Railroad discovered "unrelieved greed" and corruption in its promotion, and the study suggests that this railroad may not have been atypical.[43] Arthur Stilwell's two major railroads, in their promotional phase, do not appear to have been designed to produce only quick profits through corrupt practices, and the same appears true for the subsidiaries, though the evidence is not conclusive. Stilwell himself did not make undue financial gains even through normal and legal business operations, though he accused some of his short-lived associates of attempting nefarious schemes to swindle the holders of securities. But even if all of the promotions had been absolutely honest, the shortage of investment capital was such that securities were issued beyond the ability of the schemes to pay. Without watered stock, a new railroad's fixed charges were still at an onerous level, and speculators took advantage of this precarious state of affairs.[44]

An analysis of Stilwell's business enterprises becomes more illuminating when developed within an economic model. Model-building is a somewhat hazardous enterprise at best, even with "normal" business operations. But with a dynamic personality such as Stilwell possessed, and the

41. *Ibid.*, 185–186.

42. Cleveland and Powell, *Railroad Finance*, 14.

43. William Robinson Petrowski, "The Kansas Pacific Railroad: A Study in Railroad Promotion (Unpublished doctoral dissertation, University of Wisconsin, 1965), 250.

44. Robert L. Brandfon, *Cotton Kingdom of the New South* (Cambridge: Harvard University Press, 1967), 68–70. This study shows the impact of railroad expansion on the Yazoo River Delta and the reasons for this expansion, principally by the Illinois Central Railroad.

irrational basis upon which he formulated his promotions, the hazards are even more formidable. A model created by John Sawyer, however, comes very close to fitting Stilwell and his enterprises.[45] Sawyer developed a concept of "entrepreneurial error" which, while not completely compatible with this study, is very helpful in analyzing Stilwell and his methods. In discussing the factor of error in economic growth, Sawyer comments,

Yet one cannot read far in the history of great economic undertakings— particularly great developments in transport and the opening up of new resources, for example—without being struck by the recurrence of an apparently quite contrary phenomena: instances in which entrepreneurial error or misinformation not only is massively present, *but where it appears to have been a condition of successful enterprise.* Cases, that is, in which *mis*calculation or sheer ignorance apparently was crucial to getting an enterprise launched at all, or at least begun and completed when it was.[46]

Large financial undertakings, then, were begun based on a grossly underestimated cost, though the project would ultimately demonstrate a degree of economic utility. The most conspicuous examples, according to Sawyer, were those enterprises with heavy fixed investment and high indivisibility, where major financial commitments preceed by a long-time factor the generation of profits. Because of capital needs, the absence of immediate profits, and the developmental nature of the projects, governmental participation to complete such projects was common.

In constructing the model, Sawyer uses a hypothetical example of an entrepreneur who, having visualized the project, estimates its costs. The estimate, based on false or misleading data, is used to generate initial capital investment, generally by the use of "heroic promotional efforts." Had the actual costs been known, Sawyer postulates that the project would have died at this point. Once the project was actually begun, however, the original investors were asked for additional sums and were forced to invest far beyond their original intent. Other investors are subsequently brought in, only to be forced to contribute more capital also. Finally, either before or after all private sources are exhausted, the projector turns to government to complete the undertaking.[47]

45. John E. Sawyer, "Entrepreneurial Error and Economic Growth," *Explorations in Entrepreneurial History*, First Series (May 1952), 199–204.
46. *Ibid.*, 199.
47. *Ibid.*, 200.

Sawyer's model requires that once in operation, the project prove to be a contribution to the economic development of the community or a source of profit to the owners. "Yet to repeat and keep our model clear," he writes, "had the total investment required been accurately and objectively known at the beginning, the project would not have been begun or, if known midway, not completed."[48] This model encompasses the major attributes of Stilwell's projects: he consistently underestimated costs, constantly sought additional capital by the most flamboyant promotional efforts, pressured the original investors for more funds, and, when the investors failed to respond, the projects, in two instances, were completed by national governments. The projects were, however, economic contributions. The Sawyer model provides the framework around which the analysis of Stilwell's schemes will be constructed.

Besides a capacity for entrepreneural error, Arthur Stilwell shared other characteristics, sentiments, and traits with businessmen of the period. The most prevalent notion about business leaders, and one which these men came to believe, was the myth of the self-made man. Reinforced by the Puritan Ethic and later by Social Darwinism, the myth received widespread acceptance through such diverse advocates as the stories of Horatio Alger, the novels of Mrs. E.D.E.N. Southworth, and the public pronouncements of Andrew Carnegie. The myth described the meteoric rise of the farm or small-town youth who came to the city, perserved, and, through his commitment to the work ethic, morality, and success, became a member of the management of the firm.[49] That the cult was based on myth has been firmly established, but businessmen—including Stilwell— and a major sector of the general population believed it was true.

One aspect of the cult emphasized the stewardship of the self-made man and his public responsibility. Stilwell accepted this responsibility through his active participation in community affairs, as a Christian Scientist, and as the promoter of civic projects. For example, he founded a

48. *Ibid.*
49. For excellent analyses of the cult of the self-made man see Irvin Wyllie, *The Self-Made Man in America* (New York: The Free Press, 1966); John G. Cawelti, *Apostles of the Self-Made Man* (Chicago: University of Chicago Press, 1968); and Moses Rischin (ed.) *The American Gospel of Success* (Chicago: Quadrangle Books, 1968).

night school for disadvantaged children in Kansas City, demonstrating his beliefs in stewardship, philanthrophy, and practical education.[50]

As a largely self-educated man who acquired a veneer of culture through his own efforts, Stilwell advocated self-education vociferously. Self-education was a vital part of the cult of the self-made man. Stilwell and advocates of the cult sought to strike a balance between traditional social and religious ideals and the spirit of individual economic enterprise. Self-culture promoted these ideals, and Stilwell developed a thin layer of "popular culture," which was demonstrated in the novels, songs, and poems he wrote, in the concerts he subsidized, and the Chautauqua programs he sponsored.

As many advocates of the success cult, however, Stilwell believed that some unscrupulous businessmen took advantage of the system. He believed in, advocated, and lauded the capitalistic system which made the cult of the self-made man possible, but he favored throwing the "rascals" out. He opposed monopolies, trusts, financial manipulation, and disavowed speculative profiteering. The success cult admitted that there were some unscrupulous businessmen, but the majority were honest, energetic, service-oriented, and philanthropic.[51] Stilwell denounced the "money trust" and the "Cannibals of Wall Street" but praised men such as Andrew Carnegie and George Westinghouse. The "rascals" could best be dealt with not by federal regulation but through true *laissez faire*. Stilwell opposed federal regulation of business, as did most followers of the cult, and he thought that the market place could be purified by the businessmen themselves.[52] If this position lacked wisdom and insight, it was consistent for a successful promoter like Arthur Stilwell.

Businessmen used a variety of methods to demonstrate their personal financial achievements. As Edward Kirkland has noted, wealthy business leaders did not build mansions and erect other edifices just for an ostentatious display of prosperity or to demonstrate a lack of taste; a variety of factors motivated these men.[53] Arthur Stilwell had a handsome home

50. Kirkland, *Dream and Thought in the Business Community*, 51–82.
51. Wyllie, *The Self-Made Man in America*, 78–81; Cawelti, *Apostles of the Self-Made Man*, 192.
52. Kirkland, *Dream and Thought in the Business Community*, 121.
53. *Ibid.*, 29–49.

on Armour Boulevard in Kansas City, but it was in no sense a mansion. On the other hand, his private railway cars, where he entertained and met potential stockholders, were opulent, and the interiors were luxuriously furnished. When he traveled, which was often, he stayed in the best hotels, ate at the most fashionable restaurants, and dressed in the height of sartorial elegance. His life style was designed to manifest prosperity to those who mattered—his business colleagues and his investors.

A promoter without peer and a booster of unlimited vision, Arthur Stilwell plunged into the financial world during some of its most turbulent years. Driven by an insatiable ambition to re-establish the name of his family and to make practical and visible economic contributions and gifted with unbounded enthusiasm, Stilwell became a railroad and urban promoter. An innovator in opening new areas for economic growth, though not an innovator technologically, he made major economic contributions in the south central states. Despite massive entrepreneurial errors, and because he was able to incorporate acceptable financial methods into his schemes, he built two thousand miles of railway and founded several dozen towns, villages, and hamlets. Yet, when he arrived in Kansas City in 1886, it is doubtful that even he realized the impact he would have on that city and the region.

III

RAILS 'ROUND KANSAS CITY

WHEN Arthur and Jennie Stilwell stepped off of the train that brought them to Kansas City in 1886, they found themselves in a community that was neither a frontier town nor yet metropolis.[1] A river town by appearance, Kansas City had become, despite the mud and dust, a railroad community. After the opening of the Hannibal Bridge across the Missouri River in 1869, the city's future was secure. Local businessmen, with great ambitions, developed a remarkable real estate boom, and the speculative fever reached its height in the mid-1880s. The population actually passed the inflated 1880 census figure of 55,000. As more Yankees moved into the city from New York, New Jersey, and Pennsylvania, with the border South contributing fewer residents, the complexion of the city changed.

A highly transitory populace moved in and out of the city. Arthur Stilwell had lived there a short while in 1880 and then departed, typical of the floating population of the community. Social disorganization arose from this extreme mobility. The vicissitudes of the census figures, however, did not abate the speculation in real estate.

In 1885 the city limits were pushed to the east and south, and in the next dozen years Kansas City doubled in size, forming a large rectangle ten miles long and eight miles wide. The city had numerous neighborhoods

1. The description of Kansas City in this and subsequent chapters is taken from a manuscript copy of the soon to be published second volume of the history of Kansas City by A. Theodore Brown. Professor Brown generously lent the manuscript, for which the author is most appreciative.

39

with highly contrasting populations and living conditions. Quality Hill on the bluffs along the river in the northwestern part of the city was the best residential area and became the home of the wealthy meat-packing and grain-merchant families. The flat and dun West Bottoms below the bluffs and along the river contained the railroad yards, the foul-smelling stockyards and slaughterhouses, and a burgeoning slum. While this was the "Hell's Half Acre" of the city, another area of vice and corruption existed only slightly north and east of the central business district. The area of commerce and trade was perched on the bluff in the center of the community where the buying and selling of business property reached a feverish pitch.

Railroad promotion had been the center of financial interest for residents in the 1870s and early 1880s.[2] With the arrival of numerous railroads, however, community concern shifted to real estate, cattle, grain, and service industries. The most dramatic business in Kansas City between 1870 and 1900 was real estate, and the records of the Real Estate Association, formed in 1886, show the size of the operations; there were three hundred real estate firms in the town, or one for every ninety families. The profitability of speculation in local land and commercial properties attracted outside capital. This capital was partially absorbed in the construction and extension of numerous cablecar routes that drove the price of property even higher. Construction also boomed in business buildings, houses, and cheap flats. Contractors cut new streets through the limestone and raw clay bluffs as the city expanded to the east and south.

The Stilwells arrived at the peak of the boom. Between July 1, 1886, and July 1, 1887, real estate and property sales hit their zenith. Individual fortunes were made and lost before the market crashed. Real estate transfers reached $88 million in 1887, climbing from $40 million the year before, and from $11 million in 1885. Local traders used eastern capital

2. For an excellent study of the role of community in Kansas City railroad promotion see Charles N. Glaab, *Kansas City and the Railroads* (Madison: The State Historical Society of Wisconsin, 1962); the story of the early years of the city is found in the definite *Frontier Community Kansas City to 1870* (Columbia: University of Missouri Press, 1963), by A. Theodore Brown. Additional insight into the society of Kansas City may be obtained in Virginia Swayne's *The Dollar Gold Piece* (New York: Farrar & Rinehart, 1942), a novel concerning the real estate boom of the 1880s.

to speculate in real estate, and some men rose to prominence on the boom. Describing these men, A. T. Brown writes, "The instability and unpredictability of business life during this unsettled period in the city's life meant that a man's fortune depended not only upon talent and tangible resources, but also upon the way his projects happened to fit the timing of community growth."[3] Arthur Stilwell's sense of timing proved to be one of his strongest assets.

Attracted to Kansas City by the real estate speculation, and possessing $25,000 with which to play the market, Stilwell moved into the business community. He spent several months becoming acquainted with local residents and forming his plan of operations.[4] Perhaps these contacts made the suggestion, or perhaps he recalled the role of Hamblin Stilwell in the Rochester Savings Bank, but, regardless, Stilwell decided to form a trust company as a vehicle for real estate speculation.

The trust company movement was just getting under way at the time, and these companies were able to become involved in many lucrative operations. They could undertake financial schemes or take interests in speculative ventures, often at tremendous profits. Trust companies paid higher dividends than banks and were not restricted by banking laws in their operations. They acted as fiscal agents performing the work of trustees and served as headquarters for bondholders' and reorganization committees. The trust companies absorbed huge amounts of capital and often dealt in stocks, bonds, and real estate like private bankers. Eventually these trust companies controlled large financial assets.[5] Given the optimism about his own abilities and the future of Kansas City, Stilwell readily saw the advantages of such a vehicle.

The Real Estate Trust Company, formed in 1886, was the first of many Stilwell business ventures. With its limited capital, the Trust did not immediately engage in gigantic financial adventures. Stilwell seized, however, upon a scheme to aid the Trust in selling houses, its primary business. He combined an insurance policy with the mortgages of the homes

3. Brown manuscript.
4. Arthur E. Stilwell and James R. Crowell, "I had a Hunch," *The Saturday Evening Post* CC (December 17, 1927), 24.
5. John Moody, *The Masters of Capital* (New Haven: Yale University Press, 1919), 120–125.

he sold. If the purchaser of the home died before the mortgage was paid, the insurance policy sold by Stilwell relieved the indebtedness. The slogan of the Real Estate Trust was, "You can live in your endowment policy and raise chickens in its back yard."[6] But selling houses had a limited appeal to Stilwell, and to satisfy his ambitions he needed more capital.

During his insurance-selling days in Chicago, Stilwell acquired a number of contacts and clients in the Midwest. He confided to Jennie his plan to raise capital from these sources. Using his exuberant salesmanship capability and the lure of the thriving Kansas City real estate market, he began to seek financial support. He traveled to Saint Louis and consulted with A. A. Mosher, the agent for The Travelers in Missouri. Through Mosher he reached Judge J. E. McKeighan; Charles M. Hays, counsel for the Missouri Pacific Railroad; H. A. Lloyd, counsel for the Wabash Railway; and several other businessmen. According to Stilwell's memoirs, this group raised $180,000 for the Trust, and several members agreed to serve on the board of directors.[7] Stilwell returned to Kansas City with his list of subscribers and began to recruit local investors.

The Kansas Citian who became Stilwell's most prominent supporter was E. L. Martin, a former mayor of the city and a man with excellent contacts in the business community. A distiller and wholesale liquor dealer, he was born in Kentucky in 1842 and came to Kansas City as a young man in 1868. The son of Irish immigrants, Martin was one of the few businessmen in city politics and had become a leader of the local Democratic party. A short, dark-complexioned man, Martin proved to be a loyal friend and long-time associate for Stilwell.[8] He also gave the Trust company a local leader with a reputation for honesty. He was known as a good businessman, "sound, reliable, and safe." His credit was good and he was described by his associates as a "self-made man."[9] Stilwell came to value most highly this recruit for his team.

6. Darrell Garwood, *Crossroads of America* (New York: W. W. Norton & Co., 1948), 132–133; Stilwell, "I Had a Hunch," December 3, 1927, 168.
7. Stilwell, "I Had a Hunch," December 17, 1927, 24.
8. Kansas City *Star*, December 16, 1912, and June 4, 1944; Kansas City *Journal*, December 16, 1912; and Brown manuscript.
9. Dun and Bradstreet Collection, Jackson County, Missouri, Volume 16, Items 2.786 and 6691 (Manuscript Division, Baker Library, Harvard Graduate School of Business Administration, Boston, Mass.).

Other Kansas City businessmen would follow Martin into Stilwell's projects. Particularly important was W. S. Woods, president of the National Bank of Commerce.[10] As one of the leading bankers in the city, Woods not only added local prestige but also provided eastern banking connections.

Even with the infusion of Kansas City capital, the Real Estate Trust needed additional funds if Stilwell's ambitions were to be achieved. He decided to travel east and talk with men he had met in the insurance business and, probably, banking acquaintances of Woods. Stilwell went first to Philadelphia and called on William Waterall, a paint manufacturer. Stilwell claimed in his memoirs that the contact was made as a result of checking through lists of directors of Philadelphia trust companies, but this story seems to be the product of his romantic reminiscences.[11] Waterall did introduce him to another paint manufacturer, John Lucas but, more importantly, to Edward T. Stotesbury and John Lowber Welsh of Drexel and Company. Drexel and Company was affiliated with Drexel, Morgan and Company, and Stotesbury and Welsh were considered Morgan's railroad experts. Stotesbury represented the firm on the boards of several companies, including the Lehigh Valley Railroad, and had become enormously wealthy in his own right. Welsh was involved in the reorganization of the Philadelphia and Reading and Erie Railroads. These men, together with several Philadelphia bankers, agreed to purchase bonds in the Trust.[12] Selling the bonds for sixty-six cents on the dollar, Stilwell placed $300,000 in securities in Philadelphia. Other investors in New Haven and Bridgeport, Connecticut, purchased bonds, so that Stilwell raised some $660,000 in actual cash. Investors in Atchison and Fort Scott, Kansas, and Omaha, Nebraska, also joined the group.[13] Stilwell returned to Kansas City and entered the maelstrom of the local real estate market.

The Trust prospered during its first six months of operation. Housed

10. *The Kansas City Gateway* I (January 1903), 20.
11. Stilwell, "I Had a Hunch," December 17, 1927, 24, 26.
12. *Ibid.*: John Moody, *The Railroad Builders* (New Haven: Yale University Press, 1920), 38; Moody, *The Masters of Capital*, 185; and Stuart Daggett, *Railroad Reorganization* (New York: Augustus M. Kelley, Publishers, 1967), 108, 111, 128, and 134.
13. Stilwell, "I Had a Hunch," December 17, 1927, 26.

in a suite of offices in a downtown commercial building, Stilwell and his employees succeeded in producing profits that allowed for a 6 percent dividend. The promoter himself received a salary of $5,000 annually.[14] But this rate of return was to be short-lived, as the local real estate market collapsed at the end of 1887.

A bad crop year and the decline of the range-cattle industry in Kansas City's hinterland led to a local depression. Several of the town's leading real estate speculators were forced to declare bankruptcy or retrench in their developments.[15] The local boom in real estate collapsed, and investors began, by 1889, to place their capital outside of the city.

Recognizing that with the end of the Kansas City boom the Real Estate Trust had lost its principal market, Stilwell and his associates decided to reorganize into another corporation with authority to operate in a larger area. On February 14, 1889, the Missouri, Kansas and Texas Trust Company of Kansas City was incorporated, with capital of one million dollars. Ten thousand shares of stock with a value of $100 each were issued. The twenty men on the list of directors were primarily from Kansas City and Saint Louis, although other cities in the midwest were represented as were Philadelphia, New Haven, and New York City.[16]

The offices of the Missouri, Kansas and Texas Trust were located in three rooms of the Water Works Building. Arthur and Jennie lived nearby in the Hotel Bonaventure.[17] A subsidiary, the Missouri, Kansas, and Texas Building Company, was created with capital of $100,000 to construct homes sold by the Trust.[18] Advertisements in local newspapers pictured a typical two-story house of the period, and proclaimed:

Stop paying rent and put your monthly payments into a home. We will build on your own lot or purchase you a lot and build on monthly payments for 10 years, not exceeding fair rent, and in case of death we cancel mortgage, leaving an unencumbered home for the family.[19]

14. *Ibid.*
15. Brown manuscript.
16. Jefferson City *Daily Tribune*, February 15, 1889.
17. *Haye's City Directory 1888–1889* (Kansas City: Haye Directory Co., 1889), 655.
18. Jefferson City *Daily Tribune*, January 26, 1889.
19. The Kansas City *Star*, April 10, 1889.

The Trust received interest on the loan, profits from the subsidiary which built the house, and a portion of the life insurance premium covering the purchaser of the home. The local real estate prospects were limited, however, and Stilwell soon expanded the financial horizons of the Trust.

Within a year after the Trust began to function, Stilwell proposed that the company construct its own building to provide office space and rental income. A handsome building of red brick with terra-cotta trim was erected at Seventh and Wyandotte streets at a cost of $98,000. This building would eventually house a myriad of Stilwell promotions. The firm also began to build houses in Lincoln, Nebraska, Saint Joseph, Missouri, and Wichita, Kansas. With the aid of Drexel and Company, the Trust sold industrial plant mortgages in the East. Loans were placed to construct a stock yard, and two office buildings in Sioux City, Iowa. The Trust helped finance the water and light plant at Joplin, Missouri, and the water works in Carrollton, Missouri. One project in which Arthur undoubtedly took pride was the Stilwell Hotel built by the Trust in Pittsburg, Kansas. It was the first, though certainly not the last, project to bear his name. In three years, the Trust had become an important source of capital for the region around Kansas City, and for the community as well. By 1895, the Trust had increased its capitalization to $1,250,000 and had a surplus and undivided profits of $780,000.[20]

Although Judge McKeighan acted as head of the Trust initially, his presence in Saint Louis undoubtedly proved awkward for the Kansas City firm, and the success of the company proved that Stilwell could manage the operation. The directors elevated Stilwell to the presidency, and he became more than the source of ideas and enthusiasm. By 1892, he was issuing statements to the press on behalf of the firm, and doing so with gusto. When the Trust decided to build a large grain elevator in the East Bottoms at a cost of $180,000, Stilwell told the press that the project was still in embryo and that the plans were incomplete. While skillfully creating an aura of mystery about the project, he had, at the same time, told

---

20. Stilwell, "I Had a Hunch," December 17, 1927, 26, 96; the Kansas City *Star*, April 26, 1890 and October 30, 1895; Arthur E. Stilwell, *Cannibals of Finance* (Chicago: Farnum Publishing Company, 1912), 39–40; and Howard L. Conard, *Encyclopedia of the History of Missouri* (New York: The Southern History Co., 1901), VI, 87.

of its size and location and announced that construction bids were being received.[21] Very early in his career he became extremely adroit in using the press for his own purposes. The exuberant Stilwell would often make use of the news media to promote his projects.

As Kansas City grew in the late 1880s the number of railroads entering the city increased, and the congestion in the railway yards approached a state of chaos. Miles of tracks in yards and terminals twisted, curved, and sprawled along the Missouri River in the East and West Bottoms. A large Union Station had been constructed in the Bottoms. Access to the station was by an incline railway or by a street hung on the side of the bluff. An unattractive area of cheap hotels and pawn shops surrounded this effort to bring unity to Kansas City passenger-train operations. Industrial facilities and distribution centers added to the difficulties of interchanging railroad cars and cargoes. A number of solutions were suggested to end the confusion and congestion, including several proposals for a belt railroad around the city to link the lines entering the area. Charters had been granted to several groups of investors, but little had been done to alleviate the problems of the terminals.

In June of 1886, and in January of 1887, the state of Missouri chartered the Kansas City Suburban Belt Railway Company, and the Kansas City Suburban Belt Railroad Company. The Railway was incorporated by nine Kansas City men with authorization to issue $100,000 in stock and build a ten-mile belt line.[22] This amount of capital would not begin to construct a line through some of the most expensive land in the city, and a second charter, to the Railroad, was issued January 8, 1887. The Railroad received authority to build a line encircling the city and to capitalize at one million dollars. The incorporators included E. L. Martin and eight other businessmen.[23] The company planned to build five miles east from the Kansas City Union Depot to Blue River, then six miles south along the Blue to Brush Creek, then northwest back to the Union Depot. When the company was formed, Stilwell was neither a stockholder nor an officer.[24]

21. The Kansas City *Star*, September 27, 1892.
22. Jefferson City *Daily Tribune*, June 8, 1886.
23. *Ibid.*, January 9, 1887.
24. Minute Book, Kansas City Suburban Belt Railroad, January 5, 1887 (Offices of the Kansas City Southern Railway, Kansas City, Missouri).

Martin and his associates lacked the funds to initiate construction, and for a few months the project languished. According to Stilwell, a crisis developed over the provision that the charter would be revoked if construction did not commence by a certain date. The time sequence fails to support this dramatic situation. Stilwell did enter the scheme, however, and infuse it with his exuberance. At the meeting of the directors of the Suburban Belt on May 31, 1889, the railroad agreed to contract with Stilwell to build the line. The Kansas City Terminal Construction Company, formed by him, would receive $450,000 of the $500,000, 6 percent, 30-year bonds of the railroad, and, in addition, $900,000 in stock, to build from Second Street, east to Cecil Station near Blue River. The Missouri, Kansas and Texas Trust Company would act as trustee for the bonds.[25] The bonds were issued on July 24, and Stilwell and Martin embarked on a journey to Philadelphia to sell the securities.

Stilwell arrived in Philadelphia and entered the offices of Drexel and Company. Typically attired in a low-crowned, narrow-brimmed gray derby hat, a short, snugly-fitted oxford gray coat, and a high "poke" collar with an ascot tie held in place by a pearl stickpin, he was the personification of the prosperous promoter. To Drexel and Stotesbury he proposed to sell $1,000 bonds for $660 with a bonus of twenty shares of $100 par value stock. He explained that a contractor was already at work, that he envisioned a line linking every railroad entering the city and most of its industrial facilities, and that the business leaders of Kansas City were strong supporters of the scheme. When the subscription forms were presented, Drexel, Stotesbury, and Welsh signed for various amounts, and other Philadelphians also agreed to purchase bonds. Stilwell and Martin telegraphed Kansas City, told the contractor to continue construction, and departed for home.[26]

Arriving in Kansas City, Stilwell began to expand his list of associates. Two local lawyers, C. A. Braley, and Judge J. D. McD. Trimble were brought into the organization. Richard Gentry, a talented engineer,

---

25. *Ibid.*, May 31, 1889.

26. The Kansas City *Star*, September 28, 1947; Stilwell, "I Had a Hunch," December 17, 1927, 96, 98; Stilwell, *Cannibals of Finance*, 45; Rose McMaster, "Origin and Development of the Kansas City Southern Railway Company" (Unpublished Masters Thesis, University of Missouri, 1936), 9–10; Arthur E. Stilwell, *Forty Years of Business Life* (New York: n.p., 1926 [?]), 4.

joined the staff of Stilwell's concern. As construction of the Suburban Belt proceeded, the Trust company furnished short-term loans and provided open account advances. The Terminal Construction Company was actually a "creature" of the Trust. By November of 1889, construction of the Suburban Belt in the East Bottoms was proceeding.

The railroad altered its starting point, deciding not to construct from the Union Station, but from the foot of Broadway at the base of the bluffs in the East Bottoms. The first locomotive arrived in November, and rails were scheduled to be received very shortly.[27] A month later, Stilwell told the press he was "highly pleased" by the progress of the line. For the first time he was identified in the newspaper as "one of the company" constructing the road. The Terminal Construction Company, he told the reporter, had 500 men and 350 teams working on a huge earthen embankment beyond Martin's distillery, as the grade up and out of the Bottom was quite steep. Stilwell further related that he was off to Saint Louis on business—to sell more securities, no doubt.[28]

On December 2, he had been elected first vice-president of the Suburban Belt, and the board of directors voted to ask the stockholders to increase outstanding capital from $500,000 to $1,000,000, with the Trust company to sell the additional mortgage bonds.[29] Construction proceeded slowly, even after the stockholders authorized the additional sale of securities. By April of 1890 it was clear that the Terminal Company would not be able to construct the line, and the contract was repudiated by the railroad. The Suburban Belt assumed the assets and indebtedness of the Terminal Company and resumed construction of the line. The old bonds were canceled, new securities issued, and plans were developed to build the line six miles south along the Blue River.[30]

Stilwell and his associates either underestimated the cost of building and equipping the line, their ability to raise capital, or both, for the project moved very slowly. In May, Suburban Belt directors added two more

27. The Kansas City *Star*, November 7, 1889.
28. *Ibid.*, December 6, 1889.
29. Minute Book, Kansas City Suburban Belt Railroad, December 2, 1889.
30. The Kansas City *Star*, March 26, and April 10, 1890; McMaster, "Origin and Development of the Kansas City Southern," 10–11; H. F. Haag, "A Brief History of the Kansas City Southern Railway System" manuscript (Offices of the Kansas City Southern Railway), 28–29.

Philadelphians to the board, William Lucas and William Waterall, and the next month voted to increase the capital of the road to $1,500,000. Unlike some western railroads which had both offices and directors in the east, the Suburban Belt initially had a local board, though financed by eastern capital. Eventually, however, the board membership began to reflect the sources of capital rather than the sources of enthusiasm. Communication problems grew simultaneously, necessitating constant travel by Stilwell to the east and by the board members to Kansas City.[31]

Construction progressed slowly in the fall and winter of 1890 and the spring of 1891. Not only did the road need capital but also the construction of the belt line was tedious and costly. The grade over Second Street was about 3.5 percent, and crossings over existing lines were expensive. Several railroads protested the crossings necessitated by the belt route, and court cases had to be won before construction could proceed. Only three miles of track had been built in 1890, and none was in operation. A second-hand locomotive was employed in the construction, and it pulled a "directors special" over the line. The "special" consisted of an old coal car with board seats.[32]

In late 1891, however, the railway went into operation with twelve miles of 60- or 70-pound rail from Second Street to Brush Creek and three miles of sidings, and the line began to solicit transfer business. Power was supplied by the construction locomotive, about which little is known, and by two 0-6-0 switch engines purchased from the Baldwin Locomotive Works. Numbers 51 and 52 would provide the Suburban Belt with its principal locomotive power for several years.[33] Martin acted

31. Minute Book, Kansas City Suburban Railroad, May 9, and June 4, 1890; Thomas C. Cochran, *Railroad Leaders, 1845–1890* (New York: Russell and Russell, 1965), 54–55.

32. United States, Interstate Commerce Commission, *Third Annual Report of the Statistics of Railways in the United States* (Washington: Government Printing Office, 1891), 274; Stilwell, "I Had a Hunch," December 17, 1927, 101. The Interstate Commerce Commission *Reports* will be cited hereafter only by title.

33. "All-time Steam Roster of the Kansas City Southern," *Railroad Magazine* LXVIII (April 1957), 74. Locomotives are classified into general types by the number of wheels. The system, designed by Fredric M. Whyte, uses numerical symbols for wheels. The first numeral represents the number of leading wheels, the second figure the number of driving wheels, and the final figure the number of trailing wheels. Thus, a locomotive symbolized as 0–6–0 would have neither leading nor trailing wheels, and have six drivers. The symbol T following the digits

as president of the line and Stilwell as vice-president. The road had issued $1,500,000 in capital stock and $1,000,000 in first-mortgage, 6 percent, 30-year bonds. The Trust company acted as trustee of the bonds.[34] The cost of the road was $2,515,930.26, and the company had assets of $2,632,152.91.[35]

While construction of the Suburban Belt proceeded, Stilwell organized another railroad to build east from Blue River to Independence, Missouri. On January 23, 1891, he and his associates incorporated the Kansas City and Independence Air Line Railway Company with capitalization of $300,000, though this sum was increased shortly. The line would be built by the Kansas City Terminal Construction Company with the Trust company handling the securities. A "prospectus" issued by the construction company advertised $200,000 in bonds to be sold to build the line. The bonds of the railway were to be deposited with the Trust company as a collateral trust mortgage. The "prospectus" claimed that suburban transportation was needed between Kansas City and Independence, and that the existing system consisting of a dummy line and cable cars was overtaxed. The KCIAL promised rapid and comfortable passenger service to commuters. The Terminal Company would build and operate the line from a junction with the KCSB to Independence, and the KCSB agreed to build a passenger terminal in Kansas City which the Air Line would use. A "liberal" contract for trackage rights on five miles of the KCSB had been signed. Equipment would consist of passenger cars manufactured by the Pullman Palace Car Company and Baldwin locomotives, and service would include express trains for businessmen. The "prospectus" promised bond purchasers a return of 5 percent and 3 to 5 percent dividends to stockholders.

The financial arrangements included sale of $200,000 of capital stock in the Terminal Company which would receive $250,000 in 30-year, 5 percent bonds and $100,000 of the capital stock of the Air Line.

---

represents a tank locomotive: a locomotive which does not have a tender but carries its own supply of fuel and water.

34. *Fourth Annual Report of the Statistics of Railways*, 214; Henry V. Poor, *Manual of the Railroads of the United States* (New York: Poor's Publishing Company, 1891), 733. The *Manual* will be cited hereafter as Poor, *Manual*, date and page.

35. Poor, *Manual*, 1892, 752.

The sum of $50,000 in bonds was held for future use, and $200,000 in additional railway stock would be sold to obtain a charter and right of way. For each $100 spent by the Terminal Company, it would receive $125 in bonds and $50 in stock of the KCIAL.[36] This arrangement was quite common in the era—the use of the construction company to build the line with a collateral trust mortgage as security.

Stilwell revealed the alleged source of the name of the Air Line in his memoirs. When told by an associate that the survey of the six-mile route was the "crookedest line I ever saw," he replied, "That being the case, we'll call it the Kansas City-Independence Air Line." As usual, Stilwell got the cart in front of the horse, as passenger cars for the Air Line arrived in August of 1891, months before the railroad was completed. Legal disputes over the right of way held up the construction for a period. Financing and construction through the Terminal Company proved inadequate, and in 1892 the Suburban Belt accepted $500,000 in capital stock and $300,000 in bonds of the Air Line to complete construction to Independence.[37]

With typical overstatement and optimism, Stilwell announced plans for a passenger depot for his fledgling rail lines, a station to be called Grand Central and located at the foot of Wyandotte Street. Constructed at a cost of $65,000, the three-story structure was an impressive edifice, especially for two railroads with virtually no passenger traffic. Nevertheless, a cable-car route from the business district was extended to the site, and the station opened with great fanfare.[38] Residents of the city, visitors, and dignitaries arrived at the opening celebration in gigs, victorias, buggies, and traps to hear speakers proclaim the glories of Kansas City and its railways.

36. Records of Minutes, Kansas City and Independence Air Line Railway Company, January 23, 1891 (Office of the Kansas City Southern Railway); Jefferson City *Daily Tribune*, January 24, 1891; "Prospectus of the Kansas City Terminal Construction Company in Connection with the Kansas City and Independence Air Line," (Anderson Scrapbooks, Missouri Valley Room, Kansas City Public Library, Kansas City, Missouri).

37. Stilwell, "I Had a Hunch," December 17, 1927, 10; the Kansas City *Star*, August 4, and December 31, 1891; Haag, "A Brief History of the Kansas City Southern," 30–31.

38. The Kansas City *Star*, February 1, and October 14, 1892, and September 28, 1947. The station was razed in 1932; Kansas City *Times*, November 25, 1932.

Grand Central Station would not only receive passengers from the Suburban Belt and the Air Line, but also from another Stilwell road, the Consolidated Terminal Railroad Company of Kansas City. On May 19, 1891, the Consolidated Terminal was formed to build westward from the depot at Second and Wyandotte to the Kansas-Missouri state line, a distance of two miles. The company was capitalized at $750,000, with the stock equally divided among Martin, Stilwell, Mosher, Trimble, and four others. The capital was issued in the form of 30-year, first-mortgage gold bonds, at 5 percent interest. On August 24, 1891, the Terminal Construction Company accepted these bonds as payment for the construction of the line, and the securities were deposited with the Trust company as a collateral trust mortgage.[39] One Kansas City newspaper denounced the line and published rumors about its financial arrangements. Stilwell, as vice-president of the Terminal Company, responded to the press report:

I hope no one will connect us with such gross exaggeration. The assertions made . . . are false. It will do us harm and the railroad companies will think we are the biggest liars in the universe. . . . I trust nothing more of such character will be published.[40]

The Terminal Construction Company sold bonds for the railroad and began to build westward. Between the Second Street station and the state line the Terminal had to cross a number of existing railroads and overcome a serious grade into the West Bottoms. The narrow strip of land connecting the East and West Bottoms was occupied by the double track of the Missouri Pacific. According to Stilwell, the engineers he hired could not find a suitable crossing. He went home, wrestled with the problem, and retired to bed. "Curiously enough," he wrote in his memoirs, "even after I had fallen asleep my mind went right on with the difficult task to which I had set it." The "vision" he saw was a line crossing above the Missouri Pacific railway on a set of piers. He rushed to the office the next morning and the engineers confirmed the feasibility of the plan.[41]

39. Minute Book, Consolidated Terminal Railway Company of Kansas City, May 19, 1891 (Office of the Kansas City Southern Railway); Jefferson City *Daily Tribune*, May 22, 1891; Haag, "A Brief History of the Kansas City Southern," 29–30.
40. The Kansas City *Star*, May 23, 1891.
41. Stilwell, "I Had a Hunch," December 17, 1927, 101–102.

Dramatic, yes, but logical, no. It seems unlikely that his subconscious, lacking access to much knowledge of surveying or engineering, would provide the answer. The excellent railway engineering talent in his organization undoubtedly provided the concept needed to reach the West Bottoms.

Only one and one half miles of the Consolidated had been completed, when on July 25, 1892, it was merged into the Suburban Belt. The merger led to a new company, the Kansas City Suburban Belt *Railroad* Company, which was capitalized at $2,250,000. Work on the road to the state line continued.[42]

Stilwell pushed the Consolidated west across the Bottoms toward the Kansas line to connect with yet another project, the Union Terminal Railroad Company. Many of the major railroads into Kansas City, such as the Santa Fe, had their yards and facilities at Argentine, Kansas. To tap this possible source of traffic, Stilwell sought to build a railway from Argentine east to connect with the Consolidated and the rest of his belt line. Chartered in Missouri on March 27, 1889, the Union Terminal had remained dormant until December 30, 1891, when a Kansas charter was received and it began to construct the line with a capitalization of $3,000,000. In July of 1892, $690,000 of Union Terminal 30-year bonds were issued to the Suburban Belt for which the latter company agreed to guarantee payment of principal and interest on $2,000,000 of 5 percent bonds to complete the line. The Suburban Belt also received $1,750,000 in capital stock of the Union Terminal. As in all the Stilwell projects, original capitalization had been immediately increased to pay for construction.[43]

The Union Terminal began construction east from Argentine to a bridge across the Kaw River linking up to the Suburban Belt. Two Baldwin locomotives, 0-6-0 switchers numbers 53 and 55, were acquired in 1894, and the next year a third, number 58, arrived. Locomotive number

---

42. Haag, "A Brief History of the Kansas City Southern," 29–30; McMaster, "Origin and Development of the Kansas City Southern," 11–12; Poor, *Manual*, 1893, 794.

43. Records of Minutes, Union Terminal Railroad Company, March 29, 1889 (Office of the Kansas City Southern); Haag, "A Brief History of the Kansas City Southern," 30–31.

56, a Baldwin 2-4-4T was acquired in 1893. These four engines shifted the cars received by the Consolidated from the railroad yards, stockyards, and slaughter houses at Argentine.[44]

One goal of Stilwell's Suburban Belt was to become involved in the lucrative flour and grain business of Kansas City. The established rail lines controlled access to the grain elevators in the area, so on January 15, 1892, Stilwell formed the Missouri Elevator and Terminal Company. The company issued 1,000 shares of stock with Stilwell, Mosher, and two others owning ten shares each, with Stilwell acting as trustee for the remaining 960 shares. The Missouri Elevator Company acquired the "Star" elevator from the Second Street Improvement Company, another Stilwell enterprise, and also purchased the "Eclypse" and "Diamond" elevators. These elevators allowed the Suburban Belt access to storage facilities for incoming grain shipments. On September 8, 1892, the Suburban Belt entered into a contract with the Second Street Improvement Company to build the "Exchange" and "Sun" elevators on the railroad. The Suburban Belt agreed to pay 6 percent per annum on costs over and above insurance and taxes. All of the elevators came under control of the Suburban Belt on September 26, 1892, when the capital stock of the Missouri Elevator was acquired. Stilwell's Belt Line now had a very sizable storage facility and soon had a rather extensive grain trade in Kansas City.[45]

Meanwhile, another promotion finally became operative. On March 18, 1892, the Air Line to Independence opened for revenue traffic. The Air Line extended only 5.6 miles but had a capital stock of $300,000 and a funded debt in five percent first-mortgage bonds of $300,000. The railway had purchased three Baldwin locomotives in 1892, numbers 101, 102, and 103. They were 2-4-4T tank engines, quite useful for short hauls and switching duties. As the line was primarily for suburban passenger service, six new passenger cars had been acquired from the Jackson and Sharpe Company. The officers of the Air Line were Mosher as president, Martin as first vice president, and Stilwell as second vice president.[46]

---

44. "All-time Steam Roster of the Kansas City Southern," 74.

45. Records, Missouri Elevator and Terminal Company, January 15, and September 26, 1892 (Office of the Kansas City Southern Railway); Haag, "A Brief History of the Kansas City Southern," 31–32.

46. Poor, *Manual*, 1892, 750 and 1152; "All-time Steam Roster of the Kansas City Southern," 74.

That the Air Line was enormously over-capitalized is apparent, but the situation grew worse. The stockholders voted to increase the capital stock to $500,000 and the bonded indebtedness an additional $200,000 in second-mortgage bonds, then authorized the sale of the line to the Suburban Belt. The Suburban Belt acquired the railway, and the original investors reaped a sizable windfall in securities of the belt line. On January 24, 1893, the Suburban Belt increased its capital to $2,750,000 and authorized an exchange of stock with the Air Line on a dollar-for-dollar basis. It also guaranteed the $200,000 second mortgage.[47]

Constant expansion of the Suburban Belt had yet to produce a profit. In the year ending December 31, 1892, the line lost $36,095.53, bringing the total deficit to $76,991.60. The belt had forty miles of line in operation or near completion, but it failed to pay either operating costs or fixed charges. The investors received stock dividends of 2 percent in 1893 and again in 1894, while the capital stock was increased to $4,750,000 in the latter year. Only in 1894 did the Suburban Belt show a profit, and even then rail operations showed a loss, while miscellaneous receipts provided enough income to offset this deficit.[48]

Construction on the western extension of the belt subsidiaries slowly continued, and then was stopped because of opposition by other railroads. The Union Terminal had already purchased three locomotives, six passenger cars, and seventy freight cars for a line only three miles long. Its capitalization of $2,000,000 indicates the extraordinary costs of the line through the heavily industrialized area of the West Bottoms. The Union Terminal faced constant opposition from the Union Pacific and the Missouri Pacific railroads which opposed any loss of traffic to this upstart, and the installations of crossings where the lines intersected. One night, a large crew of men from the Terminal tore up a portion of the track of the Missouri Pacific to lay a crossing. The Missouri Pacific, hearing of this action, moved six locomotives to the site and placed them on that portion of the trackage not yet removed, simultaneously obtaining a court injunction against further action by the Union Terminal. The latter company appealed to the Kansas Supreme Court. The Kansas Court finally

47. The Kansas City *Star*, November 29, 1892; *Commercial and Financial Chronicle*, December 10, 1892, 995.
48. Poor, *Manual*, 1893, 331–332, 794–795 and 1894, 223–224; Haag, "A Brief History of the Kansas City Southern," 32–33.

decided to allow the Union Terminal to cross the tracks of the protesting Missouri Pacific and Union Pacific, a decision upheld by a federal court in Saint Louis. Construction began at once.

The linking of the Terminal and the Belt created a new route for the exchange of stock cars as well as a commuter line for packing-house employees.[49]

The new road will be a great thing for the workingmen of the packing-house districts. It will enable them cheaply and expeditiously to reach the low-priced, open, healthful suburban lands, which are now, however desireable, out of the question on account of the time required to reach them. But it is in its purely commercial aspects that the great circling belt is most striking. It reaches all of the packing houses; taps every railroad entering the city; and reaches the stockyards on both sides of the river. It reaches seven of the city's ten grain elevators, and commands three-fourths of the entire local grain business.[50]

The route to Argentine opened in 1895, and through trains were operated east to Independence. A foundry, a rice mill, and other new facilities were located on the Belt line and provided additional traffic. The Belt continued to increase its interchange of cars with lines entering Kansas City.[51]

The Air Line to Independence lost money, and Stilwell came up with a scheme to provide additional revenue. Stilwell decided to establish an amusement resort on the Air Line. He gave the site the name Fairmount Park; presumably he was influenced by the beautiful park by the same name in Philadelphia, the source of his capital. The railroad obtained a lease on fifty acres of land covered with trees and created a small lake on the property by damming a creek. As the hot winds blew across Kansas raising the temperatures in the city to unbearable levels, crowds flocked to the beach on the lake and the nearby picnic pavillion. Small bungalows were constructed and rented to vacationers, with dining facilities provided in a large hall. The absence of developed parks in Kansas City encouraged excursionists to travel to Fairmount Park. Special Sunday trains were scheduled on the Air Line to haul the pleasure seekers. Stilwell initiated

49. Poor, *Manual*, 1894, 224; *Commercial and Financial Chronicle*, November 17, 1894, 879; the Kansas City *Star*, March 25, 1895.

50. Kansas City *Times*, quoted in the *Commercial and Financial Chronicle*, March 23, 1895, 525.

51. *Commercial and Financial Chronicle, Investors Supplement*, April 1895, 70–72.

an annual horse show which was held at the park, attracting entries from Kansas City and the surrounding region. The first horse show was held in September of 1895. The boxes in the grandstand were filled with members of leading Kansas City families and officials of the various Stilwell companies. The Stilwells occupied a box where they entertained guests and stockholders in the firms. By 1896, the park had become the site of a Chautauqua, and Stilwell brought the "Great Commoner," William Jennings Bryan, to the resort. The Suburban Belt formed a subsidiary to operate the facility, but it proved unprofitable and the park was ultimately abandoned in 1904.[52]

By 1895, the Stilwell empire in Kansas City had been completed. He had built more than forty miles of belt railway from Argentine, Kansas, east across the West Bottoms to the East Bottoms and on across the north side of Kansas City to Independence. A branch extended south along the east side of the city to Brush Creek. The belt did not encircle the city but ran through the major industrial areas and connected with all the local railroads. Subsidiary enterprises contributed to the income of the Suburban Belt; particularly important were the grain elevators. The entire system had been financed by overcapitalization and by selling bonds at a discount and providing bonuses of common stock. Stilwell and his associates controlled the system through the Trust company and the Terminal Construction Company. Both of these enterprises profited from the operation; the Trust company received fees for selling bonds and for trustee work, and the construction company gained through the sale of securities and by, apparently, overcharging for construction. The city gained an important belt line, however, and the railway provided access to the city for other railroads, including several Stilwell would later promote. If the total cost of these projects had been known at the outset, it is doubtful that their securities could have been sold.

Stilwell always claimed that the Kansas City lines were not only profitable but that the investors made considerable gains through the appreciation of stock values.[53] Official reports of the earnings of the Su-

---

52. Minutes of the Fairmount Amusement Company, July 26, 1895 (Office of the Kansas City Southern Railway); Stilwell, "I Had a Hunch," December 17, 1927, 101; the Kansas City *Star*, March 30, August 12, 1893 and September 4, 1895; Kansas City *World*, July 30, 1899; New York *Times*, September 5, 1897.
53. Stilwell, *Cannibals of Finance*, 45–46.

burban Belt and its subsidiaries suggest otherwise. Between 1892 and 1902, the Suburban Belt lost $293,461.48 and the Air Line accumulated a deficit of $182,932.64. Even the Missouri Elevator and Terminal lost money—$19,758.25—as did Fairmount Park. The total ten-year deficit for the system was $1,013,111.66.[54] The failure of the projects to generate profits did not alienate the original investors or prevent them from placing more money in Stilwell's enterprises. Many of his associates were simultaneously investing in a promotion far more costly in dollars and far larger in scope; Arthur Stilwell had decided to build a railroad from Kansas City to the Gulf of Mexico.

54. United States, Interstate Commerce Commission, *Valuation Report*, LXXV, 377–378.

IV

TO THE GULF

ARTHUR STILWELL never gave credit for the conceptualization of his schemes to anyone other than himself. The idea was always his, and carrying out the project was always his work; yet any failure was consistently the fault of others. In deciding to build a railroad from Kansas City to the Gulf of Mexico, Stilwell recalled in his memoirs that the inspiration came as the result of the economic situation in the midwest and a "hunch." He wrote,

I had been reading much about the terrible financial conditions in the Middle West. Kansas and Nebraska were in distress. Mortgages were being foreclosed hourly. Corn was fifteen cents a bushel and being burned for fuel. Wheat was thirty-five cents a bushel. Farmers were having a fearful time keeping their heads above water and many of them were in dire want. What was the basis of all this suffering? . . . I analyzed every scrap of data relating to the situation I could obtain and finally made up my mind that the misery of the West was due to the unjust prices the farmers had to pay for the transportation of grain for export.[1]

It would be hard to fault Stilwell's description of the economic plight of the Midwest and Great Plains in the late 1880s and early 1890s, although his analysis of the cause is in error. Farmers were sorely pressed as falling prices of agricultural commodities and soaring credit charges

---

1. Arthur E. Stilwell and James R. Crowell, "I Had a Hunch," *The Saturday Evening Post*, CC (December 3, 1927), 168.

combined with overproduction to threaten their position in the market place. As midwestern farmers began to revolt against these conditions— other than overproduction—which were threatening their existence, they accused the railroads of grossly overcharging them to transport agricultural products. Stilwell proposed a solution to this alleged problem:

> My life's greatest resolution came to me in this hour. I, a struggling young insurance man, unknown and unheralded, would go West, build a railroad to a Southern port as an outlet for export shipments, reduce the cost of transportation at least one-third and help redeem this great stretch of territory which was staggering under the burden of corporate greed. The magnitude of the resolution did not apail me. I believed not only that the thing could be done but that I could do it. And yet I was not the world's prime egotist or an irresponsible visionary. Let me explain it in the way which seems most logical. Let me say simply that I had a hunch. . . . I had a hunch I could build a railroad. All the small successes I had gained thus far in life had found beginnings in hunches. All the more important things I was to do in later years came about the same way.[2]

Given the scope of the project and Stilwell's publicity-creating techniques, he remained unknown and unhearlded only briefly, and without his ego and vision the project would have perished. But he failed in his analysis to concede, or even mention, that the idea of a railroad from Kansas City to the Gulf did not originate with him.

From its earliest days, Kansas City grew as the result of its railroad connections. The business leaders of the community labored mightily to secure charters, land grants, and local financial subsidies for railroads in their efforts to create a city on the bluffs above the Missouri. Largely through their efforts, rail lines were obtained and the city triumphed over its less fortunate rivals. As the town promoters and businessmen of Kansas City laid out their grandiose rail schemes, one connection they plumped for was a line to the Gulf. A master transportation plan in the 1850s included such a railway, and a number of romantically named railroads— the New Orleans, Shreveport, and Kansas City and the Kansas City, Galveston & Lake Superior—were chartered.[3] William Gilpin, a promoter of epoch vision, proposed a railroad from Independence, Missouri, to Galveston on the Gulf as a means to escape dependence upon the East, a

2. *Ibid.*
3. A. Theodore Brown, *Frontier Community Kansas City to 1870* (Columbia: University of Missouri Press, 1963), 119, 126.

THE KANSAS CITY, PITTSBURG AND GULF RAILROAD

notion that prevailed until the end of the nineteenth century. Another local promoter, Johnston Lykins, argued for a north-south rail route to open the coal mining areas of Missouri and Indian Territory and the rice- and cotton-growing areas of Louisiana and Texas to Kansas City trade.[4] In the pre–Civil War period such men as Senator Thomas Hart Benton called for linking Kansas City to the Gulf, and the legislature of Louisiana in 1857 created the New Orleans, Shreveport and Kansas City railroad to connect those cities.[5] This was but one of many such stillborn railways.

In the three decades after the Civil War, Kansas City community leaders continued to call for a direct rail line to deep water on the Gulf. The future of the city rested on the expansion of its rail network and the competition each new connection would, it was hoped, bring. The hopes for competition among the railroads entering the city, however, were dashed by the growth of railroad pools and the uniform rates established by pooling agreements. As a result, community leaders attacked the "monopolistic" railroads and encouraged the construction of a new route to the Gulf of Mexico to disrupt the pools. Direct shipment of midwestern grain through Galveston or Sabine Pass, Texas, or Lake Charles, Louisiana, would, they thought, break the hold of the eastern railroads. The line to deep water became a dream of the leaders of Kansas City.[6]

The Kansas City Board of Trade sent representatives to Galveston in 1874 to make arrangements for shipping grain through that port over the Missouri, Kansas and Texas and Houston and Texas Central railroads, but the attempt to create a major export facility failed. Grain dealers and merchants nevertheless continued to send as much business as possible through the Gulf, and an effort to build a direct rail line remained a major aspect of local transportation policy.[7]

As the monopolistic tendencies of the midwestern railroads continued unabated, even after the creation of the Interstate Commerce Commission, businessmen and farmers agitated for a new railway to break

4. Charles N. Glaab, *Kansas City and the Railroads* (Madison: The State Historical Society of Wisconsin, 1962), 28, 32.

5. *Engineering News*, February 17, 1898; Rose McMaster, "Origin and Development of the Kansas City Southern Railway Company," (unpublished masters thesis, University of Missouri, 1936), 4–5.

6. Glaab, *Kansas City and Railroads*, 175–176, 187–188.

7. *Ibid.*, 177, 190–192; *The Railroad Gazette*, June 13, 1874.

the strangle hold of Kansas City's eastern connections. The Commercial Club endorsed a proposed railroad through Indian Territory and Texas to force down rates, and subsequently the Kansas City and Sabine Pass Railway was incorporated. The KCSP would be an "airline," only 700 miles long with new facilities to be constructed at Sabine Pass, a small port near the Texas-Louisiana border. As with many such schemes, this one died without a mile of track being constructed. Later, the Populist party agitated for a line to deep water, agreeing with Stilwell that the farmers were paying a premium to ship their goods and that millions of dollars could be saved.[8] Thus, one of the primary reasons for building a Gulf line from Kansas City would be to circumvent the long and costly shipment of grain to the east and lower the costs to farmers and grain dealers.

Other factors in building a line south of Kansas City would be to open up additional natural resources and to expand the trade territory of the city. In Missouri, Arkansas, and Indian Territory were large deposits of coal and in Arkansas and Louisiana were thousands of acres of timber, both areas being largely undeveloped. To farmers and businessmen in the treeless Great Plains, the opportunity to acquire access to the timber of south central and southwestern Louisiana had a magnetic appeal. The longleaf pine of Louisiana could house both the farmer and the urbanite at a much lower cost, if only transportation could be provided.[9]

Other men had tried to promote such a railway, and some with modest success, but only Stilwell would carry the project to fruition. J. B. Watkins and Company of Lawrence, Kansas, a major land broker in the Kansas City hinterland, purchased more than a million acres of timberland in Louisiana and constructed a rail line, the Kansas City, Watkins and Gulf, north from Lake Charles to Alexandria. The depression of 1893, however, brought about the failure of the Watkins Company which col-

8. New York *Times*, August 18, 1887, September 2, and December 4 and 5, 1893; the Kansas City *Star*, November 2, 1889; *The Railroad Gazette*, September 20, 1889.

9. Arthur E. Stilwell, *Forty Years of Business Life*, (New York: n.p., 1926 [?]), 5; *Engineering News*, February 17, 1898; M. H. Chamberlin, *Needed Railways in Southern Missouri and Northern Arkansas* (St. Louis: Merry & Nicholson, 1891); M. B. Hillyard, *The New South* (Baltimore: Manufacturer's Record Co., 1887), 308; Charles S. Sargent, *Report on the Forests of North America* (Washington: Government Printing Office, 1884), 537, 543–544.

lapsed the next year holding $17,000,000 in farm mortgages.[10] Even as the Watkins Company failed, Arthur Stilwell kept his project alive and expanding. "I worked with the spirit of a crusader," he wrote later. "Was I not fighting a wonderful battle?"[11] Although one Kansas City historian has stated that "The time for spectacular railroad enterprises was past," the promotion of the line to the Gulf by Stilwell proved to have all of the characteristics of a "spectacular" scheme.[12]

Stilwell and E. L. Martin dreamed of a larger rail enterprise even as they constructed the belt railways around Kansas City. Martin urged that they turn their attention to the extensive coal fields at Hume, Missouri, about eighty miles south of Kansas City. They formed a syndicate which purchased considerable acreage in the Hume area and began to seek capital to construct a railroad to their holdings. From the outset, Stilwell urged that Hume not be the terminus of the project but only a station on a longer line to Pittsburg, Kansas, or Joplin, Missouri. Attempting to temper Stilwell's ebullient enthusiasm, Martin raised the question of finance, but the promoter was not to be denied. Despite the tremendous commitment of time and treasure to the Trust company and the belt lines, a new company was formed to build a railroad south from Kansas City.[13]

On August 2, 1887, the Kansas City, Rich Hill and Southern Railroad Company was incorporated to build a line eighty miles long from Kansas City to Rich Hill, a site near Hume. Capitalization of $2,000,000 was authorized, with E. L. Martin acting as president of the company. During the next two years, the KCRHS languished as Stilwell and Martin concentrated their attention on other projects. Construction was never initiated, although portions of the road were located and surveyed.[14] Without a sizable influx of capital, the project looked hopeless.

10. Ray Ginger, *Age of Excess* (New York: The Macmillan Company, 1965), 63–69; Allan G. Bogue, "The Administrative and Policy Problems of the J. B. Watkins Land Mortgage Company, 1873–1894," *Bulletin of the Business Historical Society*, XXVII (March 1953), 56.

11. Arthur E. Stilwell, *Cannibals of Finance* (Chicago: Farnum Publishing Company, 1912), 48–50.

12. Brown, *Frontier Community*, 229.

13. Stilwell, "I Had a Hunch," December 31, 1927, 24.

14. Minute Book, Kansas City, Rich Hill and Southern Railroad Company, September 7, 1887 (Offices of the Kansas City Southern Railway, Kansas City, Missouri); Jefferson City *Daily Tribune*, August 4, 1887.

Stilwell and Martin turned to their Philadelphia and Kansas City investors for the funds to start the line south. Stilwell felt that the 20 percent commission required by New York City and Philadelphia investment houses to sell the securities would deprive the company of its profits; he decided to sell the securities himself. Once again he traveled east where he had become known as the "whirlwind stock salesman of the West." Stilwell claimed that it was not the force of his personality that made him a successful salesman, but his honesty. He placed his own money in his schemes and never sold anything, he said, unless he was convinced of its merits.[15] Regardless of the method used, he attracted enough capital to proceed with the project, and two new corporations were established to carry it out.

On November 6, 1889, the State of Missouri issued articles of incorporation to the Kansas City, Nevada and Fort Smith Railroad, and authorized capitalization of $3,000,000. Martin served as president of the company and Stilwell as vice-president, and their Kansas City associates William Taylor, Churchill White, J. McD. Trimble and William Woods served as officers or directors. Twelve Philadelphians purchased stock in the company and elected three of their number to the board of directors. Richard Gentry, a major stockholder, became the general manager and a member of the board. Martin announced that within a month construction would commence, the line would extend from Kansas City to Monett, 170 miles, rails had been purchased, and entrance to Kansas City would be over the Belt Line. Construction of the railway was to be accomplished by the Missouri Coal and Construction Company, the second new firm created by Stilwell and Martin.[16]

The Missouri Coal and Construction Company had been chartered on November 2, 1889, for the purposes of holding and improving real estate, selling mortgages, constructing and equipping railroads in Missouri and elsewhere, mining and marketing coal, and selling construction materials. Stilwell obtained a charter to deal with all aspects of his scheme. The capitalization of $800,000 was divided into 8,000 shares of $100 par value with the entire amount subscribed and one half paid. The division

15. Stilwell, "I Had a Hunch," December 31, 1927, 24 and January 14, 1928, 77.
16. The Kansas City *Star*, November 7, 1889; Minute Book, Kansas City, Nevada and Fort Smith Railroad, July 26, 1891 (Offices of the Kansas City Southern Railway).

of the stock suggests the nature of the promotion and the pivotal role of Stilwell. Martin took 850 shares, as did Woods, Gentry, and White, while other investors took from 3 to 100 shares each. Stilwell held the latter figure in his own name, but as trustee he controlled 4,316 shares. When the board of directors met six days after the company received its charter, four of the Kansas Citians resigned from the board to be replaced by three Philadelphians—William Waterall, W. H. Lucas and B. F. Hobart—and by Ezra Bowen of Burlington, New Jersey. A portion of the stock Stilwell controlled as trustee had been sold in the east, and the purchasers simply exercised their financial power. The Missouri Coal and Construction Company also acquired from the syndicate 3,000 acres of coal lands in Bates County, Missouri, near the proposed terminus of the line.[17] The new line was financed in the same manner as the belt railroads; the construction company issued a collateral trust mortgage through the Trust company, with the larger profits falling to the stockholders of the construction operation.

The directors of the Kansas City, Nevada and Fort Smith moved quickly to initiate the construction of Stilwell's "hunch." On January 10, 1890, the company signed a contract with the Missouri Coal and Construction Company to build and equip the line, with the railroad to pay $20,000 in bonds for each mile constructed. In addition, the railroad would pay the construction company $3,113,000 in stock. The KCNFS directors also voted to pay the KCRHS $240,000 for its franchise, surveys, and right of way. The construction company then purchased the stock and assets of the KCNFS for $1.00, agreeing to construct a "first-class single-track railroad," from Brush Creek, the end of the Belt Line, to Monett, Missouri. The contracts were signed by Martin as president of the KCNFS and by Stilwell as vice-president of the construction company. The latter corporation became the instrument for actually laying track and a source of income for the incorporators. The Kansas City men received rather handsome salaries—Martin received $3,000 annually, Stilwell, White, and Taylor $1,200 each, and Richard Gentry $4,000 for

---

17. Minute Book, Missouri Coal and Construction Company, November 2 and 8, 1889 (Offices of the Kansas City Southern Railway); the Kansas City *Star*, November 7, 1889.

his engineering work. The corporate labyrinth grew as the construction company voted to rent a room in the Missouri, Kansas and Texas Trust Company building for $600 a year. Again, the multiplication of corporations was proving profitable to Stilwell's original creation.[18] With a strident call for subscribers to pay their obligations, the directors adjourned the meeting, and Arthur Stilwell left immediately for Philadelphia.

The Philadelphians who would provide the capital for the construction company approved the financial arrangements but had to be sold on the project itself. Richard Gentry surveyed the line, a distance of about 125 miles, declared it could be built for $1,000,000, and issued a report which claimed that potential coal and timber revenues "looked good." A delegation from Kansas City rushed the report to Waterall, John Lowber Welsh, and E. T. Stotesbury in Philadelphia.[19] Convinced of the viability of the railroad, the Philadelphians paid their pledges, and Gentry began laying track.

The line crept slowly southward from Grandview toward Amoret. To avoid building a costly line, trackage rights were obtained on an existing railway between Grandview and Brush Creek. Gentry laid ten miles of rail by October 10, and the company purchased four passenger cars and 120 freight cars from the St. Charles Car Company and two 2-6-0 locomotives from the Baldwin Locomotive Works. Even as the line developed, Stilwell embarked on an additional project which would come to characterize all of his rail schemes; he began to promote townsites along the route.[20]

The involvement of railroad promoters in nonrailroad enterprises was characteristic of southern and western railway schemes. An additional income for stock and bond purchasers, a potential source of revenue, and a bonus for the promoter, the townsites proved financially beneficial to many involved in the railroad enterprise. By the fall of 1890, Stilwell

---

18. Minute Book, Kansas City, Rich Hill and Southern Railroad Company, January 11, 1890; Minute Book, Missouri Coal and Construction Company, January 11, 1890; McMaster, "Origin and Development of the Kansas City Southern," 15–16.

19. Minute Book, Missouri Coal and Construction Company, January 15 and 22, 1890.

20. *Ibid.*, April 28 and October 23, 1890.

began selling lots at the townsites of Amoret and Stuart City. He reported land sales of $33,500 at the two locations, a small sum, but extremely important to a project already desperately searching for capital.[21]

Gentry completed the line from Grandview to Amoret—45.6 miles —in December of 1891, but the construction company had to borrow $200,000 in order to open the railway. The officers took severe salary cuts, with Stilwell, Taylor and White receiving no compensation. By May of the next year the company was reduced to short term borrowing to finish the line to Hume. The Missouri, Kansas and Texas Trust lent the struggling construction company $55,000 at 8 percent for eight months. By October 1, the line to Hume had been completed, but financial difficulties mounted.[22]

When the board of directors of the construction company met on January 29, 1892, it was a gloomy picture the officers described. The company had acquired additional equipment, including another locomotive and 50 coal cars, but the coal business proved less than successful. Although the company owned a sizable coal mine at Amoret, the coal had proved to be of low quality and sales were minimal. A recent loan of $55,000 had been obtained from the Provident Life and Trust Company, but loans totaling $305,000 were already outstanding to that firm in addition to a debt of $255,000 at the Bank of Commerce in Kansas City. Further, operations of the company for 1891 showed a deficit. Ninety percent of the business had been northbound, consisting primarily of coal, livestock, and wheat; there was no southbound traffic. Taking on nearly every characteristic of an entreprenuerial error, the project appeared doomed, until Stilwell urged additional construction. He proposed an extension of twenty miles to a connection with the Missouri, Kansas and Texas Railroad, which at that time lacked direct access to Kansas City. The directors voted their approval, and pledged additional capital.[23]

In January and February of 1892, financial control of the construction company and the KCNFS passed out of the hands of the Kansas Citians and into the hands of the Philadelphians. The construction company directors voted to increase its capital to $3,500,000; the original

21. *Ibid.*
22. *Ibid.*, December 21, 1890, and May 26, 1891.
23. *Ibid.*, January 29, 1892.

stockholders would receive $200,000; the sum of $600,000 was earmarked for construction of 50 miles of track south of Hume; and $400,000 was set aside for an additional 50 miles of track. The Trust company would sell the stock, receiving a commission of 5 percent on the sales but would be allowed to take the total commission out of the first 10 percent of the shares sold. A copy of the decision was sent to Stotesbury and Welsh, who were elected to the boards of both the railroad and the construction company. Stotesbury's response in a letter to Martin bristled with anger concerning the sales agreement and demanded that the increase in capitalization be reduced to $2,500,000 and that the Trust company receive 5 percent on each bloc of stock as it was sold. The board met, rescinded its action of January 29, and followed the plan sent by Stotesbury.[24] Stilwell and Martin continued to direct the project; however, the purse strings were absolutely controlled by the investors in the east. A major change had indeed taken place.

On July 21, 1892, an item in the Kansas City *Star* revealed that another substantial change had taken place in the development of the Kansas City, Nevada and Fort Smith; the line would be built to "salt water." From a short, coal-hauling, feeder railway, the KCNFS would become a means for Kansas City to reach the Gulf of Mexico by a new direct rail route. This, of course, had been Stilwell's hope from the beginning.

The same newspaper account announced that a contract had been signed to build the line from Hume on to Pittsburg, Kansas. Pittsburg, an important coal-mining and zinc-smelting center, would be reached in sixty days, the optimistic report continued, and would give the KCNFS a route of 112 miles. A subsidiary, the Kansas City, Pittsburg and Western Railroad Company was incorporated in Kansas to build that portion of the line in that state. The promoters acted quickly to construct the line and put it in operation, as the city of Pittsburg was to provide a subsidy of $40,000, and, in return, the railroad agreed to locate its shops there. In the fall of 1892, the Trust company sold $300,000 in securities and, at Stilwell's urging, the money was allocated for construction of the line to Pittsburg. When bond sales accelerated in January of 1893, the directors

24. *Ibid.*, February 20, 1892; Minute Book, Kansas City, Nevada and Fort Smith Railroad, February 1, 1892.

agreed that construction from Pittsburg to Joplin, Missouri, should proceed.[25]

Even as the KCNFS extended its operations, it was clear that all was not well. Costs mounted as the line purchased land for yard and locomotive facilities in Kansas City and acquired three more Baldwin locomotives and eighty-three additional freight cars. General Manager Gentry reported that the KCNFS had a deficit of $5,968 for 1892, only somewhat less than the deficit of $7,734.11 for 1891. The line was not paying its way, and fixed charges were still being deferred. While the railroad was not proving profitable, the parent company—the Missouri Coal and Construction Company—undoubtedly was. The investors in the construction operation determined to plunge ahead, and Stilwell constantly provided ideas for further development.[26]

At the director's meeting of the construction company on December 3, 1892, Stilwell proposed that the name of the railroad be changed to the Kansas City, Pittsburg and Gulf, and that a route to deep water be built through Pittsburg, Joplin, Fort Smith, Texarkana, and Shreveport to Sabine Pass in Texas. The directors agreed, and surveyors were sent into the field. The KCPG or "Pee Gee," became the primary vehicle in Stilwell's plan to reach the Gulf.[27]

Recognizing the extraordinary costs of the expanded project, Stilwell and Martin moved to raise the substantial capital that was needed. Stilwell thought a new construction company should be created with capitalization of $2,500,000. Martin concurred but raised the practical question of where the money was to come from. The indefatigable promoter said simply that he planned to call the new operation the Philadelphia Construction Company and that the money would be acquired in that

25. Ira Clark, *Then Came the Railroads* (Norman: University of Oklahoma Press, 1958), 196; the Kansas City *Star*, July 21, 1892; McMaster, "Origin and Development of the Kansas City Southern Railway," 16–17; Minute Book, Missouri Coal and Construction Company, September 10 and December 3, 1892, and January 26, 1893.

26. Minute Book, Missouri Coal and Construction Company, January 26, 1893; H. V. Poor, *Manual of the Railroads of the United States* (New York: Poor's Publishing Company, 1892), 1040–1041. Cited hereafter as Poor, *Manual*, date and page.

27. The Kansas City *Star*, December 3, 1892; Minute Book, Missouri Coal and Construction Company, December 3, 1892.

city. The plan actually carried out, however, provided for the Philadelphia Company to purchase the Missouri Coal and Construction Company for $2,498,900 by issuing 24,989 shares of $100 par value stock. The Philadelphia Company accepted the contract between the KCPG and the Missouri Construction Company and agreed to build and equip a line to Fort Smith or beyond for a flat fee of $25,000 per mile. The railroad would pay for the construction with 6 percent gold first mortgage bonds payable at the offices of Provident Life in Philadelphia. At the meeting of the Missouri firm on August 23, 1893, Stilwell moved approval of the sale, with the proceeds to be distributed to the stockholders; the resolution was unanimously approved.[28]

During the period from January to September of 1893, work on the KCPG from Pittsburg to Joplin proceeded. Even as Stilwell traveled back and forth to Philadelphia and up and down the proposed route, he still was not credited with being the prime mover in the operation. The local press referred to the KCPG as "Martin's Road." Stilwell, however, made the financial and construction arrangements. He placed most of the Philadelphia Construction Company stock in Philadelphia, but investors in St. Louis, Boston, New York, and New Haven also purchased stock. He sold the stock for $66 per $100 share, with the Missouri, Kansas and Texas Trust receiving a $6 per share commission. He also worked with Gentry to keep construction costs low; he placed an order for steel rails with Charles N. Schwab of Carnegie Steel, paying the low price of $16 to $18 per ton. Small subcontractors did most of the grading and track laying, charging less than the major companies. He raised a $17,000 subsidy for the line in Joplin, even before the tracks had reached Pittsburg. On June 10, an excursion marked the opening of the line as several hundred citizens of Pittsburg journeyed to Kansas City, a trip that took more than six hours.[29] The scheme to reach deep water surged on.

Stilwell, Martin, and Gentry kept construction crews working on several projects as the line expanded. To secure the Pittsburg subsidy, work proceeded on the shops, roundhouse, and yards there, and, simul-

28. Stilwell, "I Had a Hunch," December 31, 1927, 24; Minute Book, Missouri Coal and Construction Company, June 7, August 2, and August 22, 1893.
29. The Kansas City *Star*, January 27, February 2, March 13 and 31, and June 6 and 10, 1893; Stilwell, "I Had a Hunch," December 31, 1927, 26; Stilwell, *Forty Years of Business Life*, 5.

taneously, work progressed on the yard and engine facilities in Kansas City. On September 1, the Joplin extension opened, and a direct trade route from Kansas City into southwestern Missouri was obtained. Undoubtedly pleased with the speed of the construction, Stilwell could also take pride in the rising gross of the KCPG. In the first eight months of 1893, the gross earnings were $101,461, compared with $35,431 in 1892. By the end of the year, the KCPG owned 106.0 miles of track and operated 187.72 miles. The road had a capitalization and debt of $2,650,000 while the cost of building and equiping the line had risen to $5,300,000.[30] The discrepancy between miles of track owned and miles operated was the result of the acquisition of two subsidiaries.

As Stilwell surveyed the route from Joplin south to Shreveport, Louisiana, it became apparent that two existing railroads could be acquired and incorporated into the "Pee Gee." The first railway to be connected with the KCPG was the Kansas City, Fort Smith and Southern Railway. This road operated from Joplin to Sulphur Springs, Arkansas, a distance of fifty-one miles. Negotiations for purchasing the KCFSS had begun in 1892, and on January 2, 1893, the KCFSS sold $825,000 in stock and $825,000 in first-mortgage bonds to the Missouri Coal and Construction Company for $742,500. E. T. Stotesbury then sold the stock of the KCFSS in Philadelphia for which the Missouri firm paid him a commission of 2½ percent.[31] The financial arrangements were typical of Stilwell's operations.

The KCFSS had been founded by Matthias Splitlog, a wealthy Wyandotte Indian. He owned a sizable tract of land south of Joplin and sought to link that city to a townsite called Splitlog he was trying to develop on his holdings. The line was formed in 1887 and constructed under the direction of Richard Gentry. When the railway opened in 1889, it immediately came to financial grief and was acquired by L. L. Bush, a railroad

30. The Kansas City *Star*, August 1 and 7, 1893; *The Railroad Gazette*, September 15, 1893; United States, Interstate Commerce Commission, *Sixth Annual Report of the Statistics of Railways in the United States* (Washington: Government Printing Office, 1894), 200, 228, 282, 332–333, and 576. The Interstate Commerce Commission Reports will be cited hereafter only by title.

31. *Engineering News*, February 17, 1898; Minute Book, Missouri Coal and Construction Company, January 26, 1893; "Report of L. A. Etter on His Trip to Port Arthur, Texas over the Kansas City, Pittsburg & Gulf RR," January 1, 1898 (Pliny Fisk Collection, Pliny Fisk Library, Princeton University, Princeton, New Jersey).

promoter. Bush, like Stilwell, planned a railway from Kansas City to Sabine Pass, but the line was only extended to Sulphur Springs. The formal transfer of the KCFSS to the KCPG took place on May 11, 1893, and through-train service from Kansas City to Sulphur Springs began the following November.[32] The "Pee Gee" marched southward.

The second short line Stilwell acquired was the Texarkana and Fort Smith Railway Company, successor to the Texarkana and Northern Railway. The T&N had been incorporated in 1885 to build from Texarkana, ten miles north into a timber area. The road also had an Arkansas charter to build across the Red River to Fort Smith. In 1889 the name was changed, and in late 1892, when Stilwell looked the line over, it consisted of twenty miles of track from Texarkana north to Wilton, Arkansas, and a steel bridge across Red River.

George Gould, son of Jay Gould, apparently feared that the entry of the KCPG into Shreveport would harm the operations of his rail properties in the region and investigated purchasing the Texarkana and Fort Smith to block Stilwell. The Kansas City promoter moved to counter Gould. In the fall of 1892, he had incorporated yet another firm, the Arkansas Construction Company, and on December 13, that Company agreed to purchase the TFS. Stilwell proceeded with great dispatch. He rushed to Philadelphia, sold $300,000 in stock in the Arkansas Construction Company "in jig time," then hurried back to Texarkana to consummate the purchase of the TFS for $210,000. Gould was thwarted.

The assets of the TFS consisted, most importantly, of the steel river bridge, the charter, and the trackage. The TFS remained under the control of the Arkansas Construction Company until November 20, 1894, when it was formally merged with the KCPG. The Arkansas Company meanwhile entered into a contract with the KCPG to build the link from Sulphur Springs south to connect with the TFS. When the formal merger occurred, the TFS had forty-four miles of track from Texarkana north to Morris Ferry. While the railway remained orphaned from the KCPG, a lone Baldwin 4-4-0, Number 5, worked the line north out of Texarkana.[33]

32. Neosho *Times*, August 25, 1887; the Kansas City *Star*, November 19, 1889, and November 21, 1893; Jefferson City *Daily Tribune*, May 11, 1893; Poor, *Manual*, 1892, 308.

33. S. G. Reed, *A History of the Texas Railroads and of Transportation Conditions under Spain and Mexico and the Republic of Texas and the State* (Houston:

Stilwell now turned to the construction of the line from Sulphur Springs to Morris Ferry.

With the opening of the railway from Kansas City to Sulphur Springs, Stilwell commanded 212 miles of track. As the line expanded, its earnings increased rapidly. The first freight train north out of Sulphur Springs included two carloads of livestock, an indication that the road was beginning to diversify its business. That the original construction was less than first rate is obvious; the grades were sharp, many short-radius curves existed, and many miles of track lacked ballast. Operating costs were high, and traffic had to be generated after the line was completed. Nevertheless, the impact on the counties in Arkansas which the line entered was significant.[34] These facts and others served as a basis for the claims being made by the "Pee Gee's" promoter.

Optimistic and romantic statements and press releases were important tools of promoters, and Stilwell became a master of the art. As the KCPG crept south into Arkansas one of the company "directors" told the press,

The lumber traffic is not the primary source of profit to which we are looking, our road running through 60 miles of the finest coal land in the southwest, and through one of the richest agricultural districts in this country. We have iron, lead, zinc, slate, manganese and other valuable minerals along our proposed route, and we are assured of a tonnage from coal alone between Kansas City and Pittsburg, Kansas, of 300,000 tons per annum. One of the principal objects of building this air line to the Gulf is to satisfy the increasing demand for a direct grain outlet, as well as the importation into Kansas City from the South of cattle, timber and ties. The money is all raised to build into Fort Smith, Arkansas, to which city we expect to be operating by January next.[35]

The language and optimism suggest that the "director" was Stilwell.

Although Martin remained president of the KCPG and the related

---

The St. Clair Publishing Co., 1941), 435–436; Stock Ledger, Arkansas Construction Company, 1892–1894, (Offices of the Kansas City Southern Railway); Rose McMaster, "Origin and Development of the Kansas City Southern Railway," 20; Stilwell, "I Had a Hunch," December 31, 1927, 24–26; *The Railroad Gazette*, April 21, 1893; the Kansas City *Star*, December 3, 1892, September 27 and November 20, 1894; "All-Time Steam Roster of the Kansas City Southern," *Railroad Magazine* LXVIII (April 1957), 74.

34. *Commercial and Financial Chronicle*, ? (1893) 422; the Kansas City *Star*, December 18, 1893; Clark, *Then Came the Railroads*, 194; H. F. Haag, "A Brief History of the Kansas City Southern Railway System," manuscript (Offices of the Kansas City Southern Railway), 21–22.

35. *The Railroad Gazette*, August 4, 1893.

enterprises except the Trust company, which was presided over by Stilwell, the latter had become the spokesman for the various schemes. With a preponderance of Kansas Citians on the boards of the companies, many believed that the firms were local institutions. In terms of the desire for constructing the rail routes, they were local developments. The sources of capital, however, were other than Kansas City. *The Philadalphia Stockholder* noted that the "Earnings of the KCPG and the KCSB continue to reflect the glowing prosperity of those railroads, in which a number of Philadelphians are interested."[36] The investors from Philadelphia were more than just "interested."

They were probably pleased with the rapid expansion of the KCPG but disgruntled with earnings. The six months ending June 30, 1893 showed an operating loss of $29.77. The line, wholly owned and operated by the Philadelphia Construction Company, operated 213.08 miles of track. Equipment included 10 passenger and 264 freight cars.[37] The ratio of equipment to trackage on the KCPG was certainly an improvement over the situation on the belt lines around Kansas City.

By 1893 the "Pee Gee" owned nine locomotives. These included two Baldwin 4-4-0s, Numbers 111 and 112, and Number 10, a 4-4-0 manufactured by the Brooks Locomotive works which had been acquired from the KCFSS when the line was purchased. All three had been owned by the KCNFS as had Numbers 627 and 628, Baldwin manufactured 2-6-0s. The road took delivery of four larger locomotives in 1893 as heavier motive power became a necessity with larger trains. Four Baldwin "ten-wheelers" (4-6-0) were purchased, and these became Numbers 270 through 273.[38] While the KCPG was not heavily endowed with locomotives, traffic did not require substantial motive power. The projected extension of the line across the Ozarks, however, would lead to substantial purchases of additional locomotives.

In order for the KCPG to build from Sulphur Springs south to join the Texarkana and Fort Smith, the railroad had to be built through Indian Territory. Permission to construct across Indian lands had to be granted by Congress. Approval was requested and received. To aid the promoters of the line, Congress later agreed that the KCPG could be built in Arkan-

36. The Kansas City *Star*, December 12, 1893.
37. Poor, *Manual*, 1894, 211, 213.
38. "All-Time Steam Roster of the Kansas City Southern," 74–76.

sas, Texas, and Louisiana before construction was completed within Indian Territory. The press reported, "Stilwell is happy."[39]

Stilwell's happiness was short-lived. Before the directors met at the annual meeting in January of 1894, the Kansas City *Star* reported that final plans for the extension to the Gulf were not completed:

The extension of the KCP&G from Siloam Springs, Arkansas to Sulphur Springs will be formally opened for traffic next Sunday, January 21. This extension completes the plans of the KCP&G Company so far made, and it now becomes necessary for the company to make further arrangements for building on south to the Gulf of Mexico. No objective point south of Sulphur Springs has been chosen and at the annual meeting of the company to be held here in a few days, this question of extending the line from Sulphur Springs south will be considered and it will be decided whether this is an opportune time to build more railway.[40]

Clearly, a crisis had been reached, and the source of the crisis was not internal, but external, for in 1893 the nation had suffered a financial panic and entered into the worst depression ever. It did not appear to be an "opportune time" for building a railway across a frontier-like section of the country.

The depression of 1893 hit farmers, workers, and businessmen alike, and strife and violence became the order of the day. President Grover Cleveland took the position that the people should support the government, but that the government would not support the people in the form of direct relief; he then dispatched federal troops to protect business and industrial property and to defeat strikes. Eugene Debs urged railroad workers to join his American Railway Union in order to aid the striking Pullman Company employees, while J. P. Morgan lent gold to the federal treasury to shore up the declining reserves. Jacob Coxey led a "petition in boots" to Washington clamoring for federal relief and was arrested for trespassing. The Populist party leader Mrs. Mary E. Lease exhorted farmers to "raise more hell and less corn," while many people borrowed money so they could attend the Columbian Exposition on the lake front in Chicago. "Pitchfork" Ben Tillman of South Carolina mesmerized his farmer constituents with demands for reform, while in Ohio William McKinley

39. The Beaver [Oklahoma] *Advocate*, March 2, 1893; undated newspaper clipping, James A. Anderson Scrapbooks (Missouri Valley Room, Kansas City Public Library, Kansas City, Missouri).
40. The Kansas City *Star*, January 18, 1894.

praised the gold standard and the high protective tariff. Henry George called for the single tax, Edward Bellamy organized "Nationalists" clubs, "Coin" Harvey sang the glories of "free silver," and Dwight L. Moody urged the people to pray. No, it did not seem to be a propitious time to build a railway.

By mid-1894, more than one hundred and fifty railroads with capitalization of $2,500,000,000 owning 30,000 miles of track were in the hands of receivers. Between 1892 and 1895, gross new miles of railway constructed each year dropped from 4,584 miles to 1,938 miles. Orders for freight and passenger cars declined as did purchases of locomotives, yet prices of railway equipment were reduced only about 7 percent.[41] The general effect of the depression on railroad entrepreneurs was to make them question the wisdom of attempting to raise additional capital. For roads with capital available, depression prices justified some purchases of equipment, if not the construction of additional mileage. "The whole tempo of railroad expansion slowed to a walk, each road glad of a respite."[42] Many of the railroad giants in the midwest and southwest collapsed, though some of the so-called "Granger" roads remained solvent through rigid economies and strong financial support. The evils of poor construction, overcapitalization, and excessive expansion were major factors leading to receiverships. The depression terminated a major period of railroad construction in the southwest.[43] Most railway men accepted these facts and sought to survive through retrenchment. A promoter, however, thrives on expansion; he cannot exist without the force of creativity strongly at work. Arthur Stilwell remembered, "inaction was the last thing in the world I contemplated."[44]

Stilwell acknowledged that the panic of 1893 gave him "serious conditions to contend with," but "a hunch came to me." "It was that I would go to Holland and raise the $3,000,000 we needed to build from Siloam Springs to Shreveport. The idea became an obsession." He had been to

41. Charles Hoffman, "The Depression of the Nineties," *The Journal of Economic History*, XVI (June 1956), 138, 141, 152–153.

42. Thomas C. Cochran, *Railroad Leaders 1845–1890: The Business Mind in Action* (New York: Russell and Russell, 1965), 105.

43. Robert Edgar Riegel, *The Story of the Western Railroads* (Lincoln: University of Nebraska Press, 1964), 305–307; Clark, *Then Came the Railroads*, 160.

44. Stilwell, "I Had a Hunch," December 31, 1927, 26.

Holland once on a vacation in the 1880s. He discussed the "hunch" with his Kansas City associates, and, although highly skeptical, they urged that he go to Philadelphia and reveal his idea to their financial benefactors. Stotesbury, Welsh, and Waterall thought he was joking. They believed that the last thing foreign investors desired was bonds in an American railway. Stilwell wore down their opposition with a torrent of words; his Philadelphia backers consented to give him power of attorney and the right to sell securities in the Arkansas Construction Company. He left for Europe in two weeks.[45]

Why Holland? Stilwell undoubtedly knew of the importance of Dutch capital in financing other American railways. James J. Hill obtained Dutch backing for the Great Northern and other railroads—the Missouri, Kansas and Texas, Chicago and Northwestern, Missouri Pacific, and Denver and Rio Grande—had sought and received financial support from Dutch bankers. The Dutch shareholders would often pay assessments when American investors refused and were therefore significant in reorganization procedures. Dutch holding companies or bureaus of administration acted as clearing houses for the securities. The Administratie Kantoren, as they were known, issued their own certificates against American stocks and bonds deposited with them. These concerns received small collection fees for gathering the dividends and interest. Circularization was a popular form of bond introduction in Holland and Germany and would be the method Stilwell would use. But although Holland had been a good field for American railway bonds, European investment in the United States in the mid 1890s had been sharply reduced.[46]

Stilwell sailed for Europe in February 1894. He knew no one in Holland, he later remembered, except a chance acquaintance from his earlier voyage, a coffee broker named John DeGoeijen. There is evidence, however, that at least one Hollander was in the Stilwell firms before 1894. As early as January 29, 1892, Jacques Tutein Nolthenius was a member of

45. Stilwell, *Cannibals of Finance*, 46–47; Stilwell, "I Had a Hunch," December 31, 1927, 26, 77.

46. Riegel, *The Story of the Western Railroads*, 138–139; Frederick A. Cleveland and Fred Wilbur Powell, *Railroad Finance* (New York: D. Appleton and Company, 1912), 29; Charles F. Speare, "Selling American Bonds in Europe," *The Annals*, American Academy of Political and Social Science, XXX (September 1907), 270–276; Hoffman, "The Depression of the Nineties," 152–153.

the board of the Missouri Coal and Construction Company. Nolthenius came to Kansas City from Holland; his family was described by the Kansas City *Star* as "wealthy."[47] Regardless of whether Nolthenius placed Stilwell in contact with DeGoeijen or the chance shipboard encounter led to their reacquaintance, the Dutchman became an agent for Stilwell's concerns.

The promoter wrote many years later that he had tried to sell the bonds on his own for two weeks after he arrived in Amsterdam, but to no avail. Sitting in his hotel room, discouraged, but always thinking, he recalled his meeting with the coffeebroker. Unable to remember the merchant's exact name, Stilwell went to the coffee exchange, obtained a list of the brokers from the doorman, and on the list he recognized DeGeoijen. Summoned to the door to meet the American, DeGeoijen remembered Stilwell and they went to lunch. Stilwell sprung his ideas on the Dutchman over the meal and overwhelmed the coffee merchant. The promoter offered him a three-year contract as Dutch agent for the Missouri, Kansas and Texas Trust Company at a salary of $5,000 a year. Stilwell would teach him to sell securities, and DeGeoijen would introduce him to Dutch capitalists and their methods. DeGeoijen accepted, an office was opened, and the two salesmen went to work.[48]

DeGeoijen proved to be an excellent choice for Stilwell. He had been born in Zwolle in 1861 and had become prosperous as a coffee broker. A popular man, DeGeoijen stood only five feet, six inches, but his warm personality made up for his deficiency in physical stature. Possessed with a charming smile, frankness, good humor, and a fine education, he won easy acceptance in Dutch businesses and households.[49]

The promoter used his best techniques on his newly found associate. "A strong believer in the wisdom of making your enthusiasm contagious, I spent hours explaining to DeGeoijen. . . . how I had set my heart on building to deep water and what it meant to the farmers of the Middle West." He told the Dutchman of the financial calamities of the farmers, which he wrongly attributed to ruinous freight rates. "In about

47. Minute Book, Missouri Coal and Construction Company, January 29, 1892; the Kansas City *Star*; September 3, 1896.
48. Stilwell, "I Had a Hunch," December 31, 1927, 77.
49. *Ibid.*; *Arkansas Gazette* [Little Rock], April 26, 1942; File 110.3, Offices of the Kansas City Southern Railway.

a week," he recalled, "I had DeGeoijen talking my own language and as much pepped up over the salvation of the Western farmers as though he and all his people traced their ancestry straight to the Mayflower."[50] De-Geoijen, imbued with his mentor's vision, urged that they contact Dutch brokers, many of whom published their own financial newspapers. The editors were introduced to the scheme and Stilwell regaled them with stories of the profits of his rail and trust operations. Stilwell decided to sell the stock in small denominations to attract moderate investors. By July, plans put into form, the advertisements were placed and sale of securities began.[51]

The Reglement Van Het Arkansas Construction Company-Syndicaat formed by DeGeoijen became the vehicle for their operations. A pamphlet printed in English and Dutch explained how the securities were to be sold. Trust certificates would be issued by the Arkansas Construction Company Syndicate for $400 United States currency or $1,000 Guilders each, secured by $360 in common and $80 preferred stock in the construction company itself. The entire issue of stocks included $4,500,000 in common and $1,000,000 preferred. The owners of the trust certificates would receive the profits from the stock on deposit as collateral at the Amsterdam office. To provide these new securities, the stockholders in Kansas City voted to increase the capital stock of the Arkansas Construction Company from $1,000,000 to $5,500,000. The promotor directed that the KCPG would issue 5 percent bonds to the construction company in payment for building and equipping the new line.[52]

While Stilwell went to Berlin to test the market there, DeGeoijen solicited Dutch investors. The initial offering sold rapidly when it was placed on the market. Sales remained good, and through the summer and early fall of 1894 Stilwell toured Germany and Holland, talking incessantly of his vision of a railroad, "straight as the crow files," from Kansas City to deep water. He made arrangements for Dutch investors to join the board of the construction company and another Hollander became a vice-

50. Stilwell, "I Had a Hunch," December 31, 1927, 77.
51. *Ibid.*
52. *Ibid.*, 77–78; Pamphlet, "Reglement van het Arkansas Construction Company-Syndicaat," and "Arkansas Construction Company Syndicate," July 13, 1894, Anderson Scrapbooks; the Kansas City *Star*, July 16, 1894.

president of the KCPG. Several investors agreed to purchase additional bonds later, when more money would become necessary. When the Dutchmen asked what percentage the promoter received, he responded, "nothing," then realized they did not believe him. Stilwell arranged for a group of auditors in Amsterdam to check the company books; they reported that, indeed, there were no personal commissions. His Dutch investors satisfied, Stilwell eagerly set sail for New York City in the fall. In New York he sought additional capital and completed legal arrangements for the transfer of funds from Holland. He had, as yet, not told his Philadelphia or Kansas City associates of his success.[53]

Stilwell strolled into the offices of Drexel and Company in Philadelphia and was presented to Stotesbury and Welsh. When he asked them to draw a draft on the Bank of Amsterdam for $500,000 they thought it was a joke. The promoter finally convinced them he was not joking—in the midst of an international depression, he had sold $3,000,000 in securities to build a railroad through western Arkansas and northwestern Louisiana. Drexel and Company began to process the papers to transfer funds from Holland to the United States, and the gleeful Stilwell, more confident in himself than ever, proceeded on to Kansas City.

The press rushed to interview him upon his arrival. Never at a loss for words, he unfolded the story of his financial triumph. Gone nearly a year, he related in detail what had transpired. The Arkansas Construction Company had increased its capital and placed large blocs of stock in Europe. Construction from Siloam Springs to Shreveport was imminent. From Shreveport south, plans were not firm, but the aim remained to build to Sabine Pass on the Gulf. Although one reporter said Stilwell talked "reluctantly" about his trip abroad, this is hard to believe. "Kansas City may well rejoice over the success of my trip," he said, "I have secured the money necessary to complete the KCP&G railway to Shreveport, Louisiana." He refused to give dates of expected completion or reveal the actual sums he had acquired, but work was in progress and would be accelerated. The funds for the line from Shreveport to the Gulf would probably be available when the railway from Kansas City to Shreveport opens, he stated. The reporter noted that Stilwell "seemed to be imbued with confidence." He could afford to be confident; he was about to build the only major railroad completed during these depression years.[54]

Upon his return to Kansas City, Stilwell began to carry out the decisions reached while he was in Europe. Jacques Tutein Nolthenius became the manager of the foreign department of the Missouri, Kansas and Texas Trust Company, and DeGeoijen became manager of the Amsterdam office and a member of the board of directors. Robert Gillham replaced Richard Gentry as chief engineer of the KCPG and the Arkansas Construction Company. Gentry claimed that policy differences caused him to resign, although he remained the largest stockholder of the KCPG in Kansas City. Gillham, a talented engineer, had introduced the cable car to Kansas City and had become chief engineer of the Metropolitan Street Railway. Gentry had earlier been a casualty of the infusion of Dutch capital; he had been replaced as second vice-president of the KCPG by T. J. Fitsingh of Amsterdam. Eastern capital too, was recognized, as Kansas Citian C. A. Braley was replaced on the KCPG board by New Yorker E. P. Merwin. The firms were obviously less and less Kansas City–oriented. The great overlapping of titles and officials in the Stilwell corporations led to their description as "like one family." One could never tell whether one were dealing with an officer of the Trust, a railroad, or a construction company. The promoter undoubtedly planned it that way.[55]

The capitalization of the KCPG had to be increased in order to issue bonds to the Arkansas Construction Company in payment for the line from Siloam Springs to Shreveport. In one of the largest expansions in Missouri history, authorized capital went from $3,500,000 to $10,000,000 in April 1894. Stilwell and other KCPG officials traveled to Texarkana and Shreveport to obtain right of way and to solicit local subsidies; they were only partially successful. To facilitate unification of the rail operation, the Texarkana & Fort Smith was merged into the KCPG, with the

54. Stilwell, "I Had a Hunch," December 31, 1927, 78; Stilwell, *Forty Years of Business Life*, 6–7; the Kansas City *Star*, December 14 and 19, 1894; Clark, *Then Came the Railroads*, 161–162.

55. "Advertisement for the Missouri, Kansas, and Texas Trust Company," John A. Prescott Scrapbooks (Missouri Valley Room, Kansas City Public Library); the Kansas City *Star*, January 25 and September 3, 1895; McMaster, "Origin and Development of the Kansas City Southern Railway," 19–20.

latter railroad issuing bonds at the rate of $25,000 per mile to pay for the former. The Arkansas Construction Company issued 45,000 shares of stock with a par value of $100 a share through the offices of Stilwell's Trust company. The Trust offices in Kansas City, Amsterdam, and London—the most recently opened branch—sold the securities at $85, giving the purchaser an initial 15 percent bonus. As the stock was sold, the Arkansas Construction Company contracted for the grading of the line. Robert Gillham rode on horseback south of Siloam Springs to the Arkansas River, surveying the route. The bridge site over the Arkansas was selected and crews of men and pile drivers went to work immediately. Because of the rugged Ozark topography, Gillham decided to shift the main line west into Indian Territory, reaching Fort Smith by construction of a branch. While Gillham planned the construction, Stilwell wined and dined the stockholders. A party of eastern investors, including men from Philadelphia, New York, New Haven, Providence, and Cincinnati were taken on a tour south of Kansas City to the Arkansas River bridge site.[56] It is not difficult to imagine Stilwell's sales talks extolling the virtues of the railroad, the territory through which it passed, and the potential profits.

Yet, it is difficult to understand why well-informed investors did not see the rising difficulties facing the KCPG. Even for a railway crossing a virgin territory in the midst of a major depression, financial arrangements appear unusual. As Stilwell so often noted, there was no floating debt. While the total cost of the railroad and its equipment had been $11,500,-000, however, revenues in 1894 totaled only $288,238. The operations for that year produced a deficit of $13,385, and again it should be noted that interest on bonds had been deferred. Other questionable procedures arise in terms of equipment purchases. For example, in November of 1895 the KCPG bought eighteen new passenger cars, a luxury it could ill afford. More money spent on ballast and trackage might have prevented wrecks, such as that which occurred on Christmas Day, 1894, when locomotive Number 12, passing over rough unballasted track near Neosho, Missouri, went off the rails, turning over on its side.[57] The figures suggest that by

---

56. *Jefferson City Daily Tribune*, April 4, 1894; *The Railroad Gazette*, October 12, 1894; *Commercial and Financial Chronicle*, November 17, 1894; "Prospectus . . . Arkansas Construction Company," Anderson Scrapbooks; the Kansas City *Star*, May 28, September 13 and December 2, 1895.

57. *Seventh Annual Report of the Statistics of Railways in the United States*,

1894 a serious "entreprenuerial error" had been made, yet the promoter constantly enticed his capitalists into commitments to further expansion. As Gillham rushed construction south toward Shreveport at the rate of one mile per day, Arthur Stilwell had to make several important decisions. Once the Kansas City-Shreveport line opened, traffic arrangements were necessary to reach the Gulf. Stilwell took a party of Dutch and English investors to Shreveport and on to Galveston, Texas, in May of 1895 to make such arrangements. By using the rails of the Houston, East and West Texas railway from Shreveport to Houston and the Galveston, Houston & LaPorte from Houston to Galveston, deep water could be reached.[58] This, of course, would be only a temporary expedient, for Stilwell had already created yet another subsidiary to build from Shreveport directly south to the Gulf.

On September 27, 1894, a charter was filed for the Kansas City, Shreveport and Gulf Railroad Company; the charter provided for a railroad from the northern boundary of Louisiana south, via Shreveport, to Sabine Pass, Texas. A contract with the Arkansas Construction Company provided for that firm to build the line from Texarkana to Shreveport, and work proceeded from both the north and the south of Shreveport. A second contract, with the Kansas City Terminal Construction Company, was signed to build from Shreveport to Sabine Pass.[59]

From the time Stilwell decided to build a railway south from Kansas City to deep water, he and those associated with him indicated that the ultimate southern terminal would be Sabine Pass, or "at some city on the Gulf of Mexico." Maps printed by the KCPG, advertisements for the line, and even the company stationery indicated that Sabine Pass was its goal.[60] Arthur Stilwell, however, began to change his mind about the southern terminus, for sometime in the late spring or early summer of 1895, he "had a hunch."

232, 318, 374–375, 630–631; the Kansas City *Star*, November 11, 1895; George Abdill, *Rails West* (New York: Bonanza Books, 1960), 116.

58. The Kansas City *Star*, May 7, 1895.

59. *Commercial and Financial Chronicle*, October 13, 1894; McMaster, "Origin and Development of the Kansas City Southern Railway Company," 24–25.

60. Stilwell, "I Had a Hunch," December 31, 1927, 24, 26; the Kansas City *Star*, September 5, 1893 and July 16, 1894.

V

ARTHUR BUILDS HIS PORT

HISTORIANS of the American city contend that the urban frontier after 1890 was not in the creation of new communities but in the exploitation of those previously established. In the years between 1860 and 1890, great opportunities for building urban communities existed, were seized upon, and a network of cities came into being. Most American cities were in existence by 1890, and with some exceptions—Miami, Tulsa, and Oklahoma City for example—few new sites grew to the minimum urban size requirement of 2,500 established in the census of 1910. The opportunities for exploitation in the urban sector, it is argued, lay in taking advantage of expanding cities, as new urban growth after 1890 tended to be centered on satellite towns or suburbs of older communities.[1] Arthur Stilwell, Henry Flagler, and other promoters were unaware, however, that the era of new cities had ended, and in their activities they carried on the important function of the promoter—the creation of urban centers.

The foundation of most western cities rested on a combination of geography, outside promotion, and local enterprise or resources. Outside promotion and local enterprise were most often directly related to railroad development, and the location and initial growth of many cities was tied to the creation of a national rail network. City promoters and real estate developers vied for the favors of the railway companies, eagerly seeking

---

1. Blake McKelvey, *The Urbanization of America* (New Brunswick: Rutgers University Press, 1963), 32; Charles N. Glaab and A. Theodore Brown, *A History of Urban America* (New York: The Macmillan Company, 1967), 109.

entrance of lines into their communities. Railroads, unbounded by previous trade routes or topography, could be built anywhere, creating cities
where they desired.[2]

From the beginning of the railroad building era, the officers of the
transportation companies were cognizant of the potential profits in land
speculation and urban growth. Surveyors moved ahead of railway construction, locating townsites and laying out lots and streets. Sales of such
sites produced large windfalls to the railroads. "Creation of new towns
was often advantageous, for it permitted a larger share of the profits from
increased land values to go directly to the railroad owners."[3] Western and
southern railroads contributed directly to urban booms in both regions,
and metropolitan growth in the "New South" often resulted from expanding railways opening new markets. Although southern railroad builders
took a parochial attitude toward what their companies were to contribute
to the city, the impact on the regional metropolises was significant; their
contribution included developing the commerce and economic activities
of the principal railway terminus.[4] In the west, however, the relations
between urban growth and railroad building were even more direct.

Railroad company "insiders" formed subsidiaries or independent
companies to acquire strategic blocks of land as potential townsites. Sometimes the railroad acquired the land for the benefit of all stockholders, but
more often the few men privy to survey data exercised their knowledge
by purchasing such locales for their personal profit. Land and timber subsidiaries of western railroads were common, and such operations became
sources of large profits.[5] In the southwest, such promotions often led to
turbulence:

New towns were born with each new rail extension. Theirs was frequently
a story of conflict, of violent boom days, and of countyseat wars as new
towns crowded out older ones and rival groups of speculators fought for
supremacy. It was a struggle for survival, with quick profits for successful

2. McKelvey, *The Urbanization of America*, 34; Glaab and Brown, *A History
of Urban America*, 112.
3. Glaab and Brown, *A History of Urban America*, 113.
4. Phillip A. Bruce, *The Rise of the New South* (Philadelphia: George Barrie
& Sons, 1905), 232; Maury Klein, "Southern Railroad Leaders, 1865–1893: Identi-
ties and Ideologies," *Business History Review*, XLII (Autumn 1968), 294.
5. Thomas C. Cochran, *Railroad Leaders 1845–1890: The Business Mind in
Action* (New York: Russell & Russell, 1965), 119–120.

promoters and a reasonable guarantee of some future prosperity for their creations. It was a mixture of sound promotion and chicanery, public service and private avarice.[6]

Avarice and unrestrained rapaciousness became two of the characteristics synonomous with the town promoter. The prototype was, of course, Mark Twain's Colonel Beriah Sellers, but the theme of the urban hucksters is found in many places. The town promoters were, generally, neither frauds nor robber barons and made major contributions to the urbanization of America. Gifted with unbounded enthusiasm and a blind faith in the future, the promoters were indispensable ingredients in the rise of the American city.[7] As one student of the promoters has written, "The influence of nineteenth-century urban promotion, although evident in the growth of larger cities, can often be more precisely delineated in the histories of smaller urban centers which may not have achieved metropolitan status but which nonetheless were successful urban enterprises."[8] Many urban promoters failed even to develop small towns successfully, but they represent a vital aspect of the process of urbanization.

From the beginning of his railroad ventures, Arthur Stilwell boomed real estate and townsites along their routes. "The buying of townsites, laying them out, naming the principal streets after the directors of the road or my friends, and booming these newly found communities as desirable places for people to locate, constituted no small part of my work," he wrote.[9] Stilwell sent Edwin Walters, a geologist and civil engineer, into the field ahead of both the surveyors and construction crews to evaluate possible townsites. From May through July of 1895, Walters traveled on foot and horseback from Siloam Springs south to the Texarkana area, a journey of 500 miles, and reported on mineral deposits, land ownership, and possible locations for town promotions.[10]

6. Ira G. Clark, *Then Came the Railroads* (Norman: University of Oklahoma Press, 1958), 198.

7. Glaab and Brown, *A History of Urban America*, 118–119; McKelvey, *The Urbanization of America*, 235.

8. Charles N. Glaab, "Historical Perspective on Urban Development Schemes," *Urban Research and Policy Planning*, edited by Leo F. Schnore and Henry Fagin (Beverly Hills, Calif.: Sage Publications, Inc., 1967), 206.

9. Arthur E. Stilwell and James R. Crowell, "I Had a Hunch," *The Saturday Evening Post*, CC (December 31, 1927), 26.

10. "Report on a Southern Trip by Edwin Walters," James A. Anderson Scrapbooks (Missouri Valley Room, Kansas City Public Library, Kansas City, Missouri).

The methods Stilwell employed to promote his townsites were typical of the period. He hired Fred Hornbeck, a Kansas City real estate man, to become head of the land division of his railroads. A shrewd operator, Hornbeck argued that the way to make money in real estate was to get in ahead of construction, buy large tracts, divide the land into smaller sub-divisions, and sell at a profit when the railroad arrived. When Stilwell sold railroad securities in Holland, he also obtained Dutch financial support for some of Hornbeck's land schemes. Stilwell and his investors were making some money on land before Hornbeck joined the operation, but he influenced future sales and increased profits. Hornbeck purchased large advertisements in newspapers lauding the towns and their "perfect climate" and hired public relations men and journalists to write stories about the potential metropolises. Real estate men in Iowa, Minnesota, Wisconsin, and Nebraska were authorized to sell lots and acreages for the Stilwell companies. Colonists were recruited by circulars and by excursions on that part of the railway which had been completed. The techniques proved highly successful.[11]

Stilwell's first efforts at town promotion were on the Kansas City, Nevada & Fort Smith in 1890. As that line extended south toward Hume, Missouri, Stilwell located two new towns, Amoret in Bates County and Stuart City in Cass County. The latter never developed, but the former consisted of a few stores, houses, and the "Stratford Inn," a hotel owned by the Missouri Coal and Construction Company. Although Stilwell's firms boomed Amoret, it failed to become more than a rural trading center. Its population reached only 215 by 1900 and increased less than 100 by the following census.[12] As the Kansas City, Pittsburg and Gulf, the successor of the KCNFS, pushed south, other townsites were located in Missouri. Stilwell named the sites for his financial supporters, hence the towns of Drexel, Stotesbury, and Merwin and a community which did grow to some extent, Amsterdam. Only the latter had more than 100 residents by 1900, and none had as many as 1,000 people by 1960.[13]

11. The Kansas City *Star*, September 28, 1947; Clark, *Then Came the Railroads*, 189; William R. Draper, "Kansas City Southern," *Railroad Magazine*, XLIV (October 1947), 21.
12. The Kansas City *Star*, October 25, 1890; *Thirteenth Census of the United States* (Washington: Government Printing Office, 1913), II, 1071.
13. *Ibid.*

There would be greater success when the KCPG penetrated Arkansas and Hornbeck took over the real estate operation.

The first Arkansas town located by Stilwell was Gentry, in Benton County, named for Richard Gentry the chief engineer and a large investor. The town came into existence under the auspices of the Arkansas Townsite Company, a Stilwell firm. George M. Craig became Hornbeck's agent for Gentry, and the team advertised the site as a future division point on the KCPG. When the town did not boom, the division point was moved across the state line into Indian Territory where the promoter located the first town named for himself.[14]

Stilwell, Indian Territory, became a division point on the KCPG. Located thirty miles south and west of Siloam Springs, the town first appeared on a map in 1895. By 1900 the population was variously reported as only 300 or 500, but it did have a sizable railroad operation. An eight-stall, brick roundhouse with a sixty-five-foot turntable, a coal chute with a trestle approach, a water tank, depot, and five-track yard meant a number of railroad employees would be stationed there. The town developed several businesses, churches, and a population comprised largely of Cherokee Indians in whose nation it was located.[15] Stilwell would grow to almost 2,000 people by 1960. The other two KCPG towns in Indian Territory, Howe and Spiro, however, remained small villages.[16]

Stilwell's successes as a developer were minimal until the railroad crossed back into Arkansas. At this point, he began to recognize the significant role being played by his Dutch investors, and the first of many towns with Dutch names was founded; in honor of Queen Wilhelmina of Holland, Stilwell named the townsite Mena. Located in Polk County, the site was approximately midway on the western border of Arkansas and

14. *K.C.S. Current Events*, II (July 1903), 7; Manuscript, George M. Craig Papers (Historical Files, Port Arthur Chamber of Commerce, Port Arthur, Texas).

15. Charles N. Gould, *Oklahoma Place Names* (Norman: University of Oklahoma Press, 1933), 67; *The Railroad Gazette*, October 11, 1895: the Kansas City *Star*, September 30, 1895; *The Indian Chieftain* (Vinita, Indian Territory), January 20, 1900; Samuel Morse Felton, "Report on the Kansas City, Pittsburg & Gulf Railroad," July 15, 1899 (Manuscript Division, Baker Library, Harvard Graduate School of Business Administration, Boston, Mass.).

16. Clark, *Then Came the Railroads*, 202; George H. Shirk, *Oklahoma Place Names* (Norman: University of Oklahoma Press, 1965), 107. Howe was named for one of the Philadelphia investors, Dr. Herbert M. Howe.

only fifteen miles from Indian Territory. With track still forty miles away, Stilwell told Hornbeck to begin to boom the town. Hornbeck planted stories in newspapers throughout the midwest describing the glories of Mena, which was also to be a KCPG division point. The climate was ideal, the trade possibilities unlimited, and the opportunities for speculation were excellent, the puff pieces and advertisements suggested. Stilwell directed the track layers to attempt to lay one mile of track each day, and stories appeared daily reporting the progress of the railroad gangs. Excursions took prospective colonists to the end-of-track where they were transferred to wagons for the remainder of the journey to the site. Before the KCPG reached Mena, more than 1,000 people were already camping there.[17]

Public interest mounted as the publicity campaign rolled on, and 5,000 excursion tickets were sold in one week. Maps of the town suggest that Queen Wilhelmina was not the only person honored. Stilwell's Kansas City & Mena Improvement Company, the site developers, named streets for Gillham, Martin, and others, while two large parks were designated for Stilwell and Janssen, a Dutch investor. Hornbeck arranged for each person buying a lot in Mena to receive one free round trip ticket from Kansas City to the town, including three days in a Pullman sleeper and three meals each day in a Pullman diner. Buyers were required to make downpayments of only 50 percent on lots valued at less than $200 and 33⅓ percent for property in excess of that amount. Stilwell inserted a provision in the deeds of all real estate sold that 2½ percent of the value went to a school building fund, and by March of 1897, the school fund contained more than $6,000.[18] The townsite auxiliary was proving highly profitable.

Stilwell later claimed that the Mena townsite had cost only $6 per acre and that all the profits from the real estate operation went into the treasury of the construction company. One of Stilwell's business associates

17. *Commercial and Financial Chronicle*, June 27, 1896; Stilwell, "I Had a Hunch," December 31, 1927, 78.

18. *Ibid.*; Stilwell, *Cannibals of Finance* (Chicago: Farnum Publishing Company, 1912), 55; "Woodland Addition to Mena, Arkansas," advertisement, George M. Craig Papers (San Jacinto Museum, San Jacinto, Texas); the Kansas City *Star*, June 27, 1896 and March 8, 1897.

disputed this, claiming that the promoter, Hornbeck, and their associates reaped large personal rewards. W. R. Draper contended that "Hornbeck told me the townsite of Mena and one or two other deals paid the syndicate a profit of $150,000 inside of six months."[19] In the absence of any business records connected with the townsites—and even if they existed there is no guarantee they would be accurate—one would suspect that there is more truth in Hornbeck's alleged statement than in Stilwell's claim.

Within a few years, Mena became a thriving trading community. By 1898, there were 2,500 people in the town which could boast an electric plant, a water works, and a telephone system; a sizable lumbering operation in the area created employment, and the orchard and nursery business was getting under way. At the turn of the century, Mena possessed a flour mill, two newspapers, the seat of the county government, and 3,423 people.[20] The town would not, however, add more than 1,000 new citizens in the next sixty years.

On his surveying trip in the summer of 1895, Edwin Walters noted towering Rich Mountain, standing 1,300 feet above the future site of Mena. Walters described the beautiful view, the cool fresh air, and the nearby springs and suggested that the top of the mountain would make a fine place for a pleasure resort. The woodlands of the surrounding Ouachita Mountains were a hunter's delight, abounding in deer, bear, and turkey. A plateau of ten acres on the top of the mountain was ideal for the resort Walters suggested, and during July 1897, one of the hottest summers on record in Kansas City, Stilwell announced that Rich Mountain had been renamed "Mount Mena" and that an inn would be built at the top of the peak. A stage road would be constructed from the KCPG station to the summit, and Mount Mena would become, he declared, Kansas City's "Mount Manitou." George Craig, one of Hornbeck's young salesmen, took over the Mount Mena property. A massive rock hotel building was

19. Draper, "Kansas City Southern," 21–22; Arthur E. Stilwell, *Forty Years of Business Life* (New York: n.p., 1926 [?]), 7.

20. *Annual Report of the Kansas City, Pittsburg and Gulf Railroad for the Fiscal Year 1897–1898*, 7; R. P. J. Nolthenius, *Nieuwe Wereld* (Haarlem: H. D. Tjeenk Willink & Zoon, 1900), 20; Dallas Tabor Herndon (ed.), *Centennial History of Arkansas* (Chicago: The S. J. Clarke Publishing Company, 1922), I, 901–902.

constructed on the summit at a cost of $100,000. Named the "Wilhelmina Inn," the hotel had 35 rooms, including a suite for the Queen who never came to visit. The rooms with their large oak beams and lace curtains, and the dining room's cut glass and fine cuisine would, it was hoped, make the inn attractive to tourists. The "Inn" failed to prosper, however, and it became a music school, was abandoned, then was rebuilt by the Arkansas Publicity and Parks Commission in 1962; once again it operates as a resort and a refuge from the hot, dry summers of the Great Plains.[21] Although Queen Wilhelmina did not come to Arkansas, Stilwell continued to sprinkle Dutch names along the western side of that state.

South of Mena, Stilwell created the sites of Janssen (later renamed Vandervoort), and DeQueen, as well as Gillham (named for the KCPG chief engineer), and Grannis (for investor C. E. Grannis) and Winthrop (for investor R. C. Winthrop). Janssen, located 22 miles south of Mena, received the Hornbeck-Craig publicity treatment but failed to attract more than a few settlers.[22] The same is true of all of the other sites except DeQueen, which did attain more than village size.

Stilwell decided to honor his friend and business associate John De-Geoijen by naming a town for him. The name was very difficult for Americans, who mispronounced it "DeQueen," and the promoter, feeling that DeGeoijen would be too much of a burden for the new town, named it DeQueen. When DeGeoijen came to the United States on his next visit he received the news about "his" town:

"How strange! [he mused.] Suppose I should name my boy John and say, 'Arthur, I have named my boy after you and called him John.' I take it you might wonder what was the matter with John's father. There is just as much sense in naming this town DeQueen after me."[23]

Apparently the response was good natured; DeGeoijen did have a son, who was named Arthur!

The DeQueen Land and Townsite Company boomed the location, contending "It is sure to make a large city." By 1900 it had a population

21. "Report On a Southern Trip by Edwin Walters," *Commerce and Finance*, January 9, 1924; the Kansas City *Star*, July 9 and 11, 1897; Draper, "Kansas City Southern," 23; Port Arthur *News*, October 16, 1952; "Visit Queen Wilhelmina State Park," Mena Chamber of Commerce.

22. The Kansas City *Star*, February 3 and 4, 1897.

23. Stilwell, "I Had a Hunch," December 31, 1927, 78–79.

of 1,200 and had become the commercial center and county seat of Sevier County. Two banks, a weekly newspaper, and numerous sawmills encouraged the development of the small town. Surviving a fire in 1899 which destroyed all but three businesses in the frontier community, De-Queen would grow to just less than 3,000 people in the twentieth century. It did not become a large city; it did become a trading and lumbering town.[24]

In 1897, as the KCPG built from Shreveport, Louisiana, south toward the Gulf, Stilwell and Hornbeck platted four more towns. The first, Zwolle, named by DeGeoijen for the Dutch town where he was born, became a very important sawmill center in the longleaf-pine district. Another site located in Vernon Parish, named Hornbeck, was a sawmill camp which became a cotton center as well, though never more than a small village. Another site, De Ridder, developed into a prosperous lumber community. Named for one of DeGeoijen's relatives, De Ridder had more than 2,000 people by 1910, most of them employed in sawmills or the large wool market. The town also became the seat of government for Beauregard Parish. By the mid twentieth century, the town had increased in size to more than 7,000 people and was the center of a large diversified agricultural area. Farther south, in Calcasieu Parish, Stilwell and Hornbeck established DeQuincy, which was named for a Dutch investor. It never became more than a small lumber village.[25]

The Louisiana towns Stilwell developed were part of a larger scheme to promote the cutting of longleaf yellow pine in the region from Shreveport to Lake Charles. The stands of pine were very extensive, and construction by the KCPG led to a lumber boom after 1897. The value of timber cut in the area more than tripled after 1900, and in some places the timber, when cut, produced fifty cords per acre. Stilwell organized a company to handle this timber business, creating traffic for the KCPG and

24. The Kansas City *Star*, April 17, 1897; Herndon, *Centennial History of Arkansas*, I, 875; *Arkansas Gazette* [Little Rock], April 26, 1942.
25. "KCS Railroad Keeps Zwolle at High Level of Prosperity," *Louisiana Municipal Review* (November 1955), 7; Shreveport *Times*, November 13, 1960; the Kansas City *Star*, May 31, 1897; Alcee Fortier, *Louisiana* (Madison: Century Historical Association, 1914), I, 319, 321, and 512; *Louisiana: A Guide to the State* (New York: Hastings House Publishers, 1941), 676–677, 679; "De Quincy Is Railway and Highway Hub of Southwest," *Louisiana Municipal Review*, (July 1954), 5, 34.

money for its stockholders. Both "developmental" and "opportunistic" investors were rewarded in this instance.[26]

Stilwell's critics declared that he had been little interested in building a railway to the Gulf and had been in the promotion largely for the profits from real estate and other operations.[27] The promoter stated that this was untrue:

> The Construction Company owned all town sites. There was not one dollar of promotion paid to me or anyone else. Each officer bought his town lots at the same price outsiders paid.[28]

Criticism nevertheless mounted and continued. George Kennan, in his biography of E. H. Harriman, wrote that Stilwell avoided established towns in order to create new communities and receive profits from town promotions. Kennan contended that the developers of the KCPG seemed to have "aimed primarily at making it a means of land speculation."[29] Kennan, of course, was defending Harriman and his relations with Stilwell and the KCPG (about which more will be said later) and reflects Harriman's attitude. That Stilwell cared only for the profits of land speculation is nonsense, but that he and others profited from such operations is undoubtedly true. The creation of towns was not his goal, but a way to raise money to build the line to the Gulf. Urban promotion experiences in Missouri, Arkansas, Indian Territory, and Louisiana prepared Stilwell for his largest and most successful scheme, a port on the Gulf of Mexico.

From its inception, Stilwell maintained that the railroad to the Gulf would terminate at Sabine Pass, Texas. Sabine Pass was located on a narrow five-mile-long passage by the same name which connected the

26. George Alwin Stokes, "Lumbering in Southwest Louisiana" (Unpublished doctoral dissertation, Louisiana State University, 1954), 43–44; Charles S. Sargent, *Report on the Forests of North America* (Washington: Government Printing Office, 1884), 536–544; *Twelfth Census of the United States, Manufacturers* (Washington: Government Printing Office, 1902), Part III, 840–841; Draper, "Kansas City Southern," 26.

27. See, for example, "Report of L. A. Etter on His Trip to Port Arthur, Texas, over the Kansas City, Pittsburg, & Gulf RR," January 1, 1898 (Pliny Fisk Collection, Pliny Fisk Library, Princeton University, Princeton, New Jersey).

28. Stilwell, *Forty Years of Business Life,* 5.

29. George Kennan, *E. H. Harriman: A Biography* (Boston: Houghton, Mifflin Company, 1922), I, 216–217.

Gulf of Mexico with a large inland body of water, Sabine Lake. The 17-mile-long lake was very shallow and muddy and provided access to the Sabine and Neches Rivers. A sizable inland trade developed from the Pass, where cargoes from oceangoing ships were transferred to lake and river boats, barges, and lighters. Newspaper articles, charters, reports in railway publications, and even company stationary indicated that Sabine Pass was the ultimate destination of the line. The first hint that this was no longer true came in January of 1894, when the directors raised the question as to the goal of future construction.[30] Stilwell later declared that he had never intended to build to Sabine Pass, and those who said he had were "absolutely incorrect."[31] Why did the promoter disavow what had clearly been his intent? His own version of what happened, written more than thirty years later, offers a fascinating answer.

As the KCPG completed its line from Kansas City to Shreveport, Stilwell decided to stop construction there, if only temporarily, and to purchase the Houston, East and West Texas Railroad. That railway operated from Shreveport to Houston, a distance of 232 miles, and was for sale for $3,000,000. Stilwell got an option to purchase the line, had his engineers inspect it, and asked the directors of the KCPG to ratify the purchase. By acquiring the HEWT, a direct connection to deep water at Galveston could be made. The directors gathered in Kansas City, ready to approve the arrangements, but Stilwell abruptly changed his mind. He recalled that he had tried to sleep the night before the directors' meeting, but a vivid dream interrupted his slumber:

The weirdest of all hunches I have ever had in my life came to me the night before the meeting was to be held. . . . I became possessed of an overpowering fear that we were planning wrongly this time in relying on the coast of the Gulf of Mexico as our principal terminus, because of the storms of tremendous violence that lashed those shores at times.

30. The Kansas City *Star*, January 11, 1893 and January 18, 1894; S. G. Reed, *A History of the Texas Railroads and of Transportation Conditions under Spain and Mexico and the Republic and the State* (Houston: The St. Clair Publishing Company, 1941), 436; Henry V. Poor, *Manual of the Railroads of the United States* (New York: Poor's Publishing Company, 1893), 339–340. Cited hereafter as Poor, *Manual*, date and page.

31. "Reasons Why Port Arthur Should Be Made a Port of Entry," pamphlet containing a copy of a telegram from Stilwell to George M. Craig, May 23, 1906 (Port Arthur Historical Society, Port Arthur, Texas).

Writing several years after the great hurricane hit Galveston, he continued,

An intuitive sense—or a hunch, as I have chosen to call it through this narrative—told me to abandon this entire project and look to a more northeasterly portion of the Texas coast for the end of our line to deep water. I did so, and there occurred to me a picture of a city with a population of about 100,000 persons on the north bank of Lake Sabine which could be connected with the Gulf by means of a canal about seven miles long. Here, in this landlocked harbor, safe from the most devastating storm the Gulf could produce, we would erect elevators and piers and create a port for the shipment of the Western farmers' export grain. It was far better than our first idea.[32]

According to Stilwell, his associates were most surprised by this abrupt departure from their original plans, and, of course, he could not divulge the reason for the change; "I was afraid to mention publicly at the director's meeting any reason for this sudden change of heart for fear that it should shock their credulity."[33] Only a few of his closest friends were told of the "hunch."

Stilwell told different versions of the "hunch" at other times. In another book he emphasized only the destructive storms of the Gulf,[34] and later the dream was described more vividly. A voice in the dream said,

Do not purchase the Houston, East and West Texas railroad. . . . Locate your terminal city on the north shore of Sabine Lake. Connect with deep water via canal from your terminal city. Build the canal the same width at the top, the same depth and the same width at the bottom as the Suez Canal. Dig it on the west shore of the lake and put the earth on the east bank to protect the canal from any storm, for Galveston will some day be destroyed.[35]

And yet, at other times, it was Sabine Pass which was going to be destroyed by storms.[36] While each version of the story is exciting or, at least, imaginative, what actually had transpired was far more practical.

In April of 1895, Stilwell, his wife, Robert Gillham, William Waterall's daughter, and Frank Henderson, a townsite agent, went to the Gulf Coast, traveling over the Southern Pacific Railroad to Sabine Pass. Unimpressed with the town, Stilwell's discomfort increased with the knowl-

32. Stilwell, "I Had a Hunch," January 14, 1928, 77–78.
33. *Ibid.*
34. Stilwell, *Cannibals of Finance*, 57–58.
35. Unidentified newspaper clipping, "Personalities of Port Arthur," scrapbook (Gates Memorial Library, Port Arthur, Texas).
36. *Engineering News*, February 17, 1898.

edge that the banking firm of Kountze Brothers owned the town and 40,000 acres of land in and around the Pass. When Stilwell entered into negotiations with Luther Kountze for access to the port facilities, problems arose. Stilwell claimed that Kountze asked $1,000,000 for his holdings and offered to put $100,000 in a bank account in Stilwell's name if he would cause the KCPG to make the purchase. Stilwell refused. "I am not for sale," he said.[37] Another version of the story says that Kountze's subsidiary which owned the land at the Pass, the Sabine Land and Improvement Company, offered to give the KCPG land for terminals, docks, elevators, and other facilities, but that Stilwell demanded a division of the profits on all property sales in the area. Highly favorable to the Kountzes, this report claimed that Sabine Pass was a splendid port, and the "natural terminus" of the KCPG.[38] One of Stilwell's own publications later suggested that the promoter had asked for 51 percent of the acreage of the Sabine Land Company if he agreed to terminate the KCPG at the Pass.[39] It seems highly implausible that Stilwell would build a railroad to a terminus he did not control, and he left Sabine Pass determined to find a more suitable—and more profitable—site.

As the train moved back north along the western shore of Sabine Lake, Stilwell and Gillham noted a large flat area east of Taylor's Bayou, a small body of water connected to the lake. Gillham became enthusiastic about the land on the lake shore, having been quite concerned about the presence of very high tides at Sabine Pass. Stilwell made two significant decisions; he dispatched Frank Henderson to nearby Beaumont to enter into negotiations for purchase of this property, and he ordered Gillham to begin engineering plans for a channel from the proposed site across the shallow lake to Sabine Pass.[40] It appears that Stilwell's "hunch" had far less to do with his decision than the fateful negotiations with the Kountze brothers.

Frank Henderson began negotiations with the Beaumont Pasture

37. Stilwell, *Cannibals of Finance*, 62.
38. "Report of L. A. Etter," January 1, 1898; Port Arthur *Herald*, December 30, 1897.
39. *The Kansas City Gateway*, (December 1902), 30.
40. Port Arthur *Herald*, March 23, 1899; Stilwell, "I Had a Hunch," January 14, 1928, 78.

Company and the firm of McFaddin, McFaddin, Weiss and Kyle for more than 40,000 acres of land. The trackage was located seventeen miles from the Gulf of Mexico along the western shore of Sabine Lake. Consisting of level prairie lands, with a gray silt and black waxy soil, the area had previously been used as a cattle range. On October 15, 1895, the Beaumont Pasture Company sold 41,850 acres to an agent of the KCPG for $6.75 an acre, and on December 14, 1895, the McFaddin concern sold the same agent an additional 4,428 acres for $25,040. Thus, by the end of the year, the promoter had acquired the site for his Gulf terminus.[41]

Stilwell lost no time in selecting the name for the new city, and once again modesty failed him, for the townsite became Port Arthur! The first public announcements about this urban promotion and its name occurred in late October and early November 1895.[42] If the directors of the KCPG or the Trust company were upset by Stilwell's unabashed self-interest in selecting the name for their terminal, they probably remained silent. One of Stilwell's associates later wrote that the directors accepted the change of plans because they were sharing in the land syndicate's profits. The promoter himself declared that the directors offered him a 10 percent personal interest in the townsite, but that he declined, saying his salary of $5,000 a year was ample compensation.[43] Clearly, however, Stilwell and his associates did have personal shares in the promotion of Port Arthur, and while their interests were "opportunistic" evidence also indicates that Stilwell's larger designs for the port were "developmental." He provided immediate profit-making possibilities in order to finance long-range projects.

Flamboyant claims, enthusiastic endorsements, and visionary predictions were the tools of the urban promoter, and Stilwell was unmatched in the business. A typical advertisement for land at Port Arthur declared,

41. Port Arthur *Herald*, December 30, 1897; M. B. Hillyard, *The New South* (Baltimore: Manufacturer's Record, 1887), 324–325; *Jefferson County Deed Records*, Volume 22, 50, and Volume 12, 64–74 (Jefferson County Court House, Beaumont, Texas) cited by John R. Rochelle, "Port Arthur: A History of Its Port to 1963" (Unpublished Masters Thesis, Lamar State College of Technology, 1969), 45; Abstract of Title, Lot No. 2, Block No. 209, Port Arthur, Texas (Mrs. James W. Ellender, Port Arthur, Texas). Cited hereafter as Ellender Abstract.

42. *Commercial and Financial Chronicle, Investor's Supplement*, October 1895, and November 2, 1895; the Kansas City *Star*, October 30, 1895, and December 23, 1895.

43. Draper, "Kansas City Southern," 25; Stilwell, *Forty Years of Business Life*, 8.

Great Cities Are Not Accidents! Nature puts them in their right place and commerce pushes them along or wipes them off the map. Neither nature nor commerce sell lottery tickets to win or lose population and business for cities. It's not chance about Port Arthur—When nature, enterprising men, capital and commerce all get together success is bound to come.[44]

The same advertisement also claimed, "Port Arthur is no place for professional boomers," which, of course, was ridiculous, for Stilwell and his friends had created two vehicles for just that purpose.

A large bloc of land around the townsite was owned by the Port Arthur Townsite and Land Company. Organized on December 4, 1895, this firm had a capitalization of $600,000, with most of the capital coming from Holland. The officers included Stilwell, E. L. Martin, Braley, and J. McD. Trimble. Another corporation, the Port Arthur Townsite Company, owned the actual site of the proposed town, about 4,000 acres, and the same men acted as trustees of the firm. The trustees were to control the company for twenty years, were to receive $2,500-a-year salaries and could be removed only by a two-thirds vote of the stockholders. The townsite company purchased its land from the land company for $12 an acre, giving the latter firm a large initial profit. Although the land company had the largest bloc, the townsite company had the more valuable holding, at least before 1901.[45]

Through the winter of 1895-1896, Robert Gillham and his crews surveyed the site at Port Arthur, laying out streets, alleys, parks, and 6,000 lots. The townsite company gave up considerable land for schools, parks, and churches. The town was "laid out in an artistic manner," with long boulevards and formal parks with Stilwell's influence evident in the selection of their names. The two main avenues were Stilwell Boulevard and Proctor Street, the latter named for investor William Proctor of Proctor and Gamble. The Dutchmen who were supplying capital were recognized by such street names as Hague, Mena Place, DeWitt, Haarlem, and Zwolle. The large park in the center of Stilwell Boulevard was called

44. The Kansas City *Star*, February 28, 1897.

45. *Port Arthur* (Houston: Anson Jones Press, 1940), 33; "The Texas Coastal Country," booklet (Port Arthur Historical Society); *Jefferson County Deed Records*, Volume 22, 50 and Volume 12, 64–74; Ellender Abstract; *Valuation Reports, Decisions of the Interstate Commerce Commission*, Vol. 75, July 1918–July 1923 (Washington: Government Printing Office, 1924), 437.

Gillham Circle, while on the other side of the site stood DeQueen Park. Once again Stilwell used his town promotion to honor and flatter his investors and associates.[46]

The land company and the townsite company rushed into print pamphlets, booklets, and newspaper copy extolling the virtues of Port Arthur. Dozens of newspaper editors, minor political figures, and businessmen were taken on excursions to the site, and their testimonials became part of the advertisements. Constant emphasis was placed on the reduction in shipping costs which the new port and the completed KCPG would bring to the midwest; Chicago and New York City were "worried," so the statements claimed. The firm of Moffett and Edwards purchased lots from the Land Company and also boomed the site. W. C. Edwards, Kansas Secretary of State; J. V. Moffett, general manager of the Rock Island Railroad Land Department; and G. M. Seward, assistant State Treasurer of Kansas purchased $250,000 in property at Port Arthur and immediately began to sponsor excursions from Kansas City. While Fred Hornbeck acted as general manager of Port Arthur land sales, George Craig moved to the site and became the local manager. Land sold quickly, and even before Stilwell made the first payment to the Beaumont interests he placed $135,000 in the treasury of the Trust company.[47]

The promoter made numerous trips to Port Arthur, usually accompanied by investors and often by foreign bondholders. Stilwell took great pride in the development of the site and in showing the area to visitors. He also received personal income from land sales. Stilwell and Craig developed "Stilwell Heights," their own "suburb" of Port Arthur, selling lots and splitting the profits. The land cost $6,840 and by 1902 they had

46. Ellender Abstract; Port Arthur *News*, March 18, 1897; Stilwell, "I Had a Hunch," January 14, 1928, 78; "Canal Harbor and Terminal Improvements," map, October 30, 1897, in *Ship Canal at Sabine Pass, Texas* (House of Representatives Document 549, House Documents Volume 68, Serial Number 3696, 55th Congress, 2nd Session). Cited hereafter as *Ship Canal at Sabine Pass, Texas.*

47. Pamphlet, Port Arthur Townsite and Land Company, 1898 (Arthur E. Stilwell Collection, Port of Port Arthur, Port Arthur, Texas), cited hereafter as the Stilwell Collection; Pamphlet, "Press Comments on Port Arthur," 1896 (Port Arthur Historical Society); Herschiel L. Hunt, *The History of Port Arthur* (n.p.: Southern Publishing Concern, 1926), 12–13; the Kansas City *Star*, December 23, 1896 and January 17, 1897; Manuscript by George M. Craig (Historical files, Port Arthur Chamber of Commerce); Stilwell, "I Had a Hunch," January 14, 1928, 78.

earned $3,815 each.[48] Jay Gould and Commodore Vanderbilt would sneer at such modest profits, but one can guess that Stilwell took as much pleasure in the name of the subdivision as in the money he earned from it.

Stilwell, Hornbeck, and Craig acted with dispatch to make Port Arthur attractive to prospective pilgrims. Fifty workmen were employed in various projects by the early spring of 1896. The laborers brought their supplies from Beaumont over a wagon road that was so bad it took an entire day for a round trip across the marshes. On Proctor Street, a saloon and a bakery sprang up, although the street was no more than two long plowed furrows. The workmen, who lived in tents and rude shelters, were plagued by hordes of ravenous mosquitoes which swarmed over the site.[49] Nevertheless, several structures of considerable size soon dominated the town.

The KCPG began to build track from Port Arthur to Beaumont, and one of the first large structures was the "Pee Gee" station. Built of wood frame and plaster, the Spanish-style building featured a tile roof, and eventually numerous palms and shrubs graced its entrance.[50] Not far from the station another large structure, the Sabine Hotel, was under construction.

By March of 1896, work had begun on the Sabine, a three-story building of seventy rooms. The front of the structure featured massive columns and a broad veranda, and surrounding the hotel was an elaborate tropical garden. Stilwell boomed the city as a winter resort, and to attract tourists a natatorium was constructed adjacent to the hotel, and a pleasure pier 2,000 feet long was built into the lake. On the pier an open-air restaurant and dance pavillion provided food and recreational activities for the hotel guests. Although artesian water supplied the natatorium, deep wells were drilled for the hotel and ultimately for the entire town.[51]

Port Arthur grew slowly in 1896 and 1897; in January of the latter year, the permanent population was only 60 to 70 people. The Sabine,

48. The Port Arthur *Herald*, May 19, and June 30, 1898; "Expenses to January 1, 1902," and George Craig to Arthur Stilwell, July 23, 1902, George Craig Papers.

49. *Port Arthur*, 33–34.

50. *Ibid.*, 156; File 110.3, Kansas City Southern Records (Offices of the Kansas City Southern Railway, Kansas City, Missouri); Felton, "Report on the Kansas City, Pittsburg & Gulf Railroad."

51. *Port Arthur*, 34, 126, 156; Hunt, *The History of Port Arthur*, 13–14.

three other hotels or boarding houses, the saloon, and two wooden homes were the only significant structures other than the railroad station. By the early fall of 1897, there were 860 people, sixteen business houses, and sixty homes.[52] There were two newspapers in the town, both of which received large subsidies from the Stilwell concerns in the form of advertisements and "manufactured" news. The growing community acquired a school building with construction provided by volunteer labor. Other visible signs of progress and community organization were the two churches, two banks, and an electric-light system. The town was incorporated in 1898, and a year later the first city officials were elected.[53] With the town's increasing visibility, Stilwell, Craig, and Hornbeck had a far more marketable item to sell.

The techniques used to promote Port Arthur were similar to those used at Mena, DeQueen, and elsewhere. Giant advertisements were placed in midwestern newspapers depicting the site, the proposed channel to Sabine Pass and the Gulf, and drawings of the Sabine Hotel and the depot. Elaborate excursion trains featuring Pullman sleepers and buffets were dispatched from Kansas City by Stilwell's enterprises or by Moffett and Edwards. Throughout the latter part of 1896 and in 1897, numerous special trains brought visitors to Port Arthur, and many of the railroad and newspaper men who accompanied the guests traveled free. The dining car menu included Gulf Coast delicacies, and Hornbeck told the prospective buyers that they would always eat like this in Port Arthur. On their arrival at the town, the guests were taken to the Sabine Hotel for further "wining and dining." A giant, memorable train arrived on March 18, 1897, with the Pullman Palace cars "Melissa," "Cremora," and "Turia," a Pullman tourist sleeper, a KCPG coach, and a dining car. Baggage car number nine on the train contained the press and facilities of the Port Arthur *News* which composed and printed its first edition on the train. Governor J. W. Leedy of Kansas and Mayor C. G. Jones of Oklahoma City were two of the dignitaries on board the excursion. The pilgrims from the train bought town lots and farm lands.[54]

One of Arthur Stilwell's "developmental" activities was to encourage

52. Port Arthur *Herald*, September 9, 1897.
53. *Port Arthur*, 156; Port Arthur *News*, November 4, 1897.
54. The Kansas City *Star*, January 19 and 27, 1897; *Port Arthur*, 35 and 39; Port Arthur *News*, March 18, 1897.

the planting of nurseries and orchards and the expansion of general agricultural production along his railways. He may have been encouraged in this direction by memories of the nurseries and orchards which had given his birthplace, Rochester, the name "Flower City," or it may have been the desire to create long-run shipping for the railroad. Regardless, he created an experimental farm at Amoret, Missouri, under the direction of Frank M. Hammon and had a number of orchards planted along the KCPG in northern Arkansas. In November of 1896, Stilwell sent Hammon to Port Arthur to establish an experimental farm of 320 acres. The farm would show potential land buyers the possibilities of the area for agricultural purposes, and the Port Arthur Land and Townsite Company offered prospective settlers ten-acre plots for small truck farms. Hammon created a beautiful farm, and by March of 1897 had laid out vegetable and flower gardens as well as fruit trees and beds of tobacco. Using the best seeds and plants available, Hammon produced bumper crops. A dairy barn was added, and blooded dairy and beef cattle were brought to the experimental farm. The farmers who bought the ten-acre plots at $20 an acre, however, discovered that there was a limited market for their produce, and many switched to the growing of rice.[55]

Rice growing had developed near Beaumont as early as 1881, but the annual production was limited. The soil, climate, and presence of artesian water were conducive to rice culture, and Stilwell, seeing the rice potential as a device to sell the almost 40,000 acres owned by his companies, directed the formation of the Port Arthur Rice Farm. Hammon wrote pamphlets and newspaper stories on rice-growing methods, and Hornbeck divided several areas of their holdings into rice farms to be sold at $40 an acre. Hammon cultivated 500 acres of rice which produced 8 to 10 barrels per acre. As interest in the crop grew some rice land was rented to tenant farmers, but most was sold. The rice farm installed a system of pumps and ditches to provide water for flooding the rice fields, charging two sacks of rice per acre for the water. The rice sold for $3.60 a barrel, so that farmers could make modest profits. Some farmers cut the rice twice, using the second cutting for hay, while others turned cattle in on the rice fields after the first cutting. Rice mills at Beau-

55. Port Arthur *News*, March 18, 1897; *Port Arthur*, 34–35; Hunt, *The History of Port Arthur*, 15; Nolthenius, *Nieuwe Wereld*, 25–27.

mont and Lake Charles purchased the crop from the Port Arthur agriculturalists.[56]

Always striving to build his schemes and to make them more profitable, Stilwell decided to bring Hollanders to Texas as rice farmers. DeGeoijen began to advertise the Port Arthur Rice Farm in Dutch journals, and Stilwell created the community of Nederland between Port Arthur and Beaumont as a settlement for Dutch immigrants. Soon a number of families arrived from Holland, and the Port Arthur *News* began publishing columns in Dutch. Although some historians have contended that southerners were basically hostile to immigrants in this era and that immigration efforts by states and railroads generally failed, this does not seem to be the case at Port Arthur. The Dutch farmers were welcomed by the "natives," and the Hollanders seemed very happy in their settlement.[57] By 1900, Stilwell's efforts to promote rice culture were paying off.

Stilwell did not initiate the production of rice in southeastern Texas, but he made a significant contribution by encouraging its expansion. In 1890 there were 135 acres of rice in the entire state, but production increased 4,800 percent by 1899, with Jefferson County the principal producer. Jefferson County, where the Stilwell enterprises represented a major property, expanded its production from 20 acres and 13,996 pounds of rice in 1889 to 5,859 acres and 5,643,194 pounds in 1899. Together, Jefferson and neighboring Orange County produced 92.7 percent of the Texas rice crop. Stilwell could be proud, and of course he was, of his contribution to this aspect of the regional economy.[58]

As important as were promoting the town, establishing the rice farm, and building the KCPG south from Shreveport to Port Arthur, without

56. Hillyard, *The New South*, 336; Port Arthur *News*, November 4, 1897 and December 3, 1898; Stilwell, "I Had a Hunch," January 14, 1928, 78; *Eighth Annual Statement of the Kansas City, Pittsburg & Gulf Railroad Company*," October 28, 1897, 8–9.

57. Stilwell, "I Had a Hunch," January 14, 1928, 78; Port Arthur *News*, November 25, 1897 and May 13, 1903; Rowland T. Berthoff, "Southern Attitudes toward Immigration 1865–1914," *The Journal of Southern History*, XVII (August 1951), 328–360; Nolthenius, *Nieuwe Wereld*, 25–27.

58. Clark, *Then Came the Railroads*, 210–211; Dermot H. Hardy and Ingham S. Roberts, *Historical Review of South East Texas* (Chicago: Lewis Publishing Company, 1910), I, 434–435; *Twelfth Census of the United States, Agriculture*, (Washington: Government Printing Office, 1902), VI, Part II, 57.

the construction of the waterway from Port Arthur to Sabine Pass none of these had meaning. The most crucial development, once the decision had been reached to form an entirely new terminus, was the completion of the connection to the Gulf. The story of this development fits the model based on entrepreneurial error almost perfectly. Arthur Stilwell had his vision; he and Gillham grossly underestimated the cost of the project, the opposition it would arouse, the time necessary to complete it, the heavy fixed investment, the initial absence of profits, and the ultimate necessity for the federal government to assume operation of the project. The original investors would see their capital lost and the waterway pass from private to public hands. The project would never have been initiated had the almost insurmountable difficulties been known, yet, it became a very significant economic asset to the region.

Stilwell and Gillham originally planned to dredge a channel from Port Arthur directly across Sabine Lake to deep water at Sabine Pass. The federal government had deepened the pass to 24 feet and constructed jetties to protect it from silt deposits. Lake Sabine had an average depth of only six feet, and silt from the Sabine and Neches rivers was constantly deposited in the lake. Gillham's engineering drawings proposed a channel seven miles long, 200 feet wide, and 25 feet deep.[59] This proposal did not differ markedly from a report issued by the Chief of Engineers of the Department of War in 1895, which suggested a similar channel across the Lake from the Pass to the mouth of the Sabine River to provide a means to ship lumber from eastern Texas and western Louisiana to the Gulf.[60] The War Department plan did not win approval, but does suggest that Gillham's proposal was feasible.

In order to dredge the channel and build docks and other navigational and shipping facilities, Stilwell created the Port Arthur Channel and Dock Company on June 16, 1896. Capitalized at $1,000,000, the channel company proposed to construct the channel, own and operate ships and steamship lines, a turning basin, wharves, warehouses and a grain elevator. The channel company purchased 2,600 acres of land between the site of Port Arthur and Taylor's Bayou from the land company and

59. *The Railway Age*, May 16, 1896.
60. "Preliminary Examination of Channel through Sabine Lake, Texas," (House of Representatives, Executive Document 275, 53rd Congress, 3rd Session).

the townsite company for development of the shipping terminal. The capital for the channel company came largely from abroad, and $500,000 in bonds were issued to each of the companies selling the land, giving them a profit of $441,229.26. When Stilwell brought a special train to Port Arthur in November of 1897, he was accompanied by DeGeoijen, A. A. Herrmann of Hamburg, Germany, and by F. Cortland Taylor, J. Pollak, and Douglas J. Neame of London, all of whom were bondholders. The Port Arthur *News* reported that at least one-fifth of the bonds had been sold in England, and an employee of the firm later reported that funds for operations were deposited in a Kansas City bank in "pounds," not dollars. Capital for initiating construction came from the Trust company, which together with the Provident Trust of Philadelphia, acted as trustee of the channel firm.[61]

Dredging of the channel began, and the Kountze Brothers immediately filed suit in federal court to block the work. The Kountzes claimed that Stilwell had not received permission from the Secretary of War to dredge the channel, and if work proceeded, silt from the lake would move through the channel, filling up Sabine Pass and the harbor owned by the Kountzes. Thus began two years of constant litigation, appearances before Congressional committees, petitions to the War Department, and expensive engineering tests and surveys. A federal court injunction stopped work on the channel and threatened the entire project. What Gillham projected to be a six-month-long construction project became a two-year nightmare.[62]

Despairing of ever clearing away the legal obstacles, and desiring to open the port as quickly as possible, Stilwell proposed a new plan: a canal around the western end of the Lake from Taylor's Bayou to Sabine Pass. He told Gillham to design the canal exactly like the Suez Canal, 188 feet

61. Minute Book, Port Arthur Channel and Dock Company, June 16, 1896 (Offices Kansas City Southern Railway); *The Railway Age*, May 16, 1896; *Port Arthur*, 33; Port Arthur *Herald*, November 18, 1897; W. A. Goodwin to William M. Deramus, May 21, 1959 (Offices Kansas City Southern Railway); the Kansas City *Star*, January 19, 1897; *Valuation Reports*, Vol. 75, 437.

62. *Port Arthur*, 41–42; Port Arthur *Herald*, January 12, 1899; Crary *versus* Port Arthur Channel and Dock Company, *Southwestern Reporter*, XLVII, 968, cited by Rochelle, "Port Arthur: A History of Its Port," 53–54; Chicago *Tribune*, November 11, 1898.

wide at the top, 74 feet wide at the bottom and 28 feet deep. To keep the spoil from the canal from entering the Lake, an earthen berm would separate the water of the canal from the water of the Lake.[63] In April 1897, the first cuts for the new canal were made. What had appeared to be an easy task, quickly done and highly profitable, was becoming difficult, time-consuming and costly, earmarks of a serious entrepreneurial error.

On February 8, 1897, Stilwell reincorporated the Port Arthur Channel and Dock Company in the State of Texas. Placing the corporation under Texas law would be beneficial in fighting the Kountze Brothers, for most Texas officials favored the project. The capitalization of the company, reflecting the rising costs of the project, was increased to $2,500,000 in bonds and an equal sum in stocks. Of the 25,000 shares of stock issued by the channel company, 10,000 were held by the Trust company, De-Geoijen had 3,072, the Amsterdam agency held 1,695, and Stilwell owned 251 and held 240 more in trust. The remainder was scattered among a number of individuals and companies. Stilwell received an additional 750 shares in February of 1899 as compensation for his efforts for the company. The initial offering of $1,500,000 in bonds, with a bonus of 50 percent in stock, was oversubscribed, but the company received constant criticism in some financial journals.[64] When the prospectus of the channel company reached the offices of the *Commercial Advertiser*, the editors complained that revenue to pay interest on the bonds was illusory, and that the burden of payment actually rested on the Trust company and the KCPG. The editors concluded that the bondholders and stockholders of the KCPG were going to be fleeced.[65] The railroad was to pay $2 per railway car handled by the channel company with a minimum guarantee of $40,000 a year. Why, asked the editors, did not the railroad own the channel and harbor? Only Stilwell could answer, and he chose not to; the arrangement was undoubtedly based on the need to find the capital he so desperately sought.

63. Stilwell, "I Had a Hunch," January 14, 1928, 78.

64. Minute Book, Port Arthur Channel and Dock Company, December 22, 1897, January 11, and February 8, 1898, and February 14 and 20, 1899; Arthur E. Stilwell to the agents of the Missouri, Kansas & Texas Trust Co., December 10, 1897, Stilwell Collection.

65. *Commercial Advertiser*, December 6, 1897, newspaper clipping in the Pliny Fisk Collection.

While litigation continued over the channel and, subsequently, the canal, Stilwell proceeded with other construction work at the Port Arthur harbor. In 1897 and 1898, a 1,700-foot lumber wharf, two general wharves and a 3,300-foot temporary export pier were constructed, as were a 500,000-bushel-capacity grain elevator, a turning basin and warehouses. More than five miles of track were built to connect the dock facilities with the KCPG track from Port Arthur to Beaumont. The export pier was an expedient to open the harbor before the canal was completed. Vessels bound for Port Arthur anchored at Sabine Pass, and lighters, pulled by tugboats, transferred goods across the lake from the export pier to the boats at the pass in a trip which took three hours. Most of the cargo was bulk, generally cotton, lumber, zinc, or flour. The literage costs were enormous, but Stilwell determined to open the port regardless of the opposition by the Kountze Brothers. The Port Arthur Channel and Dock, the Port Arthur Land Company and the Trust company each paid one fifth of the literage costs while the townsite company paid two-fifths. Only the Trust directly and the KCPG indirectly however, were able to supply the actual cash to maintain the system. The channel and dock company soon had an extensive harbor operation on its nearly 4,000-acre holding with money for the project coming from the sale of securities and advances from the Trust company.[66] Gillham's plans originally called for eight slips 1000 feet by 250 feet, a large transfer pier, a turning basin 500 feet wide, and a drydock.[67] Not all of these projects were necessary or feasible as long as the canal remained unfinished and the literage system in use.

Although Stilwell directed Gillham to design the canal along the western shore to the same dimensions as the Suez, costs were prohibitive. When two hydraulic dredges of the New York Dredge Company went to work cutting the canal, portions were dug only 18 feet deep, and the top of the waterway was only 83 feet wide. Work began in May of 1897, and dredges began excavating 5,000 cubic yards of the stiff yellow and blue clay along the route. The material excavated was piled between the canal and the lake, forming the berm. By November 1897, three more dredges

66. *Valuation Reports*, Vol. 75, 435–442; Port Arthur *Herald*, July 15 and 22, August 5, and October 7, 1897, and February 10, 1898; Felton, "Report on the Kansas City, Pittsburg & Gulf Railroad"; *Ship Canal at Sabine Pass, Texas*, Map, "Canal Harbor & Terminal Improvements."
67. *Engineering News*, February 17, 1898.

were at work, and the KCPG had to appropriate $2,500,000 for the excavation of the canal.[68] With construction proceeding rapidly, the Kountze Brothers obtained another injunction forcing the dredges to stop.

The Kountze Brothers remained determined to prevent Stilwell from building the canal and establishing Port Arthur. They realized that if Stilwell's plans were brought to fruition, their land holdings and urban scheme would be virtually valueless. Therefore, in February 1898 they appealed to Secretary of War Russell Alger to order the dredges stopped on the grounds that silt from Taylor's Bayou would flow through the canal and be deposited in Sabine Pass. The secretary ordered the work stopped until evidence was presented that the charges were untrue. J. McD. Trimble, president of the Port Arthur Channel and Dock, declared that Gillham's plans would prevent the silting of the Pass and that, after all, if such silting did occur, Port Arthur would suffer also. Preserving navigation was important to all concerned, said Trimble. When Secretary Alger agreed to allow further excavation as long as revetments in Sabine Lake prevented excavated materials from entering the lake, the Kountzes protested again. This time they charged that the channel company was acting illegally, that their work was not inspected, and that the channel company was interested only in tolls on the canal.[69]

Alger asked the Corps of Engineers to ascertain the effect of the silting, and the corps, using their own testing devices and information collected by Robert Gillham, declared that silting was minimal. Gillham placed testing instruments at Taylor's Bayou and the Pass, and they showed a silting rate of one foot every one hundred years. The chief engineer advised Alger that the channel company should be allowed to proceed.[70] Seeing that the secretary was about to remove his injunction, the Kountzes shifted the fight to the halls of Congress.

From the inception of Stilwell's plan, various congressmen and congressional committees had taken an interest in the project. During the pre-

68. *Ibid*; Port Arthur *News*, November 4, and December 9, 1897; Manuscript by George Craig (Port Arthur Chamber of Commerce).

69. J. McD. Trimble to G. D. Meiklejohn, February 21, 1898; Order from Secretary of War, R. A. Alger, March 12, 1898; B. D. Crary to Alger, March 24, 1898, in *Ship Canal at Sabine Pass*.

70. Colonel Henry M. Roberts to Brigadier General John M. Wilson, June 8, 1898; General Wilson to Secretary Alger, June 18, 1898, in *Ship Canal at Sabine Pass*; *Port Arthur*, 45.

vious year some members of the House Rivers and Harbors Committee had visited Port Arthur to inspect the canal site and dredging work. In May of 1898 that committee sent to the House floor a joint resolution inquiring of Secretary Alger about the situation at Sabine Pass. The House and Senate passed the resolution, and Alger prepared the lengthy report entitled the *Ship Canal at Sabine Pass.* Undoubtedly, the resolution was written and passed at the instigation of the Kountzes, for the wording of the inquiry is hostile.[71]

Stilwell countered the Kountze effort in two ways. First, he asked state legislatures and politicians in the midwest and south central states to memorialize Congress in favor of the canal. Arguing that freight rates would be reduced, the legislatures of Iowa and Arkansas and the Nebraska Secretary of State asked Congress to allow completion of the canal and to make Port Arthur a subport of entry.[72] Second, Stilwell went to Washington to testify before the House Ways and Means Committee, which was involved because of the port of entry question. To aid in developing Port Arthur, and to avoid long journeys to Galveston, the nearest port of entry, Stilwell asked for Port Arthur to be made a subport of entry. When Stilwell went before the Ways and Means Committee he was allotted only twenty minutes to speak. He emphasized the storms at Sabine Pass and the safety of his landlocked harbor and canal. The attorney for the Kountzes responded that Stilwell's only interests were financial and personal, that he wanted a town named for himself, and, besides, the canal was just as subject to storms as Sabine Pass. Describing the effects of the most recent storm, the attorney asked Stilwell, "What did the storm do to your canal?" "It only wet the water," he answered. The committee room rocked with laughter. The committee decided not to create a subport of entry, but it also refused to block construction of the canal.[73] The Kountzes lost another round.

Stilwell later wrote that he went to see President McKinley after the hearing, the President told him to complete the canal immediately if the results were favorable, and the canal was quickly opened. This could not

71. The Kansas City *Star*, January 30, 1897; *Ship Canal at Sabine Pass, passim.*
72. *Congressional Record* (55th Congress, 2nd Session), XXXI, Part IV, 3289, and (55th Congress, 3rd Session), XXXII, Part II, 1916 and 2036.
73. Stilwell, *Cannibals of Finance*, 63–65; Stilwell, "I Had a Hunch," January 28, 1928, 26, 83, 86.

have occurred, for many months would pass before the canal actually became operative.

In March of 1898, the Kountzes filed a series of lawsuits against the channel company. Allies of the Kountzes owned a neck of land through which the canal had to pass, and although the land had little value, the friends of the Kountzes asked $1,000 an acre for it. A year before Stilwell had requested the Texas Legislature to grant the channel company the right of emminent domain, and when this was granted in March of 1897, the Kountzes objected. The Kountze allies divided the narrow piece of land into many separate holdings, each owner refused to sell, and when Stilwell tried to use emminent domain, each went to court in a separate suit. In one case, decided by the federal Court of Appeals in New Orleans, the court ruled that the property owners would not suffer "irreparable damages," as they had claimed, and further, that the land was worth only about $6 an acre. Then Charles T. Crary, another property owner, charged that the channel company did not have the right to use emminent domain on the shore, but only in the lake. Finally, on November 21, 1898, the Texas Supreme Court ruled for the channel company. This was the sixteenth court case brought by the Kountzes, their allies, or the Sabine Land Company, and each time the channel company won. Dredges were poised to renew excavation when the court decided against a motion for a rehearing in December. The channel company now could legally proceed to cut the last two miles of the waterway.[74] Jubilant Arthur Stilwell sent a telegram:

Tell Port Arthur people they will now see the dawn of the greatest prosperity for the coming Gulf port. We rejoice with you.[75]

Not only had Stilwell finally defeated the Kountzes, after two years of Congressional hearings, engineering surveys, and court cases, but he could also take pride in the growing shipping business at Port Arthur.

74. Port Arthur *Herald*, January 12, 1899; H. P. N. Gammel (comp.), *The Laws of Texas, 1822–1897* (Austin: The Gammel Book Co., 1898), X, 1073–1074; Davis *versus* Port Arthur Channel and Dock Co., *Federal Reporter*, LXXXVII, 512–517; Crary *versus* Port Arthur Channel and Dock Company, *Southwestern Reporter*, XLVII, 968–970, all cited by Rochelle, "Port Arthur: A History of Its Port," 53–56. See also unidentified newspaper clippings, November 22, 1898, and December 28, 1898, Pliny Fisk Collection.
75. Port Arthur *Herald*, November 24, 1898.

Even as the legal battle continued, the literage system brought increased trade to the port. Stilwell created the Port Arthur and Mexican Steamship Company which inaugurated service to Mexican Gulf ports. A contract was signed with the Port Arthur-Trans-Atlantic Steamship Company to provide five 5,000-ton ships for service to Europe. In addition, the English firm of Furness, Withy and Company of London and the Dutch firm of Joseph DePoorter agreed to call at the port. The steamer *Drumelzier* arrived at Sabine Pass on January 6, 1898, received a cargo of meat, flour, corn, cotton and cottonseed oil cake, and sailed for Liverpool on the 29th, inaugurating regularly scheduled service to Europe. Additional vessels for Rotterdam and Liverpool arrived throughout 1898, and in the first six months of that year, shipping from Port Arthur equaled the previous four years at Sabine Pass. Commerce totaled 327,000 tons compared with 87,000 tons the year before. Completion of the canal would accelerate this rate even more rapidly.[76]

As the dredges moved toward each other in March of 1899, the Kountze Brothers, in a gratuitous move, signed an agreement with the channel company to interpose no further obstacles to construction of the canal, and the channel company agreed to withdraw its damage suit of $500,000 against the Sabine Land and Improvement Company. The two-year legal battle was terminated, but the Kountzes refused to admit they individually opposed the canal, saying that whatever action they had taken was as officers of the Sabine Land Company.[77] The delays which they created would cost Stilwell far more than a monetary loss.

The last one hundred feet of the canal remained to be cut on the morning of March 20, 1899. The captain of the dredge *Florida* moved his vessel forward and extracted the last piece of earth. The first ship through the waterway was the launch *Jennie,* named for Arthur's wife. A large crowd at the pier in Port Arthur held an impromptu celebration, while the formal ceremonies took place on the 25th, with Stilwell, Gillham, and other officers of the various affiliated companies presiding. The town of

76. Chicago *Tribune,* November 27, 1898; Port Arthur *News,* November 25, 1897; Port Arthur *Herald,* January 6 and 20, and February 2, 1899; *Engineering News,* February 17, 1898; *Manufacturer's Record,* March 18, 1898; Unidentified newspaper clippings, January 31 and November 22, 1898, Pliny Fisk Collection; Robert Gillham to Secretary Alger, March 19, 1898, *Ship Canal at Sabine Pass.*
77. *Wall Street Journal,* March 2, 1899.

only 1,900 people entertained 5,000 guests including the governors of Arkansas and Kansas, members of several state legislatures, and other dignitaries. The canal opened only for vessels of shallow draft, as several sections were only eight feet deep. The *Florida* and the *R. P. Clark* worked through the summer lowering the 37,700-foot canal to a uniform depth of 25 feet.[78]

Not until the following August did a deep-draft ocean vessel move through the canal. Sunday, August 13, the British ship *St. Oswald* steamed into Port Arthur, and the deep-water port officially opened. The 310-foot-long ship took an hour and twenty-five minutes to make the passage from Sabine Pass to the dock. A banquet at the Sabine Hotel honored Captain Curtis and the crew of the vessel. From the wharf and grain elevator of the channel company, the vessel took on a cargo of grain, flour, staves, and lumber. Her cargo loaded, the *St. Oswald* sailed back down the canal and on to Rotterdam.

The long-awaited opening of Port Arthur had been achieved. The city on the western shore of the Lake Sabine was connected to the Gulf by a seven-mile-long canal, and cargoes from the midwest could flow to the Gulf, avoiding longer rail shipments to the east coast. Arthur Stilwell had created for himself an urban monument. Although the operation had all the attributes of an entrepreneurial error, it had been carried to completion. A "hunch," a "dream" or a "vision," said Stilwell, but the city and the canal were real enough in 1899. With pride of creativity Stilwell wrote, "I consider the founding of Port Arthur and the construction of the Port Arthur Ship Canal my greatest achievements." Yet, while he gave Port Arthur attention, he committed much energy to his adopted home-town of Kansas City, the completion of the KCPG, and to numerous other projects, all of which became an increasingly heavy burden.

78. Port Arthur *Herald*, March 23 and 30, 1899; *Port Arthur*, 46; *The Railroad Gazette*, March 31, 1899.

VI

"STRAIGHT AS THE CROW FLIES"

ARTHUR STILWELL became a familiar figure on Kansas City streets, and his name appeared prominently in local newspapers. He adopted the city as his home, and in the midst of the depression of the 1890s the community on the bluffs of the Missouri River embraced him and his financial schemes that brought outside capital and employment to the area. Kansas City endured less social disorganization in the decade before 1900, despite the vagaries of the depression, witnessed cultural and community growth, and developed a regional reputation for its music, art, and theater. The city still suffered economically, however, from the collapse of the real estate boom in 1887, and the depression after 1893 only worsened conditions.

Throughout the Gay Nineties, Kansas City expanded and developed. The floodtide of immigrants passing through on their way west diminished, to be replaced by farmers and ranchers moving into the city, abandoning their agricultural pursuits. Charitable agencies collapsed under the terrible burden of relief obligations, forcing a change in the city's charter in 1893 to deal with growing eleemosynary responsibilities. Yet even municipal elections were scenes of turmoil and violence as the nativistic American Protective Association endorsed winning tickets in the city elections and forced the police department to drop Irishmen from its ranks. The local Roman Catholic population of 20,000 reacted negatively and violence ensued. There were, however, positive gains in the period too. The street railway system was consolidated, the water supply improved, and a system of gas lighting spread over the city. William Rockhill Nelson, crusading

114

editor of the Kansas City *Star,* led the progressive forces of the city in creating an extensive and beautiful park system.[1] Increasing concern for the urban environment in Kansas City brought out some of the best attributes of its residents, and among those concerned with civic improvements was Arthur Stilwell.

Sometime in 1894 Stilwell built, furnished, and began to maintain the Bethany Night School, one of Kansas City's pioneer social-service centers. Located at Wood and Riverview Streets near the Armour packing house in "Hell's Half Acre," the school provided evening educational opportunities for children employed during the day, with 150 to 200 children attending annually. The building also contained a library, free baths, and a daycare center for infants and younger children of working mothers. The school provided books and clothing for those children too poor to attend public schools. According to Stilwell, the $40,000 he contributed to the night school came to him as a gift from Dutch investors in the Kansas City, Pittsburg & Gulf Railroad. John DeGeoijen sent Stilwell the money, so the promoter later recalled, as a gift from the Dutch syndicate. The Dutch investors had thought Stilwell was receiving a percentage of the money from the sale of securities, and when an audit showed he did not, they were embarassed and sent the gift. He, in turn, used the money for this philanthropic purpose. The school was ultimately destroyed in the flood of 1903, but its existence for almost a decade shows Stilwell's faith in the cult of the self-made man; the successful businessman had an obligation of stewardship and civic responsibility. It also demonstrates the continuing impact of the memory of his grandfather Hamblin Stilwell, who had been a trustee of the Western House of Refuge, a home for wayward boys in Rochester. Stilwell declared that his grandfather hoped to redeem these boys, and from that trait came his own efforts at the Bethany Night School.[2]

1. Again the author is indebted to A. T. Brown for the use of the manuscript of the second volume of his history of Kansas City. Other studies which make significant contributions to the history of Kansas City in this period are William H. Wilson, *The City Beautiful Movement in Kansas City* (Columbia: University of Missouri Press, 1964); and Lyle W. Dorsett, *The Pendergast Machine* (New York: Oxford University Press, 1968); Virginia Swayne's *The Dollar Gold Piece* (New York: Farrar & Rinehart, Inc., 1942), is also an important, though fictional, view of the social history of the city.
2. Kansas City *Post,* July 20, 1907; Kansas City *World,* July 30, 1899; the

Beginning in the mid-1880s, Kansas Citians had talked of building a convention hall, but the periodic waves of enthusiasm for the project came to naught. Stilwell and other business leaders continued trying to promote the construction of such a hall. In 1895, the board of trustees of the Commercial Club asked him to become chairman of a committee to solicit funds for the building. "A man who can raise money and build a railroad in these times would be a good man to have charge of the building project," declared the club president. Stilwell accepted enthusiastically, had plans drawn for a five-story building, and organized a drive to raise $150,000. Shares were offered at $25 each, and Stilwell subscribed personally for $3,000. A contest to name the hall attracted publicity for the fund-raising drive, and as entries were submitted the Kansas City *Star* noted, "Chairman Stilwell seemed to be the ladies favorite, his name being suggested in many elegantly accoutered messages. His conferees suppressed some of the most complimentary of these notes." The contest winner would not see the building named, for the fund drive failed when pledges were not met. Two years later Stilwell offered to provide a site for a hall, leasing more than 50,000 square feet of land at Thirteenth and Central streets for a small sum. The building he envisioned would cost $75,000 and he pledged $500, the KCPG would donate $1,000 and the Missouri, Kansas and Texas Trust offered to give $3,000. Mass meetings and additional pledges supported the project, but again it failed. Finally, in 1899, a hall costing $225,000 opened, for which Stilwell, a director of the convention hall corporation, had donated $15,000. He also brought orchestras from Chicago and elsewhere to Kansas City to give free concerts at the hall. When a fire destroyed the building in April of 1900, just before the convening of the national Democratic convention, he helped raise the money to reconstruct the building which reopened in time for the convention.[3]

Kansas City *Star*, September 14, 1896; Arthur E. Stilwell and James R. Crowell, "I Had a Hunch," *The Saturday Evening Post*, CC (December 31, 1927), 78; Arthur E. Stilwell, *Forty Years of Business Life* (New York: n.p., 1926 [?]), 27–28; Arthur E. Stilwell, *Cannibals of Finance* (Chicago: Farnum Publishing Company, 1912), 188–189.

3. Brown Manuscript; the Kansas City *Star*, January 13, 16, and 23, 1895, and June 9 and 10, 1897; Kansas City *World*, July 30, 1899; New York *Herald*, September 27, 1908; Convention Hall, Stockholders Report, August 19, 1903, H. P. Wright Scrapbooks (Library, University of Missouri-Kansas City, Kansas City, Missouri).

Stilwell's civic activities encompassed several aspects of life in Kansas City. He served as first vice-president and a director of the Commercial Club. He put up $1,000 for the Stilwell Stake at the annual Horse Show at Fairmount Park. When William Rockhill Nelson organized the Western Gallery of Art, Stilwell contributed $200, promised to give at least $1,000 more if twenty other businessmen would make a similar donation, and said that on his next trip to Europe he would try to bring back a painting for the gallery. When the gallery opened, the Stilwells joined a small coterie of Kansas City's elite at a musicale held at the museum. The promoter developed an emotional attachment for his adopted home and later, when he had moved to New York, wrote, "I shall always think of you, my dear Kansas City, and still watch you from afar."[4]

Commercial developments in Kansas City also attracted Stilwell. In 1897 he announced the formation of Janssen Place, a real estate and building enterprise not far from his own residence on Thirty-sixth Street. Located between Thirty-sixth and Thirty-eighth Streets and Holmes and Locust, Janssen Place was designed as a formal, restricted housing area for the well-to-do. Modeled after the successful Van Deventer and Portland Place developments in Saint Louis, the scheme included thirty-two large lots facing a broad, flat boulevard. The north end featured a massive white limestone and bronze gate which had two eighteen-foot-wide carriage ways. The ground alone cost $100,000, and the restrictive covenant in the deeds for the lots required the structures to cost at least $10,000 and provided that no fences be erected between the houses. Stilwell formed the Janssen Place Land Company, named for Dutch investor August Janssen, and began to install the street, sewers, and sidewalks. The former cow pasture across from his home on Thirty-sixth Street was transformed into a large formal garden, but few buyers were found. Indeed, when the land company went out of business in 1906, twenty-eight lots remained unsold. The sterile formal arrangement did not attract Kansas Citians who preferred the "natural" developments which placed homes on the hills and in the small valleys in the southern part of the community. Eventually Janssen Place acquired additional residents, and today it is a beautiful neighborhood which collectively takes care of the broad lawns, the flower

4. The Kansas City *Star*, September 14, 1897, September 5, 1896, and February 27, 1897; Stilwell, *Cannibals of Finance*, 192–193.

gardens in the median strip and the limestone gates.[5] Once again, the promoter misjudged the market.

While Stilwell promoted his railroads and Port Arthur, fought with the Kountze Brothers, and made numerous trips to Europe, he kept his hand in other businesses. He formed the National Surety Company in March of 1893 and operated it for four years. The firm handled surety business for several railroads, became prosperous, and was sold in February 1897 to a syndicate which moved the company to New York City.[6] Another venture which Stilwell created was the Central Coal and Coke Company. Designed to promote coal and timber traffic on the Kansas City, Pittsburg and Gulf, this company floated $3,000,000 in preferred stock, which was sold at eighty, with an equal amount of common stock as a bonus. The men in the operation told Stilwell to take a 5 percent commission for himself, so he recalled, and he began to try and sell the securities. He failed. Although Stilwell felt he was entitled to something more for his work than the modest salaries he received from the various enterprises, this commission gave him an unfair advantage over prospective buyers. He told the directors he did not want the commission of $150,000, went back to selling the stock, and placed most of it immediately, or so he remembered. The Central Coal and Coke Company purchased widespread coal and timber lands and opened several sawmills south of Shreveport in the longleaf pine area. For Stilwell, the operation also had signficance because of the increased coal and lumber traffic on the KCPG.[7] The railroad always received his primary attention, and in 1896 and 1897 he pushed construction to the Gulf as rapidly as possible.

The Arkansas Construction Company built the Kansas City, Pittsburg and Gulf south from Siloam Springs through Indian Territory toward the townsite at Mena. Fort Smith, originally the goal of the railroad, was

5. The Kansas City *Star*, January 10 and 30, 1897; Walter B. Stevens, *Centennial History of Missouri* (Chicago: The S. J. Clarke Publishing Company, 1921), I, 900; Wilson, *The City Beautiful Movement in Kansas City*, 44; Martha Rowe Lawson, "Janssen Place (1897–1964)," *Jackson County Historical Society Journal*, (November 1964), 10–12.

6. Stilwell, *Forty Years of Business Life*, 25, 30; *Building a Great Transcontinental Railroad* (New York: n.p., 1906), 10–11; Aaron Trupin, Director of Insurance Research and Statistics, Insurance Department, State of New York, to the author, May 26, 1970.

7. Stilwell, "I Had a Hunch," January 14, 1928, 77–78.

bypassed because of the rugged terrain and was reached by a branch-line fifteen miles long. In 1895, the construction company had completed 77 miles of track from Siloam Springs to the Arkansas River bridge site at Redlands, Indian Territory, and 42 miles of the line between Texarkana and Shreveport, Louisiana. The following year the company built the rest of the route to Mena and laid track from Texarkana north while work on the Arkansas River bridge continued. That the investors in the Arkansas Construction Company earned good profits is clear; Stilwell admitted to having made $80,000 himself.[8]

To build the line from Shreveport to Port Arthur, Stilwell revived the Kansas City Terminal Construction Company. A subsidiary of the KCPG, the Kansas City, Shreveport and Gulf, held the corporate charter to build through Louisiana to Stilwell's new city on Lake Sabine, and the KCSG signed a contract with the Terminal Construction Company to build the railway. The contract provided for payment of $25,000 in bonds per mile, an equal amount in stock, plus an interest in all townsites and subsidies. The terminal company issued $3,000,000 in stock of $100 par value, and in February 1896 Stilwell went back to Europe and sold some of the stock. The distance from Shreveport to Port Arthur was 215 miles, and the line was completed in less than two years. In 1896 the terminal company built from Shreveport to Hornbeck, Louisiana, 94 miles, and from Port Arthur to Beaumont, 19 miles. Early the following year the track from Hornbeck to the Texas-Louisiana state line was completed, leaving only the bridge over the Sabine River and the track into Beaumont to be built.[9]

With construction work taking place in four locations, the KCPG constantly faced financial problems. "The Port Arthur Route," as it was now called, had to pay for right of way, grading contracts, rails, locomotives, and passenger and freight cars, without being in complete operation. At one time there were 2,000 men employed on the track gangs and hun-

8. H. F. Haag, "A Brief History of the Kansas City Southern Railway System," manuscript (Offices of the Kansas City Southern Railway, Kansas City, Missouri), 44, 49; Kansas City *World*, July 30, 1899; Stilwell, "I Had a Hunch," January 14, 1928, 77.
9. *The Railway Age*, May 23, 1896; *Commercial and Financial Chronicle*, August 24 and November 2, 1895, and *Investor's Supplement*, Vol. LXIV, 71; the Kansas City *Star*, September 21, 1895; *The Railroad Gazette*, December 27, 1895; Haag, "A Brief History of the Kansas City Southern Railway System," 49.

dreds more working on three major bridges. The difficulties of financing railway expansion in the depression of the 1890s can be seen in the fact that in 1896 Stilwell built one ninth of the total railroad mileage constructed in the country.[10]

Funds for the KCPG came from several sources. Stilwell became an expert in wringing money out of communities hungry for railroad connections. Shreveport, a town of 20,000 people, needed a rail route south to the pine country and the Gulf. Local businessmen thought that the KCPG would do for Shreveport and surrounding Caddo Parish what the Illinois Central Railroad had done for the Mississippi Valley. The city and the parish voted bonds of $325,000 to defray the costs of locating the KCPG shops in Shreveport, and the railroad agreed to locate its division headquarters there and build a union passenger station.[11] When the original survey showed the KCPG going directly from Port Arthur to Louisiana, bypassing Beaumont, Texas, that community raised $35,000 and donated land for right of way and depot grounds.[12] If Stilwell could make profits from new communities, he also knew how to extract subsidies from established towns.

Another source of funds, and of course the most important, was the sale of stocks and bonds. On December 23, 1895, the KCPG directors increased the capitalization of the railroad from $10,000,000 to $20,000,000, and Stilwell announced that the additional capital had been previously raised in Europe and Philadelphia. In October of 1896, *The Railroad Gazette* tried to establish where the Stilwell enterprises were financially, and discovered that the three construction companies— the Arkansas, Philadelphia, and Kansas City Terminal—had a total capitalization of $9,500,000. The KCPG with $20,000,000 in bonds and an equal amount of stock authorized had issued only $12,000,000 of each. The stock was quoted in Philadelphia at $18 to $20, and the bonds sold for 70 to 80. The railroad paid the construction company each time ten miles of track were completed, so that when the construction was finished,

10. The Kansas City *Star*, May 12 and 14, July 19, and December 31, 1896; *The Railway Age*, May 16, 1896.
11. *Commercial and Financial Chronicle*, May 4, 1895; *The Railroad Gazette*, July 12, 1895; *The Railway Age*, May 3, 1895; Manuscript, undated, File 110.3 (Offices of the Kansas City Southern Railway).
12. *The Railway Age*, February 15, 1896.

the latter owned the railroad, plus the townsites and bonuses. There was no floating debt, and interest remained deferred. The Dutch and Philadelphia investors seemed pleased with the progress being made.[13]

Stilwell provided the KCPG with the best passenger trains money could buy—an extravagance, but one which generated publicity and public interest. The railroad announced it was inaugurating a new train from Kansas City south to the end of track at Poteau, Indian Territory. "The Arkansas Traveler" would have the finest passenger cars, lighted by the new Pintsch gas lights and heated by steam lines from the locomotive. In addition, the cars were vestibuled, permitting easy passage throughout the train. On June 1, 1896, the first "Traveler" left Kansas City's Grand Central Station at 10:00 p.m. with a baggage and express car, smoking and chair cars, and a Pullman.[14] The railroad purchased three sets of cars for this train, which also meant more locomotives were needed.

As the KCPG built southward, traffic increased, and the steep, winding grades through the Ozark and Ouachita Mountains made heavier and larger locomotives necessary. In 1894 and 1895, the KCPG took delivery of four 4-4-0 passenger locomotives manufactured by the Schenectady Locomotive works. Also in 1895, the Baldwin Locomotive Company sold the KCPG six 2-6-0 freight engines which became numbers 21 through 26, and four 4-4-0 freight locomotives, numbers 1 through 4.[15] These purchases were necessary but only added to the financial burdens of the KCPG.

On December 12, 1896, the KCPG issued its first formal annual report. For the year ending September 30, 1896, the railroad earned $756,944.57 compared with $529,794.80 the previous year, while expenses rose to $604,250.02 from $392,918.65. Assets and liabilities were enumerated at $27,048,532.31. Average miles of track operated rose from 287 to 395, but the proportion of operating expense to gross earnings, the operation ratio, also rose from 74 percent to 79 percent. A low sum was included for maintenance of the track and equipment, a figure which would increase markedly once the line was completed. E. L. Martin gave the

13. The Kansas City *Star*, December 23, 1895; Jefferson City *Daily Tribune*, March 31, 1896; *The Railroad Gazette*, October 2, 1896.

14. Kansas City *World*, January 12, 1896; the Kansas City *Star*, June 2, 1896.

15. "All Time Steam Roster of the Kansas City Southern," *Railroad Magazine*, LXVIII (April 1957), 74–76.

president's report and predicted that when the route south of Shreveport opened the KCPG would be able to pay interest on its debts. Although the general business depression hurt the railway, the management expressed confidence in the future. By the time of the report the KCPG had 602 miles of line in operation with construction proceeding rapidly.[16] What the report failed to indicate was the poor construction of the line—most of the track lacked ballast and many areas were poorly drained—and that some reconstruction had already begun. The bridge over the Red River was condemned in 1895, and even after extensive repairs remained unsafe according to at least one engineer.[17] The report also failed to disclose that capitalization per mile jumped from $38,755 in 1895 to $79,792 in 1896.[18] Clearly, Stilwell needed to get the line completed and refinanced.

As the KCPG expanded, numerous favorable press and financial reports were published. When the bridge over the Arkansas River opened on April 24, 1896, and Mena was reached by October, large shipments of timber increased weekly earnings, which the press duly noted.[19] Through his connections with Drexel and Company, Stilwell placed highly complimentary stories in several financial journals. *The Philadelphia Stockholder,* for example, reported that Port Arthur, Texas, was booming; "Its coming importance is already rapidly increasing its population, and giving activity and value to its real estate." With regard to the KCPG, the journal declared,

If you will study the salient features of this line and give attention to the country it traverses, you will find it difficult to define its possibilities or limit the development it will awaken. Turn this proposition over in your mind, carefully consider it in all its phases, look at it from the most pessimistic

16. *Seventh Annual Statement of Kansas City, Pittsburg & Gulf R. R. Co.,* December 12, 1896; *Wall Street Journal,* December 14, 1896.

17. Samuel Morse Felton, "Report on the Kansas City, Pittsburg & Gulf Railroad," July 15, 1899, (Manuscript Division, Baker Library, Harvard Graduate School of Business Administration, Boston, Mass.).

18. United States, Interstate Commerce Commission, *Eighth Annual Report of the Statistics of Railways in the United States* (Washington: Government Printing Office, 1896), 252–253, 340–341, 394–395, and 648–649; and *Ninth Annual Report of the Statistics of Railways in the United States* (Washington: Government Printing Office, 1897), 228–229, 322, 380–381. The reports will be cited hereafter only by title.

19. Kansas City *Times,* April 25, 1896; *The Railway Age,* October 30, 1896; *Wall Street Journal,* October 23 and December 8, 1896.

standpoint, and still you will be convinced that it is one of the most natural and valuable railroad propositions recently conceived, where the energies of man have penetrated the richest storehouse of nature, and given an outlet and carrying facilities to home and foreign markets for the fabulously rich resources of a vast territory.[20]

Yet all was not well, for Stilwell received notice from his Dutch investors that they were withholding funds until after the presidential election of 1896 was resolved; they were concerned that William Jennings Bryan and "free silver" would defeat William McKinley and the gold standard.[21]

The monetary question loomed large in American politics after the Civil War, and the nomination of Bryan by the Democrats and Populists brought the issue squarely before the electorate and also brought fear to the hearts of businessmen. Men of wealth and property worried about the chances for class conflict and about the impact free silver would have on the national economy. The Republican party, under the shrewd leadership of Mark Hanna, said that all was lost if Bryan won; the only hope for the country was the preservation of the gold standard by the election of McKinley, and businessmen and financers poured thousands of dollars into the campaign. Standard Oil interests, John W. Gates, western railroad companies, and others donated money to the Chicago headquarters of the Republican party. The vast sums spent by the McKinley forces suggest the seriousness with which the gold-standard men viewed the election, and a tremendous effort was made to enlist prominent men to speak for the Republicans. A speakers bureau put 1,400 "talkers" in the field to advocate the election of the candidate, who stayed at home in Canton, Ohio, greeting delegations on his front porch. Bryan charged that the businessmen were coercing their workers into voting for McKinley, but the Republicans primarily emphasized "cheap money," and its alleged effects on the working class.[22] Prosperity was the Republican theme, and one of the most ardent supporters of McKinley and the gold standard was Arthur Stilwell.

20. *Philadelphia Stockholder*, March 9, 1896.
21. Stilwell, "I Had a Hunch," December 31, 1927, 79, and January 14, 1928, 31.
22. Paul W. Glad, *McKinley, Bryan, and the People* (Philadelphia: J. B. Lippincott Company, 1964), 166–188; Stanley L. Jones, *The Presidential Election of 1896* (Madison: The University of Wisconsin Press, 1964), 282 and 339.

The promoter faced a crisis of the most severe nature as the campaign opened in the late summer of 1896. Not only had his Dutch investors withheld their promised $3,000,000, but also for the first time there was a loss of faith in the scheme: at a board meeting, Martin, supported by the other directors, proposed a receivership. The KCPG had contracted for expenditures of almost two million dollars and had no money to pay its obligations. Stilwell objected. He proposed to go to a number of individuals and ask them for short-term loans until the election crisis passed. He wrote out a list of names—George M. Pullman, Aretas Blood, Stotesbury, Welsh, Rolla Wells, and others—and the sum of money he would ask from each of them. Martin, Waterall and the other directors stared at him incredulously. Martin protested that Stilwell was already committed to a strenuous speaking tour in the McKinley campaign, but the promoter responded he would combine the fund-raising and vote-getting efforts. The directors reluctantly authorized him to issue notes for the company, and he began his tour.[23]

Although railroad executives were often involved in politics, they usually tried to keep their companies free from openly partisan positions. Stilwell, however, began his efforts in 1896 among his employees. During the second week of August, KCPG employees received a holiday and free transportation to Fairmount Park where he spoke. The next week employees of other lines gathered at the park to hear him lecture on the problems of raising funds in Europe. He had been going to Europe for years, Stilwell related, and each time funds were harder to get because Europeans feared free silver. If silver became the basis of the monetary system of this country, he predicted that railway bonds could not be sold, and without funds, construction would end and so would employment; he preached gold and prosperity. Governor William J. Stone of Missouri, a Bryan Democrat, became incensed at Stilwell over the speeches and because Stilwell's associate J. McD. Trimble was running against the Governor as a "sound money" or "gold standard" Democrat.[24] When Stone accused Stilwell of coercing the KCPG employees, the promoter responded vigorously:

23. Stilwell, "I Had a Hunch," January 14, 1928, 31 and 70.
24. Thomas C. Cochran, *Railroad Leaders 1845–1890: The Business Mind in Action* (New York: Russell & Russell, 1965), 192–193; the Kansas City *Star*, August 16 and September 30, 1896.

A lot of fellows who never had any business experience and who couldn't make a living in any business vocation insist upon the sole right to teach finance to the people. When a man who makes finance a business chips in, they say he is a coercer of labor. Just because I employ 6,000 men I have no right to tell these men, when they ask me what I think about the questions before the country. The mission of financial enlightenment, these fellows maintain, belongs everlastingly to them.

Stilwell continued, attacking the mining companies which supported Bryan:

I could have avoided being a bad man if, instead of lecturing for sound money, I had bought a little jerk-water silver mine, I would be a saint. . . . Instead, dodgers have been scattered about calling me the blackest corporation tool in America.[25]

To make his point further, he offered to donate $1,000 to the Bryan campaign if Stone could prove his charges, but the Governor dropped the reference to Stilwell from his speeches.[26]

Stilwell did not confine his contribution to the McKinley campaign to speeches; he also published a series of pamphlets on the money question.[27] Written in the form of "fables," the pamphlets sold for 5 cents each, or 1,000 for $30.00. The fables were satirical, with such characters as "Receiving Ifican Teller," a thinly disguised lampoon of silver-Republican Senator Henry Moore Teller, saying, "The people think free silver means free silver for them. It's a catchy phrase." Free silverites in the fables praised Bryan; Thomas Watson, the Populist vice-presidential candidate; and John Peter Altgeld, the Democratic governor of Illinois who had pardoned the Haymarket Square victims and thus became a devil figure for many Americans. The fables portrayed the silver mine company owners as greedy and grasping, desiring to flood the economy with "cheap money": free silver was a free gift to the mining companies the pamphlets proclaimed. Stilwell attacked the "blue sky" claims that free silver was a panacea and loaded his political tracts with morals: "Legislation can

25. Jefferson City *Republican-Courier*, September 25, 1896.
26. *Ibid.*, October 2 and 9, 1896; the Kansas City *Star*, September 21, 1896.
27. Arthur E. Stilwell and J. E. Roberts (eds. and pubs.), *The World By the Tail with a Down Hill Pull*; *The Mystic 16 to 1*; *The Demonetization of the Mule*; *The Wise Men of Kansas* (Kansas City: Stilwell's Political Fables, 1896). A fifth pamphlet, *Parting of the Ways*, was advertised, but no copy has been located.

neither make nor unmake values," and "We can not lift ourselves up by our own boot straps." These were also the themes of his speeches.

Singing praises of McKinley and the gold standard, the promoter spoke in Joplin, Omaha, and the candidate's home town of Canton, Ohio. Although he was denounced as a "hireling of the Drexels" in Omaha, the audience of railroad workers that filled the hall offered round after round of applause. To the Railroad Men's Sound Money Club in Canton he gave his speech on gold, and that weekend he and Mrs. Stilwell were entertained at the McKinley home.[28] Having spent the better part of two days with the future president, Stilwell declared,

I saw a man with firm, steady eyes that were full of both warmth of heart and delicacy of soul. I felt that I was in the presence of a great man and a good man. Before I left Canton I was convinced that Major McKinley is the greatest living American.[29]

Stilwell discovered characteristics in McKinley that no one, except perhaps Mrs. McKinley, had discovered before or since.

Stilwell's illustrated talk on "free silver" became widely known, and large crowds came to see him on his tour of the east. He used several tables, bricks painted silver, a large tin box labeled "U. S. Mint," and dummy silver dollars. Transferring the various devices around the stage, he sought to show the results of cheap money with his crude gimickery. He needed a baggage wagon just to get his paraphernalia to the halls in which he spoke. The novelty of the speech had an appeal, and large audiences gathered in Chicago, Philadelphia, Baltimore, and Wilmington. Waves of applause greeted his denunciations of free silver as "Repudiation and hell."[30]

Stilwell's efforts in the McKinley campaign were not crucial to the election of the champion of the gold standard, for the promoter was only one of many business leaders who gave money and speeches to "save the economy." Although Stilwell claimed that he was motivated to enter politics in 1896 because of the monetary issue, it could also be that he was seeking a friendly administration in Washington which would not

28. The Kansas City *Star*, September 2 and 14, and October 22, 1896.
29. *Ibid.*, October 15, 1896.
30. *Ibid.*; the Chicago *Tribune*, November 27, 1898.

interfere with the canal work at Port Arthur. The promoter wrote later that McKinley not only tried to help him against the Kountzes at Port Arthur but also offered him the ambassadorship to Russia as a reward for his campaign efforts.[31] This seems unlikely from the contents of the correspondence between Stilwell and McKinley from 1897 to 1900. The Kansas Citian made requests and recommendations for friends concerning patronage matters and sent newspaper clippings to the President with regard to financial conditions in the midwest. In each instance, John Addison Porter, McKinley's secretary, replied saying only that the President had received Stilwell's letter; there were no direct replies from the President. The promoter did take a much less active role in the re-election campaign in 1900, when he countered the "16-to-1" free-silver campaign with a 12-to-1 "free lunch" proposal. Free silver would benefit only silver-mine owners, but free lunch, Stilwell declared, would benefit five million workers.[32] Needless to say, the idea did not become widely accepted.

With the election of McKinley in November of 1896, Stilwell rejoiced and announced that 1,500 more men would be hired to work on the KCPG south of Mena. He cabled Europe, "The free and unlimited coinage of silver has been beaten. America has voted for . . . unlimited prosperity." To his fellow citizens he proclaimed, "Kansas City is on the threshold of a new tide of success, and as soon as I am rested I will take up the banner of Kansas City again."[33]

The promoter was undoubtedly tired, for while he traveled speaking for McKinley, he also contacted numerous capitalists asking them to take short-term notes to save the KCPG. In Chicago Stilwell visited with George M. Pullman, asking the Palace Car manufacturer to take $150,000 in notes. Pullman agreed, undoubtedly doing so to save the business of the KCPG which was one of the few customers for new equipment in those depression years. Likewise, Aretas Blood, principal owner of the

31. Stilwell, *Cannibals of Finance*, 149; Stilwell, "I Had a Hunch," January 14, 1928, 72.
32. John Addison Porter to Stilwell, September 15 and November 10, 1897; March 22 and 25 and June 21, 1898; and Stilwell to William McKinley, July 5, 1900, William McKinley Papers (Manuscript Division, Library of Congress, Washington, D. C.).
33. The Kansas City *Star*, November 5, 1896.

Manchester Locomotive Works, agreed to take $450,000 in notes. Stilwell said that Blood made the loan because the KCPG had placed an order for thirty-two locomotives with his firm, the only order Manchester received that year. This has the ring of truth, as locomotive production had collapsed, but the KCPG took delivery of only 12 Manchester-built locomotives in 1897. From other investors Stilwell obtained additional loans to tide the KCPG over until the money from Holland arrived. Martin and the other directors withdrew the receivership proposal.[34]

Far more important to Stilwell than his encounter with President McKinley during the campaign was the contact he made with George M. Pullman. During the course of his conversation with Pullman about the loan, Stilwell mentioned his paternal grandfather, Hamblin, and the manufacturer revealed that Hamblin had been his friend when he resided in Rochester. According to Stilwell, Pullman knew his grandfather when they both were involved with the Erie Canal, and the railroad-car manufacturer took the Kansas City promoter home to dinner so that they could reminisce about the early days of Rochester. Pullman agreed to furnish the cars for the KCPG on good terms, and Stilwell left feeling that he had established not only a significant business relationship but had also found someone who recalled with equal affection the memory of his grandfather.[35]

During the next year Stilwell turned often to Pullman for advice and financial support. He sent Pullman a small photograph of his grandfather and an onyx paper weight, for which the manufacturer expressed gratitude, displaying both in his office. The promoter wrote to Pullman,

I must say that the day I spent with you in Chicago was one of the most pleasant days I ever spent in my life. . . . when I met you and found that . . . you had known my grandfather, I cannot tell you how it pleased me and how much I enjoyed talking with you regarding that time, which to me has the most sacred memories. When I learned that you yourself had trod, what seemed to me the sacred decks of those Old Packet Boats, my business relations to you assumed an entirely different aspect from anything I had anticipated and I could not help sending you a token commemorative of that event. I only hope that this will be the beginning of many pleasant ex-

34. Stilwell, "I Had a Hunch," January 14, 1928, 70, 72, 77; John H. White, Jr., *American Locomotives: An Engineering History, 1830–1880* (Baltimore: The Johns Hopkins Press, 1968), 450.
35. Stilwell, "I Had a Hunch," December 3, 1927, 4, and January 14, 1928, 31.

periences and I look forward to the day I can take you over our completed
road, which time is not far distant.[36]

The completion of the KCPG to the Gulf was still ten months away, but
during those months Stilwell often consulted with Pullman and did take
him over the line. The promoter needed sound financial advice, and, more
importantly, financial support.

By January of 1897, construction of the KCPG, "straight as the
crow flies," to the Gulf was progressing. The gap between Mena and
Horatio, Arkansas, remained incomplete, but track crews continued to
lay considerable rail each day. An unfortunate incident, however, brought
work to a halt. The white "mountaineers" of Polk County drove off the
Negro construction gangs, announcing that no blacks were allowed to live
in the county. When the railroad subcontractor brought in replacement
crews of Italian immigrants, they too were driven off. The introduction
of native white laborers allowed construction to proceed.[37]

The line from Kansas City to Shreveport finally opened at 3:45 on
the afternoon of March 2, 1897, when the agent for the Missouri, Kansas
and Texas Trust Company office in Berlin, Germany, drove the last spike.
The opening of the line was very important for the KCPG; it meant that
through traffic to New Orleans, Houston, and Galveston was possible for
the first time. Completion of the 556-mile railway provoked a celebration
in Kansas City, and a triumphal arch erected on Ninth Street declared that
prosperity for both cities was enhanced. A windstorm toppled the arch (an
omen of things to come?) but it was quickly rebuilt, and flags of the United
States, England, Germany, France, and The Netherlands were placed on
the arch in honor of the KCPG investors. The first freight train south included twenty-five cars of flour, and the first passenger train, the "Arkansas Traveller," followed shortly.

When Stilwell appeared before the next meeting of the Commercial
Club his efforts to speak were greeted by "applause so loud and con-
tinuous that he blushed like a school boy." With John DeGeoijen and
other Hollanders in the audience, Stilwell declared, "Kansas City did not

---

36. Arthur E. Stilwell to George M. Pullman, December 16, 1896, Stilwell Collection (Port of Port Arthur, Port Arthur, Texas).

37. Unidentified newspaper clipping, January 11, 1897, Pliny Fisk Collection
(Pliny Fisk Library, Princeton University, Princeton, New Jersey); the Kansas
City *Star*, February 9, 1897.

believe I was eloquent, but foreign capitalists did." "Port Arthur," he said, "should be the Liverpool of the United States." Stilwell, DeGeoijen, and the other foreigners then left on a ten-day inspection trip of the line to Shreveport and the site at Port Arthur.[38]

Shreveport welcomed the opening of the KCPG even more enthusiastically than Kansas City, for the railroad meant not only increased business but also additional employment for workers in the city. The KCPG shops at Shreveport were extensive, including a 20-stall roundhouse and a large repair facility. The passenger station, completed in 1898, was built by the Kansas City, Shreveport and Gulf Terminal Company, a subsidiary, and the station was used by several other railroads. The freight business also boomed, as the shipping of cotton north from Shreveport rapidly increased.[39]

The *Commercial and Financial Chronicle* noted the opening of the line with an editorial:

The opening this week of through service from Kansas City to Shreveport, La., over the line of the Kansas City, Pittsburg & Gulf, is important not only as giving another through route to the Gulf but as making a further step in the progress of an enterprise of considerable magnitude. . . . It is rather noteworthy that an undertaking of such dimensions should have been pushed through during a period of great depression in the commercial and financial world. . . . Mr. A. E. Stilwell, of Kansas City, has been the head and front of the enterprise, and it is to his perserverance and energy that its progress is due. The future of the undertaking will be watched with interest.[40]

The KCPG was progressing and on January 24, 1897, purchased the Calcasieu, Vernon and Shreveport Railway Company, a narrow-gauge logging railroad running from Lockport to Edgewood, Louisiana, a distance of sixteen miles. This timber railroad became part of the KCPG branch line to Lake Charles. The road was widened to standard gauge and extended to Lake Charles, giving the "Pee Gee" a second gulf terminus.[41]

38. Unidentified newspaper clipping, March 3, 1897, Pliny Fisk Collection; the Kansas City *Star*, March 2, 7, and 10, 1897.

39. Undated manuscript, File 110.3 (Offices of the Kansas City Southern Railway).

40. *Commercial and Financial Chronicle*, March 6, 1897.

41. Ira G. Clark, *Then Came the Railroads* (Norman: University of Oklahoma Press, 1958), 161–162; Henry V. Poor, *Manual of the Railroads of the United*

In the Spring of 1897, as work on the track between Shreveport and Port Arthur continued, a change in the officers of the KCPG took place. On March 29, Stilwell replaced Martin as president of the road. Martin had been ill for some time, and his decision to resign came as "no surprise." Stilwell wrote a more glamorous and self-praising version of the change in officers in his memoirs, claiming he was only 32 years of age at the time, although he was actually 37, and his assertion that he was the "youngest railroad president the United States had ever known," was probably not true.[42]

Stilwell faced an immediate crisis as president of the KCPG in the form of an attack on the line. The Traffic Manager of the Louisville and Nashville railroad, Y. Van Den Berg, published a report denouncing the Stilwell road.[43] Van Den Berg sent copies of his document to Holland, undermining confidence in the railroad there, and the report also circulated widely in New York City, Boston, and Philadelphia, causing concern among investors. Bonds of the KCPG fell to 70 in the market. Stilwell responded with a vigorous public-relations effort, flooding brokerage houses with facts and figures about the line, denying the charges made in the report and soliciting favorable endorsements from businessmen. The New York *Times* published a friendly story about the progress of the KCPG and its future, saying in part that the line was well financed and that traffic growth was encouraging. F. A. Gilbert, president of the Boston Electric Light Company and a director of the Missouri, Kansas and Texas Trust Company, reported on an inspection trip of the KCPG made by a group of New England investors, declaring, "I had no idea of the magnitude of the property." Stilwell traveled to Boston, issued a laudatory press release laced with facts and figures, and claimed that all was well, earnings were rising, grading on the last link in Louisiana was complete, and that

---

States (New York: Poor's Publishing Company, 1897), 198; *Valuation Reports, Decisions of the Interstate Commerce Commission*, Vol. 75, July 1918–July 1923 (Washington: Government Printing Office, 1924), 411–412. *The Manual of the Railroads* will be cited hereafter as Poor, *Manual*, date and page.

42. The Kansas City *Star*, March 29, 1897; *Commercial and Financial Chronicle*, April 3, 1897; Stilwell, "I Had a Hunch," December 31, 1927, 24.

43. There is no apparent reason for Van Den Berg's interest in the KCPG or explanation as to why he published his report. The Louisville and Nashville was not a direct competitor with the KCPG. Stilwell charged that the report was instigated by the Kountze Brothers, but this was never proven.

fixed charges were being met.[44] Yet he continued to solicit aid and advice from Pullman.

Stilwell adopted George M. Pullman as a grandfather, whether the Palace Car manufacturer accepted such a relationship or not. Constantly writing Pullman, Stilwell kept him informed of the progress of the KCPG and extended numerous invitations for trips over the railway. Business was always booming, according to the promoter, but when he was in or near Chicago he always dropped in to see Pullman about financial support or more equipment. On May 28, he sent Pullman the daily earnings report of the KCPG from January through early May and made arrangements for a joint tour of the line. Pullman and his wife arrived in Kansas City on June 10, visited the offices of the Stilwell concerns, and then embarked on an inspection trip.[45] After the visit, Stilwell wrote to Pullman,

I cannot begin to tell you how thankful I am that you have seen our property, and that the impression which I could see you had, has been removed from your mind, and that I had not exaggerated the possibilities of the road through enthusiasm. Having the high regard for you, and for your opinion which I have, it was very distressing to me that you felt I had exaggerated the road, but now I know you see it in its true light, and it gives me a great deal of quiet satisfaction each hour. I hope from now on our paths in life will lead closer together.[46]

Although skeptical before the tour, Pullman agreed to "become more interested" in the KCPG, and Stilwell immediately had a Pullman associate, Norman B. Ream, and Pullman's son-in-law, Frank O. Lowden, elected to the board of the railroad. The promoter wrote the car builder that he had received orders for $170,000 in railroad bonds and he anticipated selling $150,000 more in Boston. Yet he went to Chicago only five days after writing the letter seeking more funds and equipment.[47] Stilwell had made a drastic error in limiting the amount of money to be spent on cars and locomotives for the KCPG; only $1,500 per mile had been re-

44. The Kansas City *Star*, February 22, 1897; New York *Times*, March 22, 1897; *Wall Street Journal*, April 12, 1897; Unidentified clippings, April 21 and May 5, 1897, Pliny Fisk Collection.

45. Arthur Stilwell to George M. Pullman, February 27, May 19, and May 28, 1897, Stilwell Collection; the Kansas City *Star*, June 10, 1897.

46. Stilwell to Pullman, June 15, 1897, Stilwell Collection.

47. *Ibid.*; *Eighth Annual Statement of the Kansas City, Pittsburg & Gulf Railroad Co.*; the Kansas City *Star*, July 20, 1897.

served for equipment, a sum much too small. He therefore purchased rolling stock through equipment trusts (mortgages on the cars and loco-motives). Stilwell claimed that Pullman agreed to build 1,000 cars for the KCPG and to purchase a total equipment trust of $3,000,000. Stilwell also wrote that Pullman extended this generous offer out of loyalty to the memory of Hamblin Stilwell and because of the growing prospects of the KCPG. If Pullman did, indeed, make such a verbal arrangement, it was probably because of the potential profits and the fact that equipment orders still had not recovered from the depression. George M. Pullman was never known as a generous, warm-hearted person, even among fellow railroad men.[48]

Stilwell's analysis of the plight of the KCPG was accurate: the road desperately needed rolling stock and locomotives. The railway had nearly 800 miles of track and yet by the end of 1897 had only 72 locomotives, 36 passenger, baggage, mail, and business cars, and 4,290 revenue-producing freight cars.[49] The KCPG received nine new passenger cars in April 1897, solving that shortage.[50] The situation with regard to locomotives was alleviated during 1897, when the KCPG took delivery of a considerable number of new engines manufactured by several different companies. From the Baldwin Locomotive Works, the KCPG purchased six 4-4-0s, (numbers 101–106) fourteen 4-6-0s (320–333), and the KCSB acquired four 0-6-0 switching locomotives (59–62). The KCPG took delivery of four 4-4-0s (170–173) and eight 4-6-0s (250–257) from the Manchester Locomotive Works and twelve 4-6-0 (400–411) road engines from the Grant Locomotive Works. These large purchases seriously taxed the treasury of the KCPG; even though equipment trusts were generally used, the monthly payments on the mortgages further impoverished the uncom-pleted railroad. This burden grew even heavier in 1898 when the KCPG acquired thirty-one 4-6-0s from Baldwin (350–380) and the KCSB pur-chased two more 0-6-0s (63–64) that year and two more (65–66) in 1899.[51] These purchases were necessary. Another item of equipment, however, would be much harder to justify.

48. Stilwell, "I Had a Hunch," January 28, 1928, 89–90; Almont Lindsey, *The Pullman Strike* (Chicago: University of Chicago Press, 1964), 319.
49. *Eighth Annual Statement of the Kansas City, Pittsburg & Gulf Railroad Co.*
50. The Kansas City *Star*, April 6, 1897.
51. "All-Time Steam Roster of the Kansas City Southern," 74–76.

In 1897 the KCPG took delivery from the Pullman Palace Car Company of Car 100 which became the private "mansion on rails" used by Stilwell as president of the KCPG, and ultimately almost as legendary as the promoter himself. Stilwell always contended that his private car was exhibited at the Chicago Columbian Exposition in 1893 and was given to him by George Pullman. It's hard to believe that Pullman would give anything of such value away, and records of the company show that Car 100 was not built until 1897. Built originally as the "Campania," named after the Cunard liner, the car was constructed of mahogany and lighted by gas Pintsch fixtures. The car included a master stateroom with a private bath, a most unusual feature. The dining area contained a large buffet on which stood a silver wine cooler engraved with the initial "S." The living-room furnishings included a massive desk and a foot-pedal organ. The organ became almost as famous as Stilwell, for legend has it that on Sunday the crew of the car and, if it was in transit, the train crew were compelled to join Stilwell around the organ and after a brief church service sing "Rock of Ages," and "Lead Kindly Light." Given Stilwell's love of music and his religious beliefs, there is probably a grain of truth in the legend. Other railroad executives were known to have arranged Sunday services for employes, feeling that the services were important morale factors, and it is noteworthy that Pullman himself had a parlor organ in his private car, as well as in his home. Arthur undoubtedly determined to emulate his newly found confidant and financial ally.[52]

As spring became summer in 1897, Stilwell could travel deeper and deeper into Louisiana in his new private car. The KCPG opened to Hornbeck on June 8, some 653 miles from Kansas City, and the next month track was completed into Lake Charles. Before the bridge across the Sabine River was completed, trains were routed from Kansas City to Lake Charles where they used the line of the Southern Pacific to reach Beau-

---

52. Car 100 would serve executives of the railroad for almost fifty years, until finally falling upon evil days and becoming a dining car for work-train crews. The organ remained in the car for many years before being removed and stored at the shops in Pittsburg, Kansas. Lucius Beebe, *Mansions On Rails* (Berkeley: Howell-North Press, 1959) 9, 90, 113–114, 187, 250, and 255; Lindsey, *The Pullman Strike*, 30–31; Cochran, *Railroad Leaders*, 210–211; the Kansas City *Star*, April 4, 1937; Beaumont *Enterprise*, April 11, 1937, and July 26, 1936.

mont and then over the KCPG to Port Arthur. The first passenger train over the route took thirty-six hours to complete the journey.[53]

Constant financial problems plagued Stilwell in 1897, and additional securities had to be issued. When the Kansas City Terminal Construction Company could no longer sell its stock to complete the line through Louisiana, it was taken over by the Philadelphia Construction Company. In an effort to sell more railroad company bonds, Stilwell bombarded the agents of the Trust company with letters relating the most favorable news about the line and its traffic.[54] He wrote his agents in Boston,

I received word from Europe to the effect that if our bonds could be sent up to ninety or ninety-five there would be an unlimited amount of purchasers there, but that they could not place any at seventy or seventy-two. I came to Philadelphia and organized a movement by which the bonds went from seventy to eighty in two days, and we were surprised to see how few bonds were on the market. I hope you will do all you can in New England to aid me and keep bonds from being dumped on the market, as I feel that with a few more days work we may be able to get them to ninety, provided we can keep people from offering their holdings there.[55]

This is one of the few instances where there is evidence of security manipulation by Stilwell, and this apparently consisted of buying bonds at high prices and keeping other bonds off the market to drive up quotations.

It became necessary in August to increase again the capitalization of the KCPG, and authorization was received to issue a total of $23,000,000 in bonds. At the same time interest was beginning to fall due on bonds issued as early as 1892, causing fixed charges to rise rapidly. Stilwell sought and received permission to list both bonds and stock of the KCPG on the New York Stock Exchange. On September 11, the stockholders voted to increase the capital stock to $23,000,000, and the meeting received the best news possible.[56]

53. Unidentified newspaper clippings, June 9, and July 3, 1897, Pliny Fisk Collection; Port Arthur *Herald*, July 8, 1897.

54. *Valuation Reports*, Vol. 75, 304; Stilwell to Agents of the Missouri, Kansas & Texas Trust Company, July 2, 1897, Stilwell Collection.

55. Stilwell to Corey and Millken, July 23, 1897, Record Book, Kansas City, Pittsburg and Gulf (Offices of the Kansas City Southern Railway).

56. Unidentified newspaper clippings, August 2, and 24, 1897, Pliny Fisk Collection; Jefferson City *Daily Tribune*, September 15, 1897; *Commercial and Financial Chronicle*, September 11, 1897; New York *Times*, September 11, 1897.

At 3:30 on the afternoon of September 11, just twelve miles north of Beaumont, Texas, the last spike on the KCPG was driven, and from Kansas City to Port Arthur citizens celebrated the opening of the line to deep water. In Kansas City, Arthur Stilwell sat in his box at the horse show at Fairmount Park, holding a watch in his hand. Suddenly a loud cannon report was heard, and on the hill overlooking the show a large drapery unfolded revealing a sign with the words, "Kansas City is now connected with its own seaport, Port Arthur, by its own rails, the Kansas City, Pittsburg & Gulf. The last spike has just been driven." Great cheers rose from the crowd and the band played the "Port Arthur March." That night from the roofs of buildings in the downtown area searchlights played over Kansas City. In Mena, Shreveport, and Beaumont, festivities and jollifications marked the event, but nowhere was the excitement greater than in Port Arthur.[57]

Excursion trains from Lake Charles and elsewhere came into Port Arthur that Saturday, the pleasure pier was jammed with tourists, and restaurants and saloons did an unprecedented business. Parades and speeches, food and drink wore out the visitors and residents who went to bed in the new port oblivious to the great danger hard upon them. Early Sunday morning, a hurricane fell on the town. Fleeing from the storm, many of those still living in tents dashed into the unfinished KCPG round-house. Unable to withstand the tremendous winds, that structure soon collapsed, killing four people. The pleasure pier was damaged severely, residences were blown away, and water five feet deep swept down Proctor Street. The storm abated on Monday, and searchers found that ten people had been killed and many more were injured. Stilwell dispatched a relief train, sent $15,000 to aid the storm victims, and directed that repair work begin immediately.[58] One wonders why Stilwell's "brownies" failed to warn him that a massive storm was about to fall on his namesake, or why the city was not safe from "the greatest storms the Gulf could produce."

To make conditions worse for the KCPG, the same day the hurricane swept Port Arthur a yellow fever quarantine was established between Shreveport and the Gulf, halting nearly all rail traffic south of that city.

57. The Kansas City *Star*, September 12, 1897.
58. *Ibid.*, September 13, 1897; *Port Arthur* (Houston: Anson Jones Press, 1940), 40–41, 156.

The quarantine remained in effect for six weeks, demoralizing business along the coast. The KCPG desperately needed through traffic, and the quarantine had a devastating effect.[59] When Stilwell issued the KCPG annual report the figures belied his optimistic statements. Coal and lumber shipments north to Kansas City had increased, but the railroad faced a continuing shortage of equipment. The fixed charges that began in April and the cash payments due on rolling stock and locomotives had been paid, but delays in opening the line to Port Arthur and the subsequent quarantine had proved costly. Earnings had fallen in June, the operating ratio climbed to 80 percent, and though earnings were increasing the road lacked the income to pay interest coming due and to purchase more equipment. Stilwell had issued bonds on a plan whereby interest was paid only out of net earnings until a certain date, when, he hoped, the line would have been open for six months. Delays precluded this. Also, the trackage south of Shreveport had been built during the dry months, and when the heavy winter rains began the track became impassable. When trains that previously ran at slow speeds were stopped completely by the gumbo mud, vast sums were committed to maintainence and heavy repairs. The unballasted track, prohibitive ruling grades, and inadequate yards and terminals led to still higher operating costs.[60] The situation appeared desperate.

Stilwell continued to issue favorable reports on the line, and newspapers and financial journals carried stories by him or other KCPG officials defending the company. Stock of the KCPG was listed on stock exchanges in New York, London, Boston, and Philadelphia, and the opening of the line to Port Arthur caused the price to rise from $18 to $29 a share. Brokerages warned purchasers, however, that it was a speculative venture. Stilwell continued to run special trains to Port Arthur with potential investors being entertained in Car 100 and deluxe Pullmans. The promoter issued more bulletins to the agents of the Trust company laden with ever-exuberant prose, but Stilwell now placed most of his hope for financial support on his friend George Pullman.[61]

59. Port Arthur *Herald*, October 14 and 21, 1897.
60. Unidentified newspaper clipping, August 26, 1897, Pliny Fisk Collection; *Eighth Annual Statement of the Kansas City, Pittsburg & Gulf Railroad Co.*; Haag, "A Brief History of the Kansas City Southern Railway System," 64–65.
61. Unidentified newspaper clipping, October 15, 1897, Pliny Fisk Collection;

According to Stilwell, Pullman had agreed to build freight cars for the KCPG, take equipment bonds as payment, and lend additional money to the road to purchase equipment from other builders. A letter from Stilwell to Pullman on October 14, 1897, however, suggests that the promoter was still trying to obtain financing from the car builder. Stilwell claimed also that on the 18th he left Kansas City for Chicago to meet with the manufacturer to sign the contract for the loan, but when he arrived at the station in Chicago he heard the newsboys crying, "Full account of the death of George M. Pullman." His potential benefactor had died unexpectedly of a heart attack. Stilwell realized the effect of Pullman's death and left Chicago before the funeral. Pullman would always be an object of Stilwell's admiration, and he continually praised the manufacturer during the next thirty years.[62]

The financial plight of the KCPG was not a secret, and the viability of the railway and the value of its securities were debated in the leading financial journals. The *Statist* of London on May 15, 1897, had recommended the bonds of the KCPG, then selling in England at 75. The *Commercial Advertiser* of New York replied in a series of editorials on the railroad, saying the gross would not pay half the interest, Stilwell's traffic estimates were unrealistic, local trade would never develop, and Port Arthur would not become a significant grain outlet. The source of information cited by this negative view was the Van Den Berg report. The *Commercial Adviser* did not attack the directors of the firm, many of whom were widely known financiers, but argued that their good faith was simply misplaced, and that the *Statist* was given to "comparatively harmless eccentricities." Edward P. Merwin, a KCPG director and head of E. P. Merwin & Company of New York, responding for the railroad, invited the editor of the *Commercial Adviser* to make a trip over the line at Merwin's expense, but the editor declined the invitation to see what he referred to as the "Wildcat Road." Merwin also sent a copy of the pamphlet, "Letters of Leading Businessmen of Kansas City, Mo., refuting the Statement Published by Y. Van Den Berg Relating to Kansas City,

---

Port Arthur *News*, November 4, 1897; Stilwell to the Agents of the Missouri, Kansas & Texas Trust Company, December 10, 1897, Stilwell Collection.

62. Stilwell to Pullman, October 14, 1897, Stilwell Collection; Stilwell, "I Had a Hunch," January 28, 1928, 90–91; Arthur E. Stilwell, *To All the World (Except Germany)* (London: George Allen & Unwin, Ltd., 1915), 19.

Pittsburg and Gulf and Kansas City Suburban Belt," which defended the Stilwell properties, but the editor discounted the testimonials as parochial and without factual basis. As the attacks continued throughout 1897, their source, according to Stilwell and the officers of the KCPG, was the banking firm of Kountze Brothers. This is quite probable. There can be no debate, however, over the contention that the KCPG needed financial support.[63]

Stilwell and others agreed that the limit placed on issuing bonds at $25,000 per mile was unfortunate. The bonds sold at only 70 to 80 percent with a stock bonus, so that a second mortgage was not feasible. Although initial interest payments had been made, additional capital seemed absolutely mandatory.[64] In seeking that capital, Stilwell made a drastic error of judgment.

On one of his frequent trips to Chicago, he went to see John W. Gates, president of the American Steel and Wire Company, and a well known Wall Street "plunger." The promoter convinced Gates the KCPG was a sound investment, that he should invest in the line, and Gates accepted Stilwell's invitation to visit Port Arthur with a group of his financial friends. They made the trip; Gates then purchased 10,000 shares of stock and $100,000 or $200,000 in bonds and also agreed to provide Stilwell's enterprises with rails and other supplies, accepting bonds as payment.[65] This financial help came at a crucial time, for Stilwell had his back to the wall, but the price to be paid was high.

Stilwell also needed Gate's support for another enterprise. The promoter was in the process of creating a rail network north of Kansas City to link Omaha and Quincy, Illinois, to the KCPG. While the problems of the KCPG grew and the Kountzes held up the development of Port Arthur, the indomitable Stilwell moved to enlarge his rail empire.

63. Unidentified newspaper clippings, Wright Scrapbooks; *Commercial Advertiser*, June 7, 9, 11, and 21, 1897; Unidentified newspaper clipping, December 31, 1897, Pliny Fisk Collection.

64. Stilwell, *Forty Years of Business Life*, 10; "Report of L. A. Etter on His Trip to Port Arthur, Texas, over the Kansas City, Pittsburg & Gulf R.R.," January 1, 1898, Pliny Fisk Collection.

65. Stilwell, "I Had a Hunch," January 28, 1928, 91; Stilwell, *Forty Years of Business Life*, 14; Lloyd Wendt and Herman Kogan, *Bet a Million! The Story of John W. Gates* (Indianapolis: The Bobbs-Merrill Company, 1948), 204.

VII

ARTHUR STILWELL'S vision of prosperity for his railways never wavered, but he remained hard pressed to provide traffic and revenues for his creations. The Kansas City Suburban Belt needed additional switching contracts from railroads entering Kansas City, and the Kansas City, Pittsburg and Gulf desperately sought more interchange traffic. Stilwell originally conceived of his line to deep water as a means to transport grain at a lower cost than shipment to the east coast. If, however, the railroads in the midwest preferred to ship the grain east to connections often financially related, as indeed they did, then the grain traffic was lost. The answer was expansion, and Stilwell began to give thought to possible acquisitions north of Kansas City.

Once again he fell into a series of entrepreneurial errors, misjudging costs and revenues, borrowing heavily from investors and then seeking additional purchasers of securities. But this was not untypical of railway expansion in the latter part of the nineteenth century. Promoters often found that the only way to save that which they had created was through expansion to obtain more traffic, yet this meant more bonds were issued and fixed charges increased even more rapidly. A truly vicious cycle began, and the end was often the receivership court. Functioning within this framework, Stilwell cast his eyes on two insolvent lines north of Kansas City.[1]

1. Arthur E. Stilwell and James R. Crowell, "I Had a Hunch," *The Saturday Evening Post*, CC (January 28, 1928), 91, 94.

Operating between West Quincy, Missouri, and Trenton, Missouri, was the Quincy, Omaha and Kansas City Railway Company, a rather pathetic line from nowhere to nowhere. The QOKC did enter Quincy, Illinois, through trackage rights over the Chicago, Burlington and Quincy. Although construction of the line began in 1869, by 1895 the railroad had only 134.51 miles of track, nine locomotives, 134 cars, and a perpetual deficit. Originally named the Quincy, Missouri and Pacific, the road defaulted in 1890 and was placed in the hands of trustees: Ward W. Jacobs of Quincy and Theodore Gilman, the New York banker. The trustees were authorized to sell the road or reorganize it, yet were unable to act because of the depression. They were undoubtedly interested in any realistic proposition.[2]

Terminating about thirty miles west of Trenton at Pattonsburg was the Omaha and Saint Louis Railway which ran north from Pattonsburg to Council Bluffs, Iowa, a distance of 145 miles. Originally the Omaha division of the Wabash Railroad, the line had been sold under foreclosure on December 28, 1886, and organized as the OStL the following May. It too suffered a series of financial reversals and was placed in the hands of receivers in June of 1893. The OStL had fifteen locomotives, 453 cars, and a substantial indebtedness.[3] The receivers of this line were also interested in sale or merger possibilities.

Stilwell conceived of these lines as the basis of a larger midwestern connection for the KCPG and as revenue producers for the KCSB. He proposed that a new railroad be built from Trenton to Pattonsburg linking the QOKC and the OStl to provide a direct line from Council Bluffs to Quincy. Another railway would be built from Kansas City north to Pattonsburg to tie all of the lines to the KCPG. By constructing 100 miles of new track he would gain access to 280 miles of existing railroad as well as a direct line to Council Bluffs and Quincy and the agricultural hinterland of both communities.[4]

---

2. *The Kansas City Gateway*, December 1902; Henry V. Poor, *Manual of the Railroads of the United States* (New York: Poor's Publishing Company, 1893), 540–541. See also Poor, *Manual*, 1894, 217–218 and 1895, 235–236. Cited hereafter as Poor, *Manual*, date and page.
3. Poor, *Manual*, 1893, 509–510; 1894, 244–245; and 1895, 272–273; *The Railway Age*, June 30, 1893.
4. Stilwell, "I Had a Hunch," January 28, 1928, 91–94.

The first step in the creation of the northern system came on April 5, 1895, when articles of association for the Kansas City and Northern Connecting Railroad Company were drafted. Chartered to build from Kansas City north through Pattonsburg to the Missouri-Iowa state line, the road had a capitalization of $1,000,000. Ten thousand shares of $100 par value stock were to be issued, but the incorporators sold only 1,000 shares initially. Stilwell, J. McD. Trimble, C. A. Braley, Robert Gillham and three others each took 50 shares, paying in 5 cents per share, and Stilwell took 650 more as trustee. The promoter was elected president and immediately began seeking capital. He asked Pattonsburg and other towns along the route to provide a bonus of $75,000, and then went to Philadelphia for more funds. More bargain shares were sold for one dollar each to E. T. Stotesbury and John DeGeoijen, and Stilwell and Trimble also purchased additional shares. The directors voted to issue 30-year bonds drawing 5 percent interest at the rate of $25,000 per mile, the Missouri, Kansas and Texas Trust Company would act as trustee, and the KCSB would be paid $21,500 per mile in bonds and an equal amount in stock to build or acquire the KCNC.[5] The organization and financing followed the pattern Stilwell generally used.

For more than thirteen months the KCNC project failed to develop. Stilwell spent time on other matters, and the only activity in the organization was an increase in its capitalization to $2,000,000 in March of 1896. An initial survey of the route proceeded, but money for the KCNC simply was not available in Kansas City or Philadelphia.[6]

The situation changed abruptly on May 20, 1896, when Stilwell arrived in Kansas City after one of his periodic trips to Holland, Germany, and England. He enthusiastically announced that financing had been arranged in Europe and that construction on the KCNC would begin soon. Accompanying him and Mrs. Stilwell on their return trip were Harold D.

5. "Articles of Association," Minute Book, Kansas City and Northern Connecting Railroad Company, and minutes of meetings April 5, July 8 and September 17, 1895 (Offices of The Burlington Northern Inc., Chicago, Illinois); *The Railway Age*, May 31, 1895; *The Railroad Gazette*, May 31, 1895; the Kansas City *Star*, September 13, 14 and 21, 1895; Journal, Kansas City and Northern Connecting Railroad, March 4, 1896, Chicago, Burlington and Quincy Archives, (Newberry Library, Chicago, Illinois).

6. *The Railroad Gazette*, March 20 and 27, 1896; *Commercial and Financial Chronicle*, March 21, 1896.

THE STILWELL LINES NORTH OF KANSAS CITY

Arbuthnot of London and Philipp Schlesinger, a Berlin banker, who came to make a tour of the Kansas City, Pittsburg and Gulf. Funds for the KCNC had been obtained in London, Amsterdam, Paris, Berlin, and Hamburg, and the Missouri, Kansas and Texas Trust had opened offices in the latter two cities. The vehicle to be used to construct the line was the Missouri River Construction Company, chartered in Albany, New York, with Stilwell, Trimble, Theodore and Winthrop Gilman, E. T. Stotesbury, and George C. Thomas as directors. The same financing procedures used previously would be employed. A syndicate composed of the Missouri, Kansas and Texas Trust, Drexel and Company, Gilman, Son and Company and the European bond purchasers controlled the KCNC.[7]

To complicate the already-involved financial arrangements, Stilwell asked the Kansas City Suburban Belt to actually build the KCNC, and that company agreed, accepting the bonds of the KCNC and townsites along its route as payment. The KCNC then increased its capital again, to $3,000,000, and began to issue securities at the rate of $20,000 per mile in first-mortgage bonds and $15,000 per mile in second-mortgage bonds. Money for the construction came through the Trust company which sold the securities—for a commission, of course.[8] Despite Stilwell's optimistic pronouncements, construction did not commence in 1896.

The KCNC finally began to reach the operation stage in January 1897, when the directors voted to purchase the Kansas City and Atlantic Railway, a line operating from Haarlem, a Kansas City suburb across the Missouri River, to Smithville. The 22-mile-long railway had been chartered as the Chicago, Kansas City and Texas railway in 1887, began operating two years later, and entered reorganization in 1893. The purchase avoided duplicate construction, and the price of $225,000 was cheap enough. The KCNC signed a lease with the Milwaukee Road to use that railroad's bridge over the Missouri to reach the KCSB and Grand Central Station.[9] The KCNC began operation with two locomotives, three passen-

7. The Kansas City *Star*, May 20, 1896; *The Railway Age*, May 23, 1896; *The Railroad Gazette*, May 29, 1896; *Commercial and Financial Chronicle*, May 30, 1896.
8. Minute Book, Kansas City Suburban Belt, June 27, and July 7, 1896 (Office of the Kansas City Southern Railway, Kansas City, Missouri); Minute Book, Kansas City and Northern Connecting, June 27, 1896; the Kansas City *Star*, August 12, 1896; *The Railway Age*, August 21, 1896.
9. Minute Book, Kansas City and Northern Connecting, January 16, 1897; W. P.

ger and seventy-six freight cars, and work on the rest of the line from Smithville to Pattonsburg, 52 miles, began.[10]

Construction of the KCNC proceeded slowly. Stilwell found it very difficult to sell the bonds at 80 and finally turned to John W. Gates for help. The financier purchased one third of the bonds necessary to complete the line, taking the securities as payment for rails and other products furnished by his steel company. Not until March 10, 1898, was the last spike driven. The KCSB built the line, receiving $6,481,300 in securities of the KCNC which it sold for $1,597,300.71 in cash. The Trust company was paid more than $80,000 in commissions to sell the securities and the KCSB lost more than $24,000 on the entire operation.[11] Nevertheless, completion of the KCNC gave Stilwell a direct line from Port Arthur north to Kansas City, Council Bluffs, and Quincy.

While the KCNC was being organized, financed, and constructed, Stilwell proceeded to acquire the rest of the lines north of Kansas City. The Omaha and Saint Louis Railway receiver, John F. Barnard, co-operated with Stilwell and Drexel and Company to reorganize the railway and to place it in the hands of the Stilwell-Drexel-Gilman syndicate. The reorganization committee of the OStL agreed to sell the road at foreclosure on January 27, 1896, and accept bonds from a new company. They also agreed to an ultimate merger with the Quincy, Omaha and Kansas City. On June 11, 1896, the OStL *Railroad* Company was chartered in Missouri with capitalization of $2,592,000 to take over the *Railway*. The incorporators included Stilwell, Trimble, E. L. Martin, and a number of New Yorkers.[12] The OStL came under the control of the syndicate with the reorganization.

Trickett, *Railroad Systems of Kansas City* (Kansas City: n.p., 1900); the Kansas City *Star*, January 10, 1897; *The Railroad Gazette*, January 15, 1897.

10. State Auditor, Report of Taxable Properties, June 1, 1897, Missouri State Archives (State Historical Society of Missouri, Columbia, Missouri); *The Railroad Gazette*, September 10, 1897.

11. Unidentified newspaper clippings and advertisements, H. P. Wright Scrap-books (University of Missouri–Kansas City Library, Kansas City, Missouri); *The Railroad Gazette*, March 18, 1898; *Valuation Reports, Decisions of the Interstate Commerce Commission*, Vol. 75, July, 1918–July, 1923 (Washington: Government Printing Office, 1924), 375, 380.

12. The Kansas City *Star*, June 11, 1896 and January 10, 1897; *The Railroad Gazette*, December 27, 1895, and June 19, 1896; *The Railway Age*, May 2, 1896; *Commercial and Financial Chronicle*, January 4, March 28, May 2 and 16, 1896.

The syndicate also acquired the Quincy, Omaha and Kansas City in early 1896. They issued $1,500,000 in preferred bonds to the bondholders of the company at a rate of 70 cents on the dollar. Stilwell achieved managerial control over the line when his associate J. McD. Trimble became the trustee for the receivers. These transactions consisted largely of paper shuffling since Gilman, Son and Company controlled the QOKC.[13]

The last link necessary to unite the northern lines to the KCPG was the construction of a railroad from the end of the QOKC at Trenton, 34 miles west to the KCNC and OStL at Pattonsburg. The Omaha, Kansas City and Eastern Railroad Company, chartered in Missouri on July 23, 1896, would build the line and eventually purchase the QOKC and OStL when terms were satisfactory. The incorporators included Stilwell, Martin, C. A. Braley, Jacques T. Nolthenius, John Lowber Welsh of Drexel and Company, and Theodore Gilman Jr. of Gilman, Son and Company. The Western Construction Company and the Missouri River Construction Company contracted to build the line, and $816,000 in first-mortgage and $612,000 in second-mortgage bonds drawing 5 percent interest were issued to pay for the work. Stilwell served as president of the OKCE, Welsh as vice-president, and Gilman acted as president of the Missouri River Construction Company which was to receive $20,000 of first-mortgage bonds, $15,000 of second-mortgage bonds and $35,000 in stock for each mile of line built. Obviously the OKCE was overcapitalized, underfinanced, and a creature of the syndicate.[14]

The OKCE completed its line from Trenton to Pattonsburg on July 4, 1897, and Stilwell arrived for the last-spike celebration in his private car. Two days earlier the OKCE filed a mortgage of $14,000,000 with the Guaranty Trust Company of New York for the purchase of the OStL and the QOKC. The receivers of the two lines gave control to the OKCE and

13. The Kansas City *Star*, December 10, 1895, January 7 and June 6, 1896; *The Railway Age*, January 10, 1896; Articles of Association, Minute Book, Quincy, Omaha and Kansas City Railroad Company, May 26, 1897 (Office of Burlington Northern, Inc.).

14. Minute Book, Omaha, Kansas City and Eastern, July 23 and August 10, 1896 (Office of Burlington Northern, Inc.); Ledger, Omaha, Kansas City and Eastern, Chicago, Burlington and Quincy Archives; the Kansas City *Star*, July 25, 1896; *The Railway Age*, July 31, 1896; *The Railroad Gazette*, August 7 and December 18, 1896; *Commercial and Financial Chronicle*, August 1, 1896.

consolidated operations began.[15] Direct entry into Kansas City awaited completion of the KCNC the following year.

Stilwell's vision of a railway empire north of Kansas City did not diminish with the completion of these acquisitions. There were rumors and several public pronouncements that the OKCE would build east from Quincy to Bardstown, Illinois, providing the Baltimore and Ohio system with a direct route into Kansas City. It was also suggested that the Keokuk and Western and the Des Moines and Kansas City railways might be acquired to gain entrance to Des Moines and southern Iowa. The OKCE did enter Omaha from Council Bluffs by trackage rights over a bridge, but this was not the expansion Stilwell had in mind. The promoter announced that a railway would be built from Quincy to Peoria, and the latter city received the news with great anticipation. This scheme did not get off the ground and neither did a stillborn trackage agreement to use the Chicago, Burlington and Quincy from Quincy to Chicago—as if the CB&Q would want another rival in the area—nor did a plan to lease the Minneapolis and Saint Louis Railroad. As late as November and December of 1898, Stilwell continued making grandiose plans to enter Chicago or to build to Manitoba, Canada.[16] He should have been more concerned about the northern lines which were not functioning smoothly.

Financial conditions on the northern lines were never strong despite attempts to integrate the railways and provide through service. The roads exchanged cars and locomotives and created a bookkeeping nightmare, but this did not alleviate the rather large payments which had to be made on the equipment. Stilwell issued $485,296.56 in equipment notes in the name of the OKCE to the Pullman Palace Car Company, with monthly installments being made to pay for the 750 freight and 12 passenger cars. Steel rails were purchased to replace the iron rails of the OStL, and thousands of ties were acquired to relay much of the track of the former QOKC. The OStL made a meager profit in 1898, but the OKCE lost

15. The Kansas City *Star*, July 3, 1897; *The Railroad Gazette*, July 2, 1897; *Commercial and Financial Chronicle*, May 15 and July 31, 1897.

16. *The Railway Age*, May 16, 1896; Unidentified newspaper clippings, April 6, December 3, 1897, and January 24 and 26 and March 22, 1898, Pliny Fisk Collection (Pliny Fisk Library, Princeton University, Princeton, New Jersey); *The Railroad Gazette*, December 17, 1897; Peoria *Journal*, December 1, 1897; Chicago *Tribune*, November 27, 1898; *Journal of Commerce*, December 20, 1898.

heavily, causing merger discussions to be called off. Stilwell presided over all the lines, but they were not financially integrated. He received a salary of $200 a month from the KCNC, and if similar salaries were paid by other lines it is apparent that he was making most of his money outside his managerial capacity.[17]

Stilwell also became uneasy about his financial allies in the northern lines. Although the various enterprises kept separate accounts and there was no exchange of securities, the KCPG and the KCSB were deeply involved in the financial arrangements. As early as February 11, 1896, he took the precaution of having the KCSB stockholders elect a "permanent committee," consisting of himself, Martin, DeGeoijen, G. M. Titsingh, and Nolthenius, to prevent a railroad "hostile" to the KCSB or the KCNC from gaining control of the lines. The permanent committee filled its own vacancies and acted as trustees over the various Suburban Belt subsidiaries. Such tight control was neither possible nor, perhaps, desirable on the northern lines where fewer Stilwell allies were able to remain on the boards of directors. As financial troubles grew on the KCPG and its northern connections, one investor kept supplying more capital—John W. Gates. Stilwell should have recognized that here was a "cannibal of Wall Street" of the first order, but the promoter needed Gates's support.[18]

As has been seen, the opening of the KCPG in September of 1897 did not mean the end of a myriad of problems, only that new difficulties arose. The canal litigation continued, leading to the heavy financial drain of the pier and literage system at Port Arthur, and the yellow fever quarantine struck the railroad just as it opened for through shipments, lasting for six weeks. When the line finally reopened, business increased rapidly, particularly when the KCPG slashed rates drastically. This, however, upset the existing rate structure, and competing railroads retaliated.

The shorter route of the KCPG to the Gulf did, as Stilwell predicted, cut the cost of shipping grain and other commodities to deep water. Stil-

17. Bill Register, Kansas City and Northern Connecting, and Ledger, Omaha, Kansas and Eastern, Chicago, Burlington and Quincy Archives; *Railway Review*, September 10, 1898; *The Railroad Gazette*, April 28, 1899; Poor, *Manual*, 1898, 742–744.

18. H. F. Haag, "A Brief History of The Kansas City Southern Railway System," (Office of the Kansas City Southern Railway), 65; Minute Book, Kansas City Suburban Belt, February 10 and 11, 1896; Minute Book, Omaha, Kansas City and Eastern, December 23, 1897; Stilwell, "I Had a Hunch," January 28, 1928, 94.

well provoked other railroads further by reducing the rates even more than the new mileage warranted. Relations with other railways on the rate question previously had been one of mutual toleration at best. Before November of 1894 the railroads in Missouri had ignored the KCPG; then when Richard Gentry attended a state railroad meeting the other lines begrudgingly admitted the road existed. As the KCPG extended further south it came into direct competion with the Missouri Pacific and the St. Louis–San Francisco railroads which operated out of Saint Louis, and wholesale rate cutting began. In January of 1898, Stilwell cut the rate on grain from Kansas City to the Gulf to 12 cents per 100 pounds, while the rate from Kansas City to New York was 19½ cents. The KCPG also absorbed elevator charges. Grain traffic immediately shifted to the line, some grain companies abandoning elevators on the railroads leading to Chicago, and traffic men in that city noted the diversion of cargoes with fear and anger. The Southwestern Traffic Association declared a boycott against the KCPG, and members refused to interchange cars with the line. Stilwell vehemently protested the boycott, first by denying its existence, then by seeking alliances with like-minded railroad executives.[19] The main ally Stilwell found was A. B. Stickney of the Chicago Great Western who believed in rate cutting, competition, and laissez faire. "He felt that even private agreements to limit competition were wrong, impractical and useless"[20] and agreed to a traffic alliance with the KCPG to ship grain from the midwest to the Gulf. The Wabash and the Houston, East and West Texas railroads also ignored the boycott which soon collapsed. Stilwell declared, "They have been trying to bottle me up for some years, but have not succeeded yet." Other railroads continued policies of discrimination, however, and only by appealing to state regulatory agencies did Stilwell stop these practices.[21] The boycotts and discriminatory rates aggravated another problem for the KCPG—a massive car shortage.

The grain, coal, and lumber business intensified in the spring of 1898,

---

19. The Kansas City *Star*, November 1, 1894, and May 12, 1896; Unidentified newspaper clippings, January 11 and 14, February 10, 14, and 15, 1898, Pliny Fisk Collection.

20. Thomas C. Cochran, "Social Attitudes of Railroad Administrators," *Bulletin*, Business History Society, XVII (1943), 15–16.

21. Unidentified newspaper clippings, February 18 and 21, 1898, Pliny Fisk Collection; Port Arthur *Herald*, July 28, 1898. For Stilwell's version of the boycott

but the KCPG found itself unable to handle the traffic because of the shortage of rolling stock. The railroad simply did not have the cash to buy freight cars, and there was a limit to purchasing locomotives and cars through equipment trusts. The fifteen 4-6-0 locomotives ordered from Baldwin began to arrive as did 400 coalcars, 150 flatcars, and 489 box-cars, but at least 1,500 more boxcars were still needed. The KCPG had only 89 engines and 4,551 cars for a line almost 700 miles long. Robert Gillham reported that "A greatly increased tonnage in coal and lumber can be secured provided the power and car equipment to handle it are furnished, and arrangements should be made at once for equipment addi-tional to that now contracted for."[22] The lack of proper planning would again cost Stilwell's concern dearly, for the revenues this traffic might bring were needed for several rebuilding projects.

In the spring of 1898, heavy rains once again turned the roadbed south of Shreveport into gumbo, and the approaches to the bridge over the Arkansas River washed away. The line had to be closed for twenty-one days, and an expensive detour was employed. Another yellow fever epidemic and quarantine stopped traffic south of Shreveport.[23] Even when the weather was perfect, the line presented difficulties.

Conditions on the KCPG varied enormously from division to division and from interpreter to interpreter. Contrasting reports by Robert Gillham and hostile observers Samuel M. Felton and L. A. Etter suggests these divergences.[24] Gillham maintained that the track from Kansas City to Pittsburg had neither objectionable curves nor grades and that the second

---

see "I Had a Hunch," January 28, 1928, 86 and 89, and Arthur E. Stilwell, *Can-nibals of Finance* (Chicago: Farnum Publishing Company, 1912), 51–53.

22. *Ibid.*, 68; *Commercial and Financial Chronicle*, November 12, 1898; *An-nual Report of the Kansas City, Pittsburg and Gulf Railroad Company for the Fiscal Year 1897–1898*, 7–9.

23. Haag, "A Brief History of the Kansas City Southern Railway System," 64–65.

24. *Engineering News*, February 17, 1898, published a lengthy survey of the KCPG based on information furnished by Gillham and E. L. Martin. S. M. Felton made an intensive study of the KCPG for the New York Reorganization Com-mittee, a group hostile to Stilwell; see Samuel Morse Felton, "Report on the Kansas City, Pittsburg & Gulf Railroad," July 15, 1899 (Manuscript Division, Baker Library, Harvard Graduate School of Business Administration, Boston, Mass.). L. A. Etter surveyed the KCPG in late 1897, apparently under the auspices of several railroads and car lines operating between Chicago and New York. See

division from Pittsburg to Stilwell, Indian Territory, was well constructed and ballasted. Etter noted that the KCPG did not even enter Kansas City over its own rails, that it had trackage rights from Grandview to Brush Creek over the Kansas City, Osceola & Southern to reach the KCSB, and the latter road forced the KCPG to pay "tribute" for yard and switching services. Felton argued that the 56- and 60-pound rail was too light, the line lacked ballast, cuts and embankments were too narrow and the road-bed was poor because of utter disregard for construction specifications. The KCPG from Stilwell to Mena possessed far too many curves, the critics charged, and Gillham made no comment. Between Mena and Shreveport the largest obstacle was the bridge over the Red River which was condemned and had to be rebuilt, requiring a large cash outlay. But as Etter noted, both the Arkansas and the Red River bridges were financed separately and required the KCPG to pay tolls each time a train crossed them. The fifth and sixth divisions from Shreveport to Hornbeck and to Port Arthur were subjected to heavy use, but heavy rains turned the road-bed into a muddy mire. Gillham praised the line's oak ties which Felton reported needed replacement because of their poor quality. Felton esti-mated that to put the KCPG in good condition would cost $360,000 for ballasting, $883,000 for trackage to reduce grades and curves, and $120,000 for sidings and spurs.

When Gillham and Martin furnished *Engineering News* with their data, they gave inflated figures for cars and locomotives owned by the KCPG by including equipment of the KCSB and its subsidiaries. In the next annual report Gillham agreed that there was a serious car shortage, a point emphasized by both Felton and Etter. Felton stated that the 45 passenger cars needed $12,165 in repairs, while freight cars needed $196,865 in repairs, automatic couplers, and air brakes. The KCPG did use the passenger cars of the old Kansas City–Independence Airline as there was no longer any passenger service over the KCIAL; a trolley line had taken away all of the traffic.

Both Martin and Gillham took pride in the shops, yard, and passenger

---

"Report of L. A. Etter on His Trip to Port Arthur, Texas, over the Kansas City, Pittsburg & Gulf R.R.," January 1, 1898, covering letter by F. L. Pomeroy, General Manager of the Red, White & Midland Lines, and G. J. Grammer, Traffic Manager, Lake Shore and Michigan Southern Railway Company, to Harvey Fisk & Sons, February 1, 1898, all Pliny Fisk Collection.

station at Shreveport which Felton also praised as modern and well arranged, though lacking in tools for the shops. The shops at Pittsburg received low marks from Felton who thought they were poorly arranged, that tools were inadequate, and that perhaps a whole new shop in a different town was necessary.

While Felton, who was known as a "savior" of weak railroads, gave the KCPG few positive comments, Etter thought that "the scheme of the Kansas City, Pittsburg & Gulf seems to have been well conceived." He agreed that grain shipped to Port Arthur went more cheaply than to New York but noted that maritime insurance rates to Europe were triple those from the east coast.

Who was correct? Was Stilwell's line as poor as Etter and Felton charged, or were they tools of opposition forces? Could Martin and Gillham be objective about the KCPG? The answer to the latter question was, obviously, no; their views reflected Stilwell's perpetual optimism and a desire to avoid seeing the weaknesses of the road. Felton, on the other hand, desired engineering and operational perfection and the changes he asked for were too drastic; wholly new shops, for example, were not necessary. The KCPG was a pioneer railroad through a wilderness most of its length, not a major trunk line from Chicago to New York. Etter offered some keen insights into the overlapping financial arrangements which created obligations the KCPG could not possibly pay. The primary problems of the KCPG were not engineering but financial.

Stilwell and Martin issued brave reports concerning the earnings of the KCPG and its related lines, but official statements to the Missouri Railroad Commission in October 1898 showed a loss of $153,325. During the national financial recovery in 1898 Stilwell tried to force up the price of KCPG securities on the stock exchange, hoping for an influx of capital, yet most brokers still warned their customers against the securities. Discrepancies existed between the company's financial statement and an audit by Price, Waterhouse, Inc., and the latter suggested that the KCPG could not pay interest charges of $844,812.50 and car trust payments of $550,000 each year. On equipment and locomotives the line owed $2,236,682.57, and Felton concluded that the only answer was to raise rates, which Stilwell adamantly refused to do.[25] As the sounds of impend-

25. Unidentified newspaper clipping, October 22, 1898, and Grammer to Fisk,

ing calamity broke over his head, the promoter followed the procedure he had used before: he called for more expansion.

In an understatement of enormous proportions, the *United States Investor* said that Stilwell saw things "through rather highly colored glasses," but perhaps he actually avoided seeing the inevitable. With his usual talent for publicity, he announced that a line of steamers had been formed to operate from Port Arthur to South America—the Missouri, Kansas and Texas Trust needed a connection for a giant new project in the Republic of Colombia, a 300-mile railway from the Magdalena River to the capital at Bogotá. While he claimed surveyors had been dispatched, nothing more was heard of the "hunch." Meanwhile, he continued making pilgrimages to Port Arthur, taking Dutch, French, and English investors to see the town and his enterprises. His most recent scheme was the Port Arthur Fish and Oyster Company which tried, unsuccessfully, to ship live oysters to Kansas City in special tank cars manufactured by the Pullman Company. The oysters perished from the heat and the rough trip.[26] Nevertheless, whether it was oysters or the earnings of the KCPG, he retained his optimism:

The prospects for our road were never brighter than they are today. I hear all sorts of rumors of receiverships, big floating debts, etc., but the facts in the case are that the Kansas City, Pittsburg, & Gulf is today earning its full interest and has the larger part of the money in the bank to meet its October coupons. It has no floating debt.[27]

Brave talk indeed, but the truth was otherwise. Adverse reports on the KCPG were printed and reprinted throughout the fall and winter of 1898–1899, saying that a receivership was inevitable. Financial journals which had been openly hostile toward the KCPG and Stilwell began to say "I told you so," and dismissed all reports by Stilwell or Gillham as fraudulent.[28]

The promoter and his engineer went to New York in November of 1898, stayed there for several weeks, and continued making visits there

February 1, 1898, Pliny Fisk Collection; Felton, "Report on the Kansas City, Pittsburg & Gulf Railroad."

26. *United States Investor*, March 5, 1898; Unidentified newspaper clipping, March 31, 1898, Pliny Fisk Collection; Port Arthur *Herald*, January 13, May 19, and June 30, 1898; Chicago *Tribune*, November 27, 1898.

27. *Commercial and Financial Chronicle*, September 3, 1898.

28. *Commercial Advertiser*, October 25 and 26, and December 7, 1898.

through early 1899, seeking new capital for the railroad. The first plan was a merger with the Chicago and Alton Railroad to give the KCPG entrance into Chicago. On the strength of this rumor, the stock of the "Pee Gee" rose, only to fall again.[29] After trying numerous sources of capital and receiving only negative responses, even Stilwell concluded that reorganization was inevitable.

Inadequate capital, prosperity, and competition drove the KCPG to the brink of disaster, and Stilwell responded, like other railroad entrepreneurs in similar circumstances, with proposals for expansion; this had not been successful. The KCPG and its affiliates could not meet their obligations, and, like 65 percent of all the American railroads between 1893 and 1898, moved toward the receiver's court. Ostensibly, receivership was an arrangement devised to protect the interests of persons from whom the railroad had borrowed money. The receivership would bring together the scattered interests of investors, conserve the property, and put the enterprise on a more responsible basis. A receivership, followed by reorganization, usually meant turning bonds into stock to reduce fixed charges (interest). The causes of insolvency were numerous, but in the case of the KCPG they included the fixed charges, burdensome leases, faulty construction, the rate war, and insufficient working capital.[30]

There were great dangers to the promoter who led his enterprise into a receivership. A promoter like Stilwell could, with only a modest personal investment, control the railroad with prestige and influence, but when shares of the enterprise were openly traded on the stock market at low prices, the management and the promoter were vulnerable to raiding. Two of the crucial aspects of business management were securing adequate financial resources and maintenance of good relations with existing and

29. *Journal of Commerce*, November 15, 1898; Port Arthur *News*, December 3, 1898; Port Arthur *Herald*, December 8, 1898; Lloyd Wendt and Herman Kogan, *Bet a Million! The Life Story of John W. Gates* (Indianapolis: The Bobbs-Merrill Company, 1948), 204–205.

30. John Moody, *The Railroad Builders* (New Haven: Yale University Press, 1920), 41; John Franklin Crowell, "Railway Receiverships in the United States," *Yale Review*, VII (November 1898), 319–330; Robert Edgar Riegel, *The Story of the Western Railroads* (Lincoln: University of Nebraska Press, 1964), 305–307; Stuart Daggett, *Railroad Reorganization* (New York: Augustus M. Kelley, Publishers, 1967), 339; Frederick A. Cleveland and Fred Wilbur Powell, *Railroad Finance* (New York: D. Appleton and Company, 1912), 215–226.

potential stockholders.[31] Stilwell's major error in the receivership was bringing into the process men such as E. H. Harriman, John W. Gates, and Ernest Thalmann, who were not impressed by him, had no faith in his operation of the line, and desired to gain control of the KCPG for themselves. He had thrown his creation into the hands of the "cannibals of Wall Street."

Stilwell spent most of January and February of 1899 in New York City and Philadelphia trying to refinance the KCPG. Gillham and Trimble joined him as did representatives of the Dutch and English stockholders. A refunding scheme, devised by John Lowber Welsh, E. T. Stotesbury, and John DeGeoijen, proposed to consolidate the various properties, raise the price of the securities, sell surplus bonds which remained in the treasury of the railroad, and use the proceeds to purchase needed equipment. The reorganization plans excluded the northern lines. In order to obtain financing for the scheme, John DeGeoijen asked Wall Street lawyer Ernest Thalmann to head a refunding committee; Stilwell reacted with wounded pride, expressing fear for the future course of such a committee.

The promoter had gone to Kansas City thinking his long-time associate Welsh would head the reorganization effort, but when he returned to Philadelphia he discovered that DeGeoijen had brought Thalmann into the plan. The Dutchman hired Thalmann, a member of the legal firm of Ladenburg, Thalmann and Company, a financial ally of Standard Oil Company, for $50,000 and promised to put an additional $260,000 into the KCPG to help it operate through the reorganization. The committee then began to advertise its existence and to distribute information about its progress.[32]

The committee proposed to replace all of the old 5 percent bonds with a new larger issue of 4 percent bonds, thereby reducing fixed charges and creating liquidity. The new working capital would enable the road to purchase equipment, and consolidation with the KCSB and the Port

31. Thomas C. Cochran, *Railroad Leaders 1845–1890: The Business Mind in Action* (New York: Russell & Russell, 1965), 62–63; Arthur H. Cole, "An Approach to the Study of Entrepreneurship: A Tribute to Edwin F. Gay," *Journal of Economic History*, VI (Supplement, 1946), 6.

32. *Wall Street Journal*, January 14, 1899; Port Arthur *Herald*, February 2 and 19, 1899; Stilwell, *Cannibals of Finance*, 70–71; Stilwell, "I Had a Hunch," January 28, 1928, 91; New York *Times*, March 24, 1900; *Journal of Commerce*, January 27, 1899.

Arthur Channel and Dock Company would eliminate terminal charges. The committee urged bondholders to deposit their securities with them, so that refinancing could be accomplished. Stilwell, unhappy that the northern lines were being dropped out of the plan and fearful of Thalmann's growing control, asked Welsh to offer an alternative proposal to include all of the allied railways. Publicly, the promoter vehemently declared there would be no receivership and that he was making a heavy personal investment in KCPG stock.[33]

Stilwell's descriptions of events the last week of March and the first week of April are filled with villains, deceit, and his own courage. He wrote that Thalmann planned to issue a negative and misleading report on the KCPG, drive down the stock, make large purchases himself, and gain control of the railroad. When Stilwell angrily confronted the Wall Street lawyer, he told Thalmann that he would prevent this attempt to rob the stockholders. On Easter Sunday morning, the 2nd of April, however, he picked up the newspaper and found that Thalmann had thrown the KCPG into receivership over a $44 printing bill. Yet, on the same page of the newspaper he saw a large drawing of Jesus Christ, and "this calm face still pointing upward, still peaceful . . . nerved me on to greater triumphs over self and material conditions."[34] He would continue to fight the "cannibals of finance."

The facts are quite different. At 11:30 P.M. on April 1st, C. E. Grannis, a long-time Stilwell associate and a heavy investor in the KCPG, went to Missouri Circuit Judge James Gibson and asked for a receivership for the KCPG, with Trimble, Martin, and Gillham as receivers. After midnight in his home, Stilwell admitted to a reporter, "It is a friendly receivership," and "It is for the sake of carrying on the reorganization plans." The local press reported that it was a coup d' etat by Stilwell to block Thalmann from going to the Saint Louis federal court. The press reported that the failure of the opening of the canal at Port Arthur and the equipment shortage led to the crisis. The reason for acting secretly on

---

33. *The Railroad Gazette*, February 3, 1899; "Agreement of Readjustment and Consolidation," March 13, 1899, Pliny Fisk Collection; *Wall Street Journal*, March 25, 1899; the Kansas City *Star*, March 30, 1899.

34. Stilwell, "I Had a Hunch," January 28, 1928, 94; Stilwell, *Cannibals of Finance*, 71–77.

the first of April was that $575,000 in interest had fallen due at the State Trust Company in New York City. Although this act kept Stilwell in control, it was a practice denounced by some critics of railway finance as "monstrous"; the officers who led a railroad to default were the last ones who should be named receivers, so they said.[35]

This was also the position of Thalmann, the State Trust, and some other bondholders. On April 6, Elihu Root, attorney for the State Trust, filed suit in federal court in Saint Louis for new receivers, claiming the state court in Kansas City was prejudiced and that officers of the company should not be receivers. When the Saint Louis court accepted jurisdiction, Stilwell immediately left Kansas City for New York. Thalmann continued to act as head of the reorganization committee, but Stilwell and DeGeoijen moved rapidly to prevent that committee from gathering more securities and to have bondholders withdraw those previously deposited. This action took on additional importance when the federal Circuit Court named two new receivers, S. W. Fordyce and Webster Withers. The court asked Gillham to stay with the company as general manager, but he resigned. The appointment of Withers, a former Collector of Internal Revenue, and Fordyce, former receiver and president of the Saint Louis Southwestern Railroad, was viewed as a complete victory by Thalmann. Most financial observers felt that the New York committee headed by Thalmann had complete control, and, based on the report by S. M. Felton which the committee had ordered, it moved to take over the line. Felton reported that the KCPG needed $2,224,702 just to stay in operation, and the New York committee, now enlarged to include E. H. Harriman and James Stillman, drew up a new financial plan.[36]

Stilwell realized that several crucial errors had been made, for he had originally invited Harriman into the reorganization effort, and the inclusion of Stillman further suggested the presence of Standard Oil money.

35. The Kansas City *Star*, April 2 and 3, 1899; Port Arthur *Herald*, April 6, 1899; New York *Times*, April 3, 1899; *Journal of Commerce*, April 3, 1899; Simon Sterne, *Recent Railroad Failures and Their Lesson* (New York: [Reprinted from *The Forum*], 1894), 13–14.

36. The Kansas City *Star*, April 6, 7, 27, and May 10, 1899; New York *Times*, April 7, 11 and 28, 1899; *Journal of Commerce*, April 7 and 27, 1899; *Wall Street Journal*, April 10 and 20, 1899; Felton, "Report on the Kansas City, Pittsburg & Gulf Railroad."

To make matters worse, Welsh went along with the New Yorkers, and the Thalmann-Harriman-Stillman forces began buying up KCPG bonds to strengthen their position.

Stilwell did not intend to allow his creation to slip out of his hands without a fight. Some of his Philadelphia supporters like Samuel Shipley and Winthrop Smith also desired to block the New Yorkers as did De-Geoijen. A Philadelphia reorganization committee was organized with another plan to issue new bonds and stock in return for the old bond-holder's equity. The stock was to be assessed $10 per share to raise $2,300,000 for improving the line and paying the equipment trust indebt-edness. The Philadelphia group, promising to work with the new receivers and the courts, realized that crucial to their contest with the New York committee was winning the support of the Dutch bondholders who held $12,000,000 in securities and the Germans who had $5,000,000. With great success, Stilwell and DeGeoijen began to woo the European investors away from Thalmann.[37]

Throughout the summer and early fall of 1899, the New York and Philadelphia committees fought to gain support. The receivers meanwhile were forced to issue $800,000 in certificates to keep the line operating. The New Yorkers bought the receivers' certificates, strengthening their position. Stilwell, desperately seeking financial support, turned to John W. Gates. Gates, who had invested large sums in the KCNC, the northern lines, the KCPG, and the Missouri, Kansas and Texas Trust, purchased additional shares in the KCPG, at Stilwell's invitation, and asked for a reorganization of the Philadelphia committee to reflect his interest. The committee added Gates associates William Edenborn and Max Pam to its membership and created a voting trust to represent the committee con-sisting of Stilwell, Gates, Edenborn, DeGeoijen, August Herkscher, Her-man Sielcken, and Shipley. Without realizing the consequences, Stilwell allowed Gates to gain the upper hand on the Philadelphia committee.[38]

37. New York *Times*, April 18 and May 1, 1899; *Journal of Commerce*, April 18 and 19, 1899; the Kansas City *Star*, April 10, 1899; *Wall Street Journal*, April 19, 1899.

38. *Journal of Commerce*, July 31 and August 1, 1899; New York *Times*, June 26, 1899; "Plan and Agreement For The Reorganization of The Kansas City, Pittsburg & Gulf Railroad Company And Its Terminal Companies," August 17,

John W. Gates, better known as "Bet a Million" Gates, had been born in Illinois in 1855, became a hardware dealer, and then a barbed wire salesman. Introducing the latter product in Texas, he made a fortune, founded a series of wire and steel companies, and by 1898 had become a leading steel producer. A short, fat, "Falstaffian" character, Gates infringed on patents, watered stock, manipulated securities, and became an inveterate gambler. He lost $550,000 playing the horses at Saratoga on one day, and won back $300,000 playing faro the next. Described as a "freebooter," "swashbuckler," and "charlatan," Gates played with corporations the way he played cards and the horses. With William Edenborn, a talented steelman operating his American Steel and Wire Company, and Max Pam, an able Chicago lawyer handling his legal problems, Gates constantly sought new companies into which to plunge, and Stilwell's various enterprises were ripe for the picking.[39]

With the support of Gates and most of the Dutch bondholders, the Philadelphia committee obtained a majority of the securities by fall, but at the same time the KCPG was entering another crisis. In order to attract tonnage, the receivers cut rates to the Gulf just as Stilwell had, a device, the *Wall Street Journal* suggested, to force another railway to purchase the KCPG. To make the receivers rescind the rates, a number of roads boycotted the KCPG, causing the receivers to seek court orders forbidding this practice. Some competitors simply abolished joint tariffs to penalize the KCPG, others denied them freight cars. Restraining orders from federal courts ended the boycott, but wholesale rate cutting ensued.[40] The rate war made it even more imperative that the reorganization be effected immediately.

1899 (Bureau of Railway Economics Library, Association of American Railroads, Washington D. C.).

39. *Who's Who in America* (Chicago: A. N. Marquis & Company, 1903), 437–438, 548; Stewart H. Holbrook, *The Age of the Moguls* (Garden City: Doubleday & Companies, Inc., 1953), 145–147, 342–344; Matthew Josephson, *The Robber Barons* (New York: Harcourt, Brace & World, Inc., 1962), 426, 446; Edwin Lefevre, "John Warne Gates," *Cosmopolitan* XXXIII (September 1902), 535–538.

40. The Kansas City *Star*, August 18 and 19, 1899; New York *Times*, August 19, and 29, 1899; *Wall Street Journal*, August 11, 16, 19, 22, 29, and October 6, 1899; *Journal of Commerce*, August 3, 16, and 17, 1899; *The Railroad Gazette*, October 20, 1899.

The contest between the New York and Philadelphia committees continued, and their advertisements, financial journal editorials, and statements by the committees made the entire affair public knowledge. The chief difference in the two proposed reorganization schemes was that the Philadelphia committee included the Suburban Belt and the Channel and Dock Company properties while the New York plan did not. The former called for $80,000,000 in new securities, while the latter planned to issue only $75,000,000. The New Yorkers said the KCPG was too weak to carry the terminal companies, but the Dutch stockholders, being heavy investors in both terminal operations, supported the Philadelphia committee. The *Wall Street Journal* told its readers to sell their bonds in the KCPG immediately to take advantage of the high price generated by the fight over control of the road. Rumors were current in both cities that Stilwell would regain control over the KCPG and that the Philadelphians had won.[41]

Stilwell and the journals did not know that Gates and Harriman, tired of the financial pressures of the reorganization struggle, had accepted a compromise which included an agreement to squeeze out the promoter. The two financial tycoons signed a contract whereby Gates would sell half of his holdings to Harriman and a new committee would be created representing both interests; however, Gates would name two thirds of the committee membership. By the latter part of October the press reported that Stilwell had been ousted from the reorganization procedure. His place in the voting trust went to Harriman, and DeGeoijen resigned to be replaced by James Stillman. An immediate consequence of the compromise was an increase in railroad rates in the south central states, as Stillman represented the Rockefeller interests on the Missouri, Kansas and Texas Railroad, while Harriman controlled the Chicago and Alton, the Union Pacific, and the Illinois Central; and all of these lines had been fighting the KCPG over rates. No longer would the KCPG be a "great disturber of the general peace," as it had been under Stilwell, declared the *Wall Street Journal*. The Gates, or Philadelphia Committee made few concessions to the Harriman, or New York Committee, with the terminal lines in Kansas City immediately incorporated into the KCPG and the

41. New York *Times*, September 1 and 3, 1899; *Journal of Commerce*, September 1, 1899; *Wall Street Journal*, September 23 and October 14, 1899.

Port Arthur operation to be assumed later. The Gates-Harriman compromise plan gave the KCPG cash for operation and equipment but cast the northern lines adrift.[42] Arthur Stilwell's airline to the Gulf had new management.

Stilwell claimed that the alliance between Gates and Harriman came about when the promoter refused to join Gates in throwing the northern lines into bankruptcy. When Gates proposed to make a killing on the securities, Stilwell threatened to expose him; Gates then removed Stilwell from the Philadelphia committee and from the presidency of the KCPG. This is, of course, possible and, given Gates's ruthlessness, quite probable, but it is also true that Harriman wanted Stilwell ousted from all of the railways, and that could have been his price for the compromise. Stilwell, however, could take solace in the fact that most Southern railways had been taken over by Wall Street and that few independent lines survived by 1900. He was not alone in losing a railroad, for others, short of funds and verging on bankruptcy, had turned to receiverships and the financiers.[43]

As late as December 9, 1899, Gates promised to retain Stilwell as president of the reorganized KCPG, but when the reorganization occurred Stilwell was not an officer of the firm. On March 19, 1900, the Kansas City Southern Railway Company was incorporated to acquire the KCPG, its subsidiaries, the Kansas City terminal lines, and to obtain control of the Port Arthur facilities. At a public sale in Joplin, Missouri, the Reorganization Executive Committee bought the line at a foreclosure sale. A seven-man, five-year voting trust took over the new railway, with Gates in control. The trust was altered later, and Harriman, Otto Kahn and George Gould were added as members, but Gates could not get along with his

---

42. "Agreement made and entered into this twenty-fifth day of October 1899 between John W. Gates, as party of the first part, and Edward H. Harriman, as party of the second part," and "Modified Plan and Agreement For The Reorganization Of The Kansas City, Pittsburg & Gulf Railroad Co. And Its Terminal Companies, Philadelphia, November 7, 1899," Pliny Fisk Collection; *Valuation Reports*, Vol. 75, 348; *Wall Street Journal*, October 27, 30, and November 6 and 16, 1899; New York *Times*, October 29 and November 15, 1899.

43. Stilwell, *Cannibals of Finance*, 78–83; For a general view of southern railroads see John F. Stover, *The Railroads of the South* (Chapel Hill: University of North Carolina Press, 1955), and for a specific example see Maury Klein, *The Great Richmond Terminal* (Charlottesville: University Press of Virginia, 1970).

allies. When the trust ended, he and the Dutch investors acquired the Harriman interests. Later, when Gates dropped out, Lenore F. Loree became president of the KCS serving for many years.[44]

Stilwell and Harriman exchanged public charges, each blaming the other for mismanaging the railway. Harriman's biographer, George Kennan, argued that Stilwell had built the road only for townsite profits and that when Harriman took over the management, through the voting trust, the line was in terrible condition. According to Kennan, Harriman rebuilt the track and bridges, restored confidence in the securities of the company, and turned deficits into profits. What Kennan fails to explain is why the Dutch investors preferred a man like Gates to Harriman and why respected railway experts such as William Ripley accused Harriman of mismanagement. Stilwell claimed he had been robbed, that Harriman allowed Port Arthur to deteriorioate, and that only under Loree did the KCS actually prosper.[45] Never did the promoter deny that he and his friends made money in the old KCPG; in fact, he admitted that W. S. Woods, E. L. Martin, Richard Gentry, and others each made about $300,000, and when he sold his holdings in the KCS in 1902, he reportedly owned $270,000 in securities.[46]

Arthur Stilwell lost the air line, "straight as the crow flies," to the Gulf, but the KCS was a major contribution to the regional economy. The line became an important means to ship export grain, and after World War Two its significance grew. The Marshall Plan, the Korean War, and wheat shipments to India and the rest of Asia caused the port to live up to Stilwell's hopes. In northern Arkansas, the fruit tree and nursery businesses expanded, as did the production of rice around Port Arthur. Numerous towns Stilwell created which never became metropolises remain as minor economic and political centers. The Kansas City Southern Railway under the successive management of Lenore Loree, Harvey Couch, and William Deramus not only became profitable but has consistently had one of the

---

44. Port Arthur *Herald*, December 9, 1899; *Wall Street Journal*, March 19 and 23, 1900; New York *Times*, March 17, October 27 and 31, 1900, November 7, 1901, April 21, 1904, May 9 and 11, 1905; George Kennan, *E. H. Harriman: A Biography* (Boston: Houghton, Mifflin Company, 1922), I, 219–224.

45. *Ibid.*, 214–231; Stilwell, *Forty Years of Business Life*, 9, 25–32.

46. Wendt and Kogan, *Bet a Million!*, 204–205; Arthur E. Stilwell, *Forty Years of Business Life*, (New York: n.p., 1926 [?]), 24–25; Stilwell, "I Had a Hunch," January 28, 1928, 89.

lowest operating ratios in the country. In 1939, a merger with the Louisiana and Arkansas Railway gave the KCS a direct line from Shreveport to New Orleans and access to Dallas. An industry leader, the KCS became one of the first railroads to diversify through incorporation of a holding company. Stilwell would have been proud that for years the flagship KCS passenger train to Port Arthur was called "The Flying Crow," and when the streamlined "Southern Belle" to New Orleans went into service, one of the Pullman cars was named "Arthur E. Stilwell." But these developments and rewards came years after his disappointments of 1899 and 1900.

When Stilwell earned the enmity of Harriman and Gates, the former also deposed him as president of the KCPG's northern affiliates. Control of the Kansas City and Northern Connecting was lost when the Kansas City Suburban Belt was forced to give the KCNC securities it had acquired for building the line to the Trust company to pay its debts to that institution. Gates held KCNC stocks and bonds himself and also, temporarily, controlled the Trust company. As president of the KCNC, Stilwell tried in October of 1899 to reorganize the line, but failed, and the next month Gates gained control of all but Stilwell's seat on the board of directors. Harriman, Gates, and the receivers of the KCPG asked for a receivership for the KCNC on January 2, 1900; Stilwell was removed from the board in April; and on May 20, 1901, the KCNC was foreclosed. Similarly, Gates took over the Omaha, Kansas City and Eastern in September of 1899, a receivership followed in January, and the OKCE also suffered foreclosure in 1901. Under the receivership, the KCNC, OKCE and Quincy, Omaha and Kansas City were operated as one line, and on January 22, 1902, they were purchased by the Chicago, Burlington and Quincy Railroad. The previous October the Wabash Railroad purchased the Omaha and Saint Louis from its receivers. Stilwell's contribution had been to provide Kansas City with a new railroad to Quincy which later gave the CB&Q an additional route across northern Missouri. Despite Stilwell's claim that investors in his railways failed to suffer losses, the second-mortgage bonds on the KCNC were never redeemed, and the other securities were heavily discounted in the reorganization.[47]

47. *Ibid.*, 94; Minute Book, Kansas City Suburban Belt, July 20, 1899; New York *Times*, October 18, 1899, June 4, 1901; *The Railroad Gazette*, October 20, 1899, June 7, 1901; Minute Book, Kansas City and Northern Connecting, November 2, 1899 and April 4, 1900; Minute Book, Omaha, Kansas City and Eastern, Septem-

Arthur Stilwell presided over at least fifty-two companies in 1898, but the institution which held them together was the Missouri, Kansas and Texas Trust Company. The Trust made substantial profits and its resources had grown to $5,106,457.98. With Gates acquiring more and more of the Trust company securities, the directors voted to change the name of the firm to the Guardian Trust, increase its stock to $2,500,000, and relocate the head office in Chicago. Stilwell and his wife moved to Chicago in July 1899, hoping at that time to save the Trust and the KCPG. Six months later the promoter resigned as president of the Trust, and Gates took over. When the Kansas City Southern evolved out of the old KCPG, Guardian Trust sued the KCS for money advanced to the KCPG and KCSB, and a long legal fight ensued. The finances of all these companies were, however, so mixed as to be "unintelligible." Stilwell always claimed that several hundred thousand dollars was owed the Guardian. Nevertheless, the Trust also went into receivership, and in 1903 its assets were sold, the purchasers being representatives of the stockholders of the Arkansas Construction Company. The liquidation process did not end until the 1920s, and although the evidence is not precise, it appears that the investors did not lose in this scheme.[48]

The most profitable Stilwell operations for which there are records were the Port Arthur land companies. These companies had total sales of $441,229.26, with profits of at least $292,229.16. Stilwell remained a trustee of the Port Arthur Townsite Company until June of 1901, when the company was taken over by George Craig, acting for John Gates who had purchased stock in the firm from William Taylor, John Lowber Welsh, and E. T. Stotesbury. The original Dutch investors maintained their majority position, however, and from 1905 until 1912, when the firm was liquidated, controlled it through their own manager, Jan Van Tyen.[49]

ber 26, 1899; Poor, *Manual*, 1900, 517–518 and 1902, 405 and 494; Richard C. Overton, *Burlington Route* (New York: Alfred A. Knopf, 1965), 268–269.

48. *Wall Street Journal*, April 13, 1899; "11th Annual Statement of the Missouri, Kansas and Texas Trust Company, October 26, 1898," Wright Scrapbooks; the Kansas City *Star*, July 15, 1899; Kansas City *World*, July 30, 1899; Stilwell, *Cannibals of Finance*, 78, 84–85; Stilwell, *Forty Years of Business Life*, 1–16, 30–31; Port Arthur *Herald*, November 11 and December 30, 1899; *Valuation Reports*, Vol. 75, 304, 375.

49. *Ibid.*, 437; New York *Times*, April 27 and 29, 1901; E. O. Haight to George Craig, June 20, 1902, and July 23, 1904, and William S. Taylor to Craig, June 20,

Ironically, the townsite company profited greatly from a boom even Stilwell's "brownies" failed to forsee; on January 10, 1901, just fifteen miles north of Port Arthur, the famous Lucas gusher blew in, opening the Spindletop oil field.

Captain Anthony F. Lucas had been drilling on a salt dome at Spindletop when a rumbling noise and a vibration in the drill stem heralded the coming of the gusher. When the well "blew in," oil shot 200 feet in the air and ran wild for nine days. More than 50,000 barrels of oil escaped each day, covering the area in a heavy black glaze. The gusher inaugurated a boom, and by 1905 there were 1,200 wells in the area which had produced 33,000,000 barrels of oil. Out of this field came several major oil companies, including Gulf Oil Corporation, Magnolia Petroleum Company, Humble Oil Company, as well as the Texas Company in which John W. Gates and George Craig were active participants. The companies desired massive shipping facilities, and Port Arthur's future was secured. Both Gulf and Texaco built refineries at Port Arthur, linked the oil wells to the city with pipelines, and began to use the Port Arthur canal to export petroleum products. Cheap water transportation proved vital to the development of Spindletop and other oil fields in the area. One third of the total petroleum output of the Gulf Coast field was transported over the canal; five oil companies contributed 98 percent of the water-born shipments through the canal in 1906. As Rupert Vance wrote, "Port Arthur is 100 percent oil," and "Man, not nature, made the Texas Gulf ports."[50]

The men who built Port Arthur were Arthur Stilwell and John W. Gates, but oil provided the basis for the city's growth. After Stilwell took Gates to Port Arthur, the latter returned, bought land, and made other investments. Through George Craig, Gates became involved in a bank,

---

1905, George M. Craig Papers (San Jacinto Museum, San Jacinto, Texas); Port Arthur *News*, May 13, 1903, May 13, 1905; Herschiel L. Hunt, *The History of Port Arthur* (n.p.: Southern Publishing Concern, 1926), 6.

50. Louis J. Wortham, *A History of Texas* (Fort Worth: Wortham-Molyneaux Company, 1924), I, 183–186; Harold F. Williamson and Ralph L. Andreano, *et al.*, *The American Petroleum Industry*, Vol. II, *The Age of Industry* (Evanston: Northwestern University Press, 1963), 20, 81–89; Arthur M. Johnson, "The Early Texas Oil Industry: Pipelines and The Birth of an Integrated Oil Industry, 1901–1911," *The Journal of Southern History*, XXXII (November 1966), 519; Rupert B. Vance, *Human Geography of the South* (Chapel Hill: University of North Carolina Press, 1932), 346–347.

rice mill, and public utilities, and eventually built a large home on the lake front. Although Stilwell dropped out of the Port Arthur development by 1902, Gates continued to reside in the town periodically and became its principal benefactor. He gave the community a hospital, library, and college, but after Gates died his family demonstrated little interest in the town. Nevertheless, Port Arthur grew as the expanding refineries and the rising petrochemical industry buoyed up the local economy. The thousand or so residents of 1900 grew to 7,663 in 1910, to 50,902 by 1930 and 66,676 in 1960, with a present metropolitan population of more than 100,000. The city suffered neglect and economic distress from 1925 to 1955 but has subsequently witnessed renewed growth. It has been suggested that it would have been more fitting to have named the city for John Gates, but Stilwell, not Gates, located the city and promoted it, and Stilwell conceived the city's most significant asset, the canal.[51]

After the canal opened for ocean-going vessels, business increased, but the dramatic growth of canal traffic came after 1901. The lumber and grain shipments were surpassed by petroleum and then virtually disappeared as significant commodities on the waterway. The Channel and Dock Company had, however, gone into receivership on September 10, 1900, and on June 7, 1902, was sold to a subsidiary of the KCS, the Port Arthur *Canal* and Dock Company, for $500,000. John Gates, through the railroad, controlled the waterway. Gates and the oil company executives desired that the federal government take over the canal, deepen it, and extend it up the Neches River to Orange and Beaumont.[52]

The federal government, beginning in 1898, considered purchasing the canal and extending it, and residents of Port Arthur and the oil companies lobbied for such action. They also desired to make Port Arthur a port of entry to avoid the necessity of going to Galveston to clear customs. The local congressman, opposing such action, was defeated in 1904. The Kountze Brothers, still fighting the Port Arthur development, worked strenuously to block any federal support of the canal. But as the oil traffic reached enormous size on the waterway, the petroleum companies exerted

51. *Port Arthur* (Houston: Anson Jones Press, 1940), 5–6, 51–53; Hunt, *The History of Port Arthur*, 17–18; *The Texas Almanac* (Dallas: A. H. Belo Corporation, 1967), 176; *Commerce and Finance*, January 9, 1924.

52. Port Arthur *News*, May 13, 1903; *Port Arthur*, 54–55, 156–157; Port Arthur *Herald*, July 28, 1900.

much energy in seeking governmental intervention, and several Texas congressmen and senators became ardent advocates of legislation to create a port of entry. Finally, in 1906, the various interests involved reached an agreement whereby the federal government would create a port of entry and extend the canal, and John Gates and the Kansas City Southern Railway agreed to give the waterway, but not the terminal, to the government. President Roosevelt signed a bill to that effect on June 19, and the Secretary of War accepted the canal on December 13. Gates had lobbied for the bill, Stilwell sent telegrams in support of his namesake, and George Craig maintained, years later, that considerable sums of money changed hands in Washington to grease the legislative wheels.[53]

By 1908 the canal had been extended to Beaumont and Orange, and Port Arthur had become the thirteenth largest port in the United States in value of exports. Oil and petroleum-related products remain the principal exports of Port Arthur. The general-cargo business dropped off dramatically shortly after 1900 and did not recover until 1964 when the newly created Port of Port Arthur Navigation District began to build and operate a modern cargo facility. Ironically, the site selected for the new terminal was the exact spot where Arthur Stilwell had built his export pier in 1897.[54] A plaque on the terminal building dedicates the facility to Stilwell's memory, and high above the docks one of the world's largest computer-operated traveling gantry cranes carries in giant letters the name "Big Arthur."

Although the development of Port Arthur, the Kansas City, Pittsburg and Gulf Railroad, and the construction of the canal to the sea bear all

---

53. *Congressional Record* (55th Congress, 2nd Session), Vol. XXXI, Part I, 782–783; (56th Congress, 1st Session), Vol. XXXIII, Part I, 693; (57th Congress, 1st Session), Vol. XXXV, Part I, 184 and 2347 and Part V, 4998, 5268 and Part VI, 5288; (59th Congress, 1st Session), Vol. XL, Part VII, 7792–7795 and Part X, 9157; *Port Arthur a Port of Entry* (House of Representatives, House Report No. 4555, 59th Congress, 1st Session); "Reasons Why Port Arthur Should be Made a Port of Entry," Arthur Stilwell Collection (Port of Port Arthur, Port Arthur, Texas); Port Arthur *Herald*, November 29, 1905, January 18 and 25, 1902, July 27, 1906; Senator J. W. Bailey to John W. Gates, June 21, 1902, George Craig to Senator James H. Berry, March 21, 1902, and Craig to George N. Bliss, April 16, 1906, all in Craig Papers; Manuscript by George M. Craig (Historical Files, Port Arthur Chamber of Commerce, Port Arthur, Texas).

54. *Port Arthur*, 157; Port Arthur *News*, February 4, 1908; John R. Rochelle, "Port Arthur: A History of Its Port" (Unpublished Masters Thesis, Lamar State College of Technology, 1969), 5–6.

the earmarks of entrepreneurial errors, they ultimately proved of benefit to the people of the south central states. One would need to respond positively to Arthur Stilwell's question, "Have I not the right then to take my place as a benefactor of my times?[55] Yet 1900, the beginning of a new century, was a very troubled year for Stilwell, for he had lost his creations, the work of a dozen years. His friends, fearing he would not recover, felt he needed cheering up, and they decided to hold a dinner to honor the promoter and city builder. What they did not know was that Arthur Stilwell had had another "hunch."

55. Stilwell, *Forty Years of Business Life*, 9.

VIII

TO MEXICO AND THE ORIENT

ARTHUR AND JENNIE STILWELL decided to take a vacation. After he resigned from the presidency of the Guardian Trust, they left Kansas City
and went to Old Point Comfort, Virginia, to rest. Jennie, as always, provided her husband with understanding, sympathy, and encouragement,
but even she was shocked at a sudden change in his appearance. Arthur
had been reading a newspaper article by the columnist George Ade who
wrote "If a man is cross-eyed it is a great detriment; if a man is hump-
backed it is an act of God; but if a man wears side whiskers it is his own
fault." Stilwell, who had long cultivated a luxurious growth of side
whiskers in an attempt to add an element of maturity to his visage, went
to a mirror, contemplated his appearance, and in an outburst of courage,
lathered his face and shaved off one of the "pork chops." Jennie came
into the room, saw what had happened, and said, "You can't go out that
way, you'll have to shave the other side off now." Arthur agreed, and was
soon smooth of cheek. He left the house, met an acquaintance who,
startled, blurted out, "I've heard about your trouble, but I didn't know it
was anything like as serious as this."[1] Other friends realized how much
Stilwell had lost—both his railroads and his whiskers—and when he and
Jennie returned to Kansas City a number of civic leaders decided to hold
a testimonial dinner to cheer up the promoter. Yet even Stilwell's closest

---

1. Arthur E. Stilwell and James R. Crowell, "I Had a Hunch," *The Saturday
Evening Post*, CC (February 4, 1928), 38.

169

associates failed to recognize the indomitable spirit of the forty-year-old railway builder.

On the evening of February 10, 1900, more than 200 men filled the banquet room of the Midland Hotel to show their appreciation for Stilwell's contributions to Kansas City. The decor of palms, rubber plants, and American flags formed the background for an "elaborate and perfect" meal. A series of laudatory testimonial speeches was followed by "three cheers for Stilwell" and the presentation of a large silver loving cup from the "Citizens of Kansas City." The promoter, in a highly emotional response, thanked his friends, neighbors and business associates. "I would much prefer to have the friendship of Kansas City," he said, "than to be president of the Pittsburg and Gulf." With regard to his misfortune, he said, "I have no complaint." The guests must have nodded in appreciation of his lack of bitterness, then they probably jumped in their seats, for Stilwell announced, "But, I have another project in mind."[2]

I have designed a railroad 1600 miles long which will bring the Pacific Ocean 400 miles nearer to Kansas City than any other present route. Not only that, but it will be 1600 miles nearer to Central and South America than San Francisco is. . . .[3]

The details of the scheme would be revealed in a few days, he stated, and the dinner adjourned. Undoubtedly some of the guests left in confusion, others in dismay and many hopeful that another profit-making project was about to get under way.[4]

The next morning the promoter went to the National Bank of Commerce to describe the project to his allies W. S. Woods, Churchill White, and W. A. Rule, officers of the bank. He intended to build a railroad from Kansas City southwest across Oklahoma Territory and Texas to the Rio Grande, then on to Chihuahua, Mexico, over the Sierra Madre to a port on the Gulf of California, Topolobampo, where a terminal facility, Port Stilwell, would be constructed. From Port Stilwell, ships would sail to Central and South America and the Orient. Port Stilwell would be closer to Kansas City than San Francisco and would open up the rich trade of

2. The Kansas City *Star*, February 11, 1900; the Kansas City *Journal*, February 11, 1900.
3. Stilwell, "I Had a Hunch," February 4, 1928, 38, 44.
4. *Ibid.*; New York *Herald*, September 27, 1908; Arthur E. Stilwell, *Forty Years of Business Life* (New York: n.p., 1926 [?]), 16.

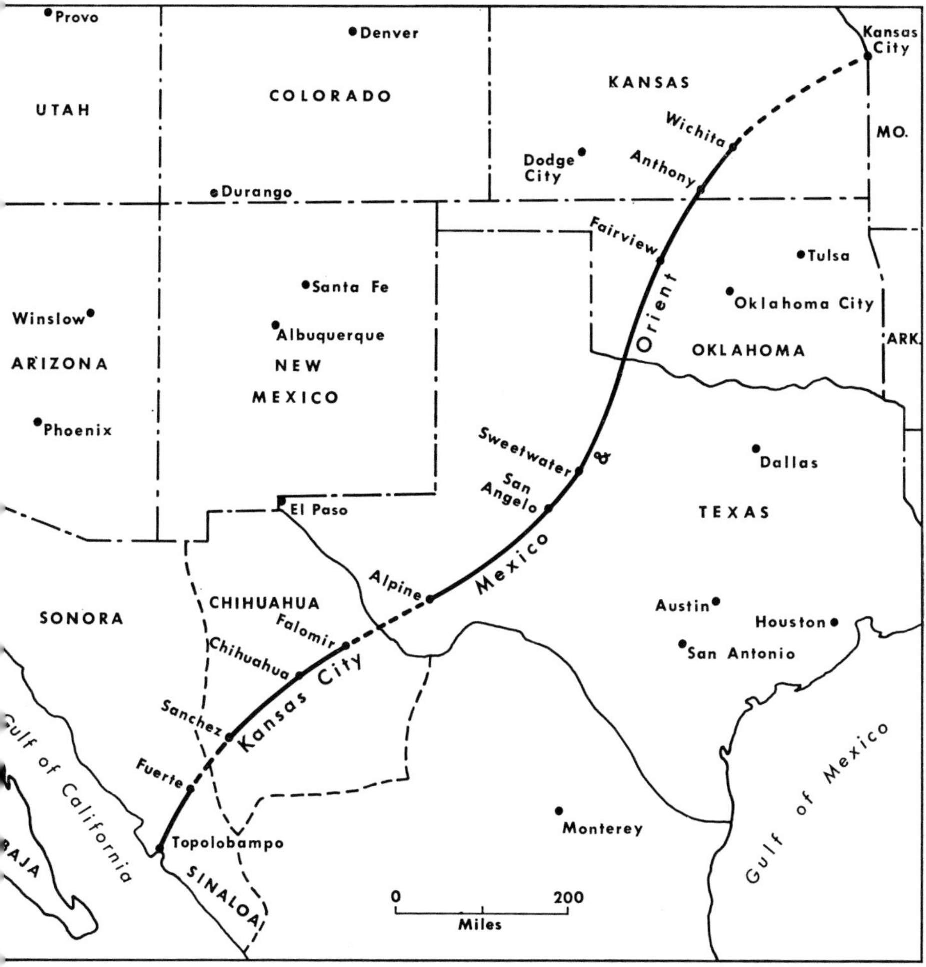
Provo
Denver
UTAH
COLORADO
KANSAS
Kansas City
Wichita
MO.
Dodge City
Anthony
Durango
Fairview
Tulsa
Santa Fe
Oklahoma City
Winslow
Albuquerque
Orient
ARK.
ARIZONA
NEW MEXICO
OKLAHOMA
Phoenix
Sweetwater
&
Dallas
San Angelo
El Paso
TEXAS
Mexico
Alpine
CHIHUAHUA
Austin
SONORA
Falomir
Houston
Chihuahua
San Antonio
Kansas City
Sanchez
Gulf of California
Gulf of Mexico
Fuerte
Monterey
Topolobampo
BAJA
SINALOA
0
200
Miles
UWM Cartographic Services

THE KANSAS CITY, MEXICO AND ORIENT RAILWAY

the Far East to the middlewestern United States.[5] Woods listened, then told the others that they had profited from Stilwell's railroad to Port Arthur and the affiliated enterprises and that he would subscribe $100,000 to the scheme on the basis of this oral presentation. His associates agreed to subscribe various amounts, giving Stilwell a financial base of $500,000.[6] They were not impractical men, these Kansas City bankers, yet they agreed to contribute money to this seemingly visionary notion. Why would men of substance place money in this latest "hunch"? The answer is that the idea was not new, it was not Stilwell's, and it had been discussed in Kansas City for many years.

Fabled Mexico, "treasure chest of the western hemisphere," had long provided adventurers with dreams of wealth. From the time of the Spanish conquistadores to the writings of Alexander von Humboldt, the public had been told of the riches of the mines and other natural resources of Mexico. Within the United States a prominent and vocal body of politicians and businessmen had long urged the conquest of Mexico either by military or economic power, and movements to separate the northern Mexican states of Sonora, Sinaloa, and Chihuahua were common after 1880. Other Americans, somewhat less avaricious and jingoistic, desired to settle in Mexico as farmers, ranchers, or businessmen, and several utopian communities were founded as well as the more successful Mormon settlements.

Coupled with this dream of Mexican wealth was the lure of commerce with the Orient. From the China trade of the Yankee Clippers to the opening of Japan by Admiral Perry, Americans saw in the Orient not only wealth but also a fertile field for the missionary. Victorian homes were filled with Japanese and Chinese bric-a-brac as the rage for things Oriental swept the country. How might this commerce be developed? Many clamored for colonies, others for a canal through the Isthmus of Panama; still others favored the opening of new trade routes. The latter concept intrigued Arthur Stilwell who proposed a rail line to the Gulf of California, creation of a new port, and the inauguration of new shipping

5. *Ibid.*; Arthur E. Stilwell, *Cannibals of Finance* (Chicago: Farnum Publishing Company, 1912), 98–99.
6. *Ibid.*; Stilwell, "I Had a Hunch," February 4, 1928, 44; Stilwell, *Forty Years of Business Life*, 17; W. R. Draper, "Promoting the Orient," *Railroad Magazine*, L (November 1949), 109–110.

routes to the Far East. Along the railroad the promoter hoped to develop mining and other enterprises.[7] His plan differed only slightly from a scheme long publicized by Albert Kinsey Owen.

Albert Owen was born in Chester, Pennsylvania, about 1848, the son of a Quaker physician. He spent his childhood at New Harmony, Indiana, at the utopian colony founded by Robert Owen. Although not related to the English socialist, Albert Owen became devoted to utopianism. He ultimately became a civil engineer and a surveyor for railroad builder General William Palmer. Palmer hired Owen to survey a rail route in Mexico, and when the work ended Owen wandered about the northern tier of states, reaching the harbor at Topolobampo in 1872. The harbor had been visited by the United States sloop-of-war *Jamestown* three years earlier, and a tentative survey had been made at the request of Dr. Benjamin R. Carman, a large landowner at Mazatlan. Owen came away from Topolobampo dreaming of a utopian colony serving as the port for a railroad to the United States. By 1874 Owen was in Virginia proposing a railroad from Norfolk to Topolobampo. He received a charter for the Southern Settlement Society which proposed to create a colony at the port on the Gulf of California. Owen gave numerous speeches and published tracts and pamphlets about his project, but few colonists were recruited. The next year Commander George Dewey surveyed Topolobampo, and his report praised the undeveloped harbor as the finest south of San Francisco. Armed with Dewey's report, Owen continued his efforts to raise funds for the community, and in 1881 he obtained a Massachusetts charter for the Texas, Topolobampo and Pacific Railroad and Telegraph Company. Associated with the venture were such diverse personalities as politicians Benjamin Butler, U. S. Grant Jr., and the old reformer Wendell Phillips. A "Greenbacker," free trader, and advocate of women's suffrage, Owen attractd a sizable following of radicals and reformers.

Owen decided to create a colony at Topolobampo based on "integral co-operation." The colonists would have no private wealth, and even the railroad would be a socialistic venture. Several hundred colonists moved to the port site, and for twenty years the little band struggled to survive.

7. David M. Pletcher, *Rails, Mines, and Progress: Seven American Promoters in Mexico, 1867–1911* (Ithaca: Cornell University Press, 1958), 1–5. This is an excellent study of the whole phenomena of American investment and promotion in Mexico, and the chapter on Stilwell is well conceived.

The scheme was to be financed by the Credit Financier of Sinaloa, which sold stock in the enterprise, but by 1887 interest waned. Owen came to Kansas City in 1888, spoke of a new project, the Kansas City, Presidio del Norte and Topolobampo Railroad, and interested Christian B. Hoffman, a flour-mill owner, in the scheme. Hoffman organized the Kansas Sinaloa Investment Company to raise funds for the colony. Owen had previously acquired a Mexican charter for the railroad as well as land concessions for the railway and the port. A dispute developed, however, between the utopians and Hoffman with regard to the profits from the scheme, and throughout the 1890s the conflict raged. By 1898 the colony had virtually disappeared.[8]

Kansas City had made other contacts with northern Mexico in the decade ending in 1900. Robert S. Towne of the Kansas City Smelting and Refining Company had opened a silver mine in Mexico and brought the ore to his smelter in Argentine, Kansas. A delegation from Sonora visited Kansas City in 1890, and an international bank was formed to stimulate trade. The proposed rail line to the Gulf of California also received public and governmental attention in Mexico.[9]

As early as 1859, the state of Chihuahua granted a concession for a railroad from Presidio del Norte (now Ojinaga) to the port of Guaymas on the Gulf of California, and in 1868 a second charter provided for a railway to be constructed to a point between Guaymas and Mazatlan, presumably Topolobampo. Although these schemes did not come to fruition, in 1891 Enrique Creel, a Chihuahua businessman, incorporated the Chihuahua and Pacific Railroad and received from the Mexican government a concession from Chihuahua to the coast at Topolobampo. The leading *Cientifico* of his home city, Creel later became Foreign Minister of Mexico in the government of Porfirio Diaz. Under the direction of Alfred A. Spendlove, general manager of the Chihuahua Mining Com-

8. *Ibid.*, 106, 108, 118 and 140; Thomas A. Robertson, *A Southwestern Utopia: An American Colony in Mexico* (Los Angeles: The Ward Ritchie Press, 1964), 19–59; Sanford A. Mosk, "A Railroad to Utopia," *The Southwestern Social Science Quarterly*, XX (December 1939), 243–258; New York *Times*, March 11, 1881 and October 1, 1892; Clarence O. Senior, "The Kansas City, Mexico and Orient Railroad," (Unpublished Masters Thesis, University of Kansas City, 1942), 45.

9. Marvin D. Bernstein, "The History and Economic Organization of the Mexican Mining Industry, 1890–1940," (Unpublished Doctoral Dissertation, University of Texas, 1951), 322–324; Pletcher, *Rails, Mines, and Progress*, 268–269, 273–274.

pany, construction began. A reorganization in 1897 brought into the company Grant B. Schley of New Jersey, who found the capital to push the line west across the mountains to Minaca, a distance of 124 miles. Two years later Owen negotiated with Creel to have the Chihuahua and Pacific extended to his dying colony at Topolobampo.[10]

Creel and Owen were unable to complete the railway, largely because of the immense difficulty of constructing track across the Sierra Madre, the spine of the continent. Stilwell proposed to conquer the mountains with trestles, bridges, and tunnels, but the costs would be enormous. Offsetting the massive capital outlay, according to Stilwell, were the mineral wealth from the mines, the profitable fruit and vegetable crops from the Fuerte River Valley north and west of Topolobampo, and the prospective trade with the Orient. Topolobampo was a natural fjord harbor, but a shallow and dangerous bar lay offshore. The inner harbor extended inland nine miles with 2¼ fathoms at low mean tide, but although the twisting channel into the harbor was easily navigated, enormous dredging would be necessary to open the entrance.[11] Railroad construction across the plains of Oklahoma, Texas, and from the Rio Grande to Chihuahua would be easy compared with the mountain trackage and the work on the harbor. Others might shrink at such prospects, not Arthur Stilwell.

Stilwell always acted as though no one else had ever thought of a direct railway connection from the midwest to the Gulf of California, and press reports often stated, "it started as an idea in Mr. Stilwell's mind." When the project was announced one reporter declared that Stilwell had the idea two years before but had been too busy to pursue it. Another story appeared in one of Stilwell's puff pieces saying that the conception came to him after he read a report advocating a canal across the Isthmus in Nicaragua. Years later one of the promoter's former associates recalled

10. Fred Wilbur Powell, *The Railroads of Mexico* (Boston: The Stratford Co., Publishers, 1921), 104–105; Pletcher, *Rails, Mines, and Progress*, 201, 206–217, and 268–269; Senior, "The Kansas City, Mexico and Orient Railroad," 54–55; Robertson, *A Southwestern Utopia*, 77–83, 125; John Leeds Kerr with Frank Donovan, *Destination Topolobampo: The Kansas City, Mexico & Orient Railway* (San Marino, California: Golden West Books, 1968), 17, 50.

11. Powell, *The Railroads of Mexico*, 8; Stilwell, "I Had a Hunch," February 4, 1928, 46; *The Railway Age*, March 20, 1903; P. L. Bell and H. Bentley MacKenzie, *Mexican West Coast and Lower California* (Washington: Government Printing Office, 1923), 6, 17, 25, 52, and 74–76.

that Stilwell had talked to Owen about the Topolobampo route, and even the most cursory newspaper reader in Kansas City in the 1890s would have known of Owen's scheme. In his conversations with investors on the "Port Arthur Route," particularly those in England, Stilwell may have heard of the project, as English and American investors in Mexican mines and railways moved in the circles where he had contacts.[12]

General cultural, economic, and political influences on Stilwell and his contemporaries included the international impact of imperialism and the race for colonies and conquest. For Americans, the annexation of Hawaii, the Spanish-American War, the acquisition of the Philippines, the "Open-Door Policy" in China, and political rivalry with Japan in the Pacific intensified the general interest in trade, missionary work, national growth, and manifest destiny. English investors would share in the general imperialistic sentiment, the economic invasion of Mexico, and the desire for a balance of power in the Pacific. The Mexican government under Diaz and the *Cientificos* labored mightily to attract foreign investors as a means to modernize the country and enhance their personal wealth and political power. National and international developments were highly propitious for the railway to Mexico.[13]

Yet, the project bore all of the earmarks of another "entrepreneurial error." Stilwell failed to consider the massive cost of crossing the Sierra Madre, the barren terrain the railway would cross in both countries which would scarcely produce any traffic, and the large quantity of equipment necessary for a railroad more than 1,600 miles long. He grossly overestimated earnings, particularly the mineral traffic and the nonexistent Far Eastern trade. Topolobampo was much closer to the midwest than San Francisco, but it was farther to Japan and much farther to the Orient than

12. *Building a Great Transcontinental Railroad* (New York: [from the *Financial World*], 1906), 19; *El Reno* [Oklahoma] *News*, February 22, 1900; *The Kansas City Gateway*, December 1902; Senior, "The Kansas City, Mexico and Orient Railroad," 55; Jules Davids, "American Political and Economic Penetration of Mexico, 1877–1920," (Uunpublished Doctoral Dissertation, Georgetown University, 1947), 174, 182.

13. There are numerous studies of the phenomena of imperialism at the turn of the century. For an excellent summary of the ideology of expansionism see David Healy, *U. S. Expansionism: The Imperialist Urge in the 1890s* (Madison: University of Wisconsin Press, 1970).

from the California port. Besides, Kansas farmers and Texas cattlemen had few exports for China and desired less in imports. The fabled China trade was just that—a fable. Further, Stilwell failed to consider the vagaries of dealing with a foreign government, particularly a government which was losing the support and confidence of its people. But he differed little from other dreamers. In his study of seven promoters in Mexico, David Pletcher wrote, "Apparently the basic mistake of the promoters was that they oversimplified their problem and either minimized or completely ignored certain serious obstacles."[14] Yet Stilwell not only convinced himself of the viability of the scheme but also convinced some very thoughtful and respected businessmen, bankers, and railroad executives.

Stilwell announced the formal organization of the Kansas City, Mexico and Orient Railway Company on February 17, 1900, and made public the scheme to link Kansas City with the Gulf of California. Shortly thereafter Arthur and Jennie departed for Chihuahua. There he met with Enrique Creel who agreed to incorporate his Chihuahua and Pacific into Stilwell's railway through a trackage agreement and to become a vice president of the KCMO.[15]

When the Stilwells arrived in Mexico City, two members of the Diaz family met them at the railway station and escorted them to their hotel. They told Stilwell that the President had sent them; the promoter wondered how Diaz knew he was coming. He received an appointment with Diaz, who told him that the governors of several states in the United States and some bankers had sent him telegrams before Stilwell's arrival. The promoter said his associates had arranged for the messages, although it resembles one of his own techniques. Stilwell told Diaz he wanted a railway concession from Presidio del Norte to Chihuahua, and the President replied that such a railroad had been included in the master plan established by the general railroad law of 1899. The promoter also asked for a subsidy of $5,000 per mile from the Mexican government. These requests were not unusual in Mexico, and Diaz had long sought foreign capital through concessions and subsidies. Since 1880 this had been Mexican policy, and the result had been a massive increase in railway

14. Pletcher, *Rails, Mines, and Progress*, 302.
15. New York *Times*, February 18, 1900; Stilwell, *Cannibals of Finance*, 99–101; Stilwell, "I Had a Hunch," February 4, 1928, 44.

mileage. Diaz accepted Stilwell's terms, and an agreement was drawn up in April 1900.[16]

Diaz expressed great enthusiasm for the railway and related to Stilwell the history of other attempts to build such a line. The President felt that the railway would open the mineral and timber resources of northern Mexico to further development, not to mention the additional maneuverability that such a railroad would provide for the army and his rurales. The existing railways, or those under construction, extended north from Mexico City to El Paso, Laredo, or Nogales, but there was no east-west route across the Sierra Madre. Completely captivated by the charming Diaz, Stilwell felt that the President would be his constant supporter. One of the promoter's associates recalled Diaz's saying that the KCMO was, "The greatest railway project of the age."[17]

What the President told Stilwell about the law of 1899 providing for the concession and subsidy was true, but the President issued only a preliminary decree in April. Under Mexican law the concessionarie received a lease for a definite period of years, and, although the railway would be built with private funds, at the end of the time period the railroad reverted to the state. The concession was neither a corporate charter nor a grant of funds, but a contract for an undertaking deemed mutually beneficial to the Mexican government and the private developers. The KCMO concession provided for a 99-year lease on a right of way 70 meters wide from Presidio del Norte to Chihuahua and free importation of construction materials for five years. Stilwell agreed to begin construction in two months, complete the line in four years, and post a bond of 32,000 pesos. Freight and passenger rates were fixed, but the exact subsidy figures were not, and later contracts provided for five different subsidy rates with an estimated total of $3,500,000 gold. The Stilwell concession, reputed to be one of the most favorable ever granted, was signed on July 27. The following November the KCMO formally received the concession previously granted to the Chihuahua and Pacific, giving Stilwell a right of way across the entire country. Although there is no evidence that President Diaz participated financially in the KCMO, when Stilwell returned to Kansas City he was accompanied by Alonzo Fernandez, Diaz's nephew and son of the gov-

16. *Ibid.*; Powell, *The Railroads of Mexico*, 1, 7.
17. Stilwell, *Forty Years of Business Life*, 17–18; Stilwell, *Cannibals of Finance*, 101–106; the Kansas City *Star*, April 28, 1900.

ernor of the Federal District, and by Lorenzo Elizaga, Diaz's brother-in-law.[18] The promoter wisely brought into his project the leading politician and banker in Chihuahua as well as some of Diaz's relatives.

While in Mexico, Stilwell also met with Albert and Marie Owen. There is some conjecture that they had met earlier, and at least one report contends that the promoter went to Topolobampo to see the utopian colonizer. During their conversation they drafted a contract, arranging for Stilwell to buy Owen's concession at Topolobampo. Owen would receive part of the subsidy from the Mexican government and stocks and bonds of the KCMO as payment. In the contract, signed in Mexico City on April 21 and witnessed by two of Stilwell's associates, W. W. Sylvester and A. S. Witherbee, Stilwell promised to pay Owen on a graduated scale, based on the mileage of the KCMO as it was constructed.[19]

Shortly after the promoter arrived in Kansas City he began to organize the railway and raise money for construction. His local associates provided some capital and several served on the board of directors. The railway had been incorporated with capital authorized at only $1,000,000, yet Stilwell announced that expenditures for constructing the railroad would be $27,000,000, obviously underestimating actual costs by many millions. The charter authorized the railroad to build from Kansas City to Wichita, across western Oklahoma Territory and west Texas to Presidio, Texas, on the Rio Grande with branches to Del Rio and Brownsville.[20] Now all the promoter needed was twenty-seven million dollars, or more.

Stilwell intended to use the Guardian Trust Company to finance the KCMO, and on May 18, 1900, he won back the presidency of the company. The board of directors decided on June 15 to finance the line to

18. Powell, *The Railroads of Mexico,* 167–168; Pletcher, *Rails, Mines, and Progress,* 269–270; Senior, "The Kansas City, Mexico and Orient Railroad," 60–61, 64; Mosk, "A Railroad to Utopia," 258; *Breve Historia del Ferrocarril Chihuahua al Pacifico* (Mexico City: Secretaria de Obras Publicas, 1961), 35–36; the Kansas City *Star,* April 27, 1900; *Memoria De La Construccion Del Ferrocarril Chihuahua al Pacifico* (Mexico City: Secretaria de Obras Publicas, 1963), 23.

19. Kerr, *Destination Topolobampo,* 54–55; Robertson, *A Southwestern Utopia,* 125–126; Pletcher, *Rails, Mines, and Progress,* 270–271; Senior, "The Kansas City, Mexico and Orient Railroad," 55–58.

20. Stilwell, *Forty Years of Business Life,* 18; *The Railroad Gazette,* February 23, March 9, and April 20, 1900; Arthur L. Carnahan, "Kansas City, Mexico, and Orient Railroad Company of Texas and its Predecessors," *Southwestern Historical Quarterly,* LIV (April 1951), 492.

Mexico. The Guardian would sell 30 to 35 million dollars of KCMO bonds which were to be given to the construction companies Stilwell had formed; the manner of finance was to be the same as used on the Kansas City, Pittsburg and Gulf. With his reinstatement as president of the Trust at a salary of $20,000 a year, and with the director's approval of the security issue, Stilwell felt that all was well.[21]

On November 30, however, his old nemesis John W. Gates threw the Guardian into receivership. Stilwell saw another plot by Gates, E. H. Harriman, and Ernest Thalmann, but Gates probably acted to save the assets of the Guardian and to divide them up among the stockholders, of whom he was one of the largest. Also, Gates probably hoped that the receivership might end a suit filed by the Guardian against the Kansas City Southern, which he controlled. In any event, the liquidation of the Guardian lasted for years, and a continuing proxy fight ensued between Gates and Stilwell and his associates. The promoter argued that the receivership and liquidation harmed "the widow and orphan, the poor and the weak," but also admitted he owned one seventh of the capital stock of the Trust.[22] It became obvious that another vehicle would be necessary to finance the railroad.

Within sixty days after the receivership, the United States and Mexican Trust Company of Delaware was created. Chartered on February 1, 1901, the company was authorized to enter the general trust business. Its prospectus announced capitalization of $2,500,000, and several Mexican nationals were listed as members of the board. Stilwell distributed many letters advertising the new company and sent numerous telegrams to his contacts in Europe. Subscribers of stock were required to pay only 40 percent before June 15, and within a few weeks several hundred thousand dollars had been pledged. The Trust and the KCMO were "more or less identified," and those who pledged support realized the primary business would be selling railway and construction company securities.[23]

---

21. Port Arthur *Herald*, May 26, 1900; *Commercial and Financial Chronicle*, July 7, 1900; *The Railway Age*, July 6, 1900; Stilwell, *Forty Years of Business Life*, 19.
22. *Ibid.*, 19–20; Stilwell, *Cannibals of Finance*, 24; Pletcher, *Rails, Mines, and Progress*, 271–272.
23. H. P. Wright to T. Y. Hoffman, March 21, 1901, and Prospectus of the United States and Mexican Trust Company, H. P. Wright Scrapbooks (University

Stilwell created two other firms to build the KCMO, the Union Construction Company and the International Construction Company which would accept railway bonds for their work. Stock in the construction companies would be sold to provide the cash for rails, rolling stock, right of way, and other expenditures, while the United States and Mexican Trust Company would hold the bonds of the KCMO in a collateral trust mortgage. The Union, capitalized at $10,000,000, would build the railway from Kansas City to Lone Wolf, Oklahoma Territory, and the International, capitalized at $31,000,000 would build from Lone Wolf to Topolobampo. For each mile of track the construction companies were to receive $15,000 to $18,000 in KCMO bonds, $16,000 in preferred stock, and $12,000 or $12,500 in common stock. Because of the high cost of construction in Mexico, the International would receive a bonus of $2,500,-000, the subsidies from the Mexican national and state governments, two thirds of the townsites and stock in various timber and mining companies. The sums of $10,000,000 for equipment and $15,000,000 for terminal facilities were set aside for future use; Stilwell did not want a recurrence of his experiences with the KCPG. The Mexican subsidies amounted to $3,550,000 in 5 percent federal bonds for work in the Sierra Madre, $7,000 per kilometer west of the mountains, plus $600,000 in State of Chihuahua 5 percent bonds and $200,000 in State of Sinaloa 5 percent bonds.[24]

In order to raise money to initiate work Stilwell began to sell the securities of the two construction companies and to create a maze of subsidiary corporations whose securities were offered as a bonus. He presented to prospective buyers the most inviting array of securities. Upon completion of the construction of the KCMO, each owner of 100 shares of Union Construction Company would receive

$18,000	KCMO	First-mortgage, 4 percent bonds
$18,000	KCMO	4 percent preferred stock
$16,000	KCMO	Common stock
$ 6,666	KCMO	townsite stock.

of Missouri–Kansas City Library, Kansas City, Missouri); Stilwell, *Cannibals of Finance*, 114–115, 119.

24. Pletcher, *Rails, Mines, and Progress*, 282; Edward Dickinson, "Second Report to J. Crosland Taylor," July 11, 1912 (Manuscript Division, Baker Library, Harvard Graduate School of Business Administration, Boston, Massachusetts).

In other words, for an investment of approximately $13,000 the stockholders would receive securities with a face value of $58,666. Similarly, purchasers of 100 shares of International Construction would receive

$17,225	KCMO	First-mortgage, 4 percent bonds
$16,940	KCMO	4 percent preferred stock
$12,600	KCMO	Common stock

and, as a bonus, holders of each share of stock would receive

5.5	shares,	Mexican Timber Field Company
20	shares,	Rio Grande Coal Field Company
800	shares,	Mexico & Orient Town Site Company
10	shares,	Chihuahua and Sinaloa Development Company
20	shares,	Sierra Madre Development Company,

or a total par stock value of $56,402 for each 100 shares of International stock.[25]

If this myriad of corporations failed to entice buyers, Stilwell offered stocks in the Western Tie and Lumber Company, the Kansas City Outer Belt and Electric Railroad (the latter being the terminal company in Kansas City), the Tri State Development Company, the Fuerte Valley Mining Company, and many others.[26] Despite Stilwell's unquestioned ability to sell stocks and bonds, he could not interest more than a few buyers in the project. Undaunted, he placed all of the unsold securities in a collateral trust and began to issue new KCMO first-mortgage collateral trust bonds at 5 percent.[27]

The promoter determined at the outset not to go to Wall Street for funds. He turned first to those who had supported the KCPG, and many pledged to purchase stock. He then went to towns along the proposed route, giving speeches, selling stocks, and requesting subsidies. Yet, the sums raised were pitifully small for such a gigantic undertaking. Following the pattern he had established with the KCPG, he determined to go to Europe to secure the funds he needed.

European investors had long placed capital in Mexico, hoping to

25. William Z. Ripley, *Railroads: Finance & Organization* (New York: Longmans, Green and Company, 1915), 16–17, 48; Senior, "The Kansas City, Mexico and Orient Railroad," 68–69.

26. Pletcher, *Rails, Mines, and Progress*, 273; J. Fred Rippy, *Latin America and the Industrial Age* (New York: G. P. Putnam's Sons, 1944), 161–162.

27. Senior, "The Kansas City, Mexico and Orient Railroad," 68.

receive a portion of the fabled riches of that country. While the French had been burned badly by the Maximillian fiasco in the 1860s, British investors continued to send large sums to Mexico. But, as J. Fred Rippy wrote, they

received no more than a meager income from their Mexican investments and a good many suffered losses. A handful of speculators, bankers, mineowners, engineers, oilmen, and exporters were amply rewarded, but the United Kingdom as a whole could not have greatly benefited. Heartbreaking disappointments were far more numerous than bonanzas.[28]

Nevertheless, British interest in Mexico remained keen, and particularly appealing was the new concept of an ocean-rail-ocean route to Australia, using railroads across the United States or Mexico. Stilwell decided to take advantage of his English contacts and this continuing interest in Mexico.

In the fall of 1901, he and Jennie sailed for England to remain there until the following spring. He made contact with a number of men who had invested in the KCPG, and they, in turn, introduced him to other interested persons. D. J. Neame, Lewis Rendell, and J. Crosland Taylor were his initial contacts, and through them he met Sir Alfred Newton, Lord Mayor of London; George A. Touche, the Sheriff of London and Chairman of the Midland Railway of Western Australia; Lord Monson, former attaché at the Paris Embassy; and a number of brokers and businessmen including Cecil Braithwaite, Harold Arbuthnot, J. S. Braithwaite, Walter Chinnery, and Granville Farquahar. These men formed the London Finance Committee of the KCMO with Taylor as secretary. In March Stilwell returned to Kansas City, bringing several members of the London committee with him. Following a dinner honoring Stilwell and his guests, he took the party to Mexico to see the territory through which the railway would pass. On this, the first of many such tours, the Englishmen agreed to make large purchases of stock.[29]

Stilwell and his party went back to England, and during the next few

28. J. Fred Rippy, *British Investments in Latin America, 1822–1949* (Minneapolis: University of Minnesota Press, 1959), 103–104.

29. Pletcher, *Rails, Mines, and Progress*, 282–283; Stilwell, *Cannibals of Finance*, 119–121; Program, Complimentary Dinner, March 14, 1902, Wright Scrapbooks; Arthur Stilwell to George M. Craig, and Stilwell to George M. Crary, May 2, 1902, George M. Craig Collection (San Jacinto Museum, San Jacinto, Texas).

months the promoter sold more securities. On August 7, 1902, he gave a dinner at the Hyde Park Hotel for the "Friends of the Kansas City, Mexico & Orient Railway Company," at which he described at length the glories of Mexico and the "Port Stilwell Route."[30] The publicity generated by Stilwell and the social and economic position of his associates raised eyebrows in London and led to an inquiry directed to the English minister in Mexico City, George Greville. In response, the minister wrote,

I met [Stilwell] . . . with his English Court composed of Lord Monson, Mr. Chinnery and others who certainly seemed to be under the spell; indeed the Arabian nights could not present a more brilliant and dazzling picture than [Stilwell's description of] the line of country between Chihuahua and the Pacific.[31]

So successful had been this style of promotion that Stilwell began commuting from London to Kansas City to Mexico City and back, marshaling bravado, good wine, and religion to sell his securities.

Between 1902 and 1911 Stilwell made many of these tours, generally entertaining guests from England but often including prospective investors from the United States. Occasionally some Germans or Dutchmen joined the party, but their total investment remained small. Stilwell entertained his guests in KCMO Car 100, a private car similar to that which he had used on the KCPG. Car 100 had a large painting on its sides depicting the flags of Mexico and the United States intertwined and contained many of the features of its predecessor, including a small organ. Placed at the rear of the train, the car was open to all of the guests each evening.[32] One Englishman who visited the car reported the following:

There is, in Mexico again, the case of Mr. Stilwell, a most ardent Christian Scientist, who is constructing a great railway down from Kansas City to the State of Sinaloa. He is in the habit of conducting parties of Americans and other magnates through the country, and when they are sitting round him in his private car he will discourse upon the future of his railway very glowingly and afterwards give very lucid answers to financial problems. After this he gives them each a book of Christian Science hymns, and with his

30. Craig to Stilwell, July 23, 1902, and Stilwell to Craig, August 8, 1902, Craig Collection; Program, reproduced in Francis Leverett, "Arthur E. Stilwell, 1859–1928," (Unpublished Masters Thesis, University of Texas, 1955).

31. Quoted in Pletcher, *Rails, Mines, and Progress*, 284–285.

32. *Commercial and Financial Chronicle*, September 27, 1902; Lucius Beebe, *Mansions on Rails* (Berkeley: Howell-North Press, 1959), 265; New York *Herald*, September 27, 1908.

secretary playing the harmonium he leads the voices; and it is delicious when those corpulent old gentlemen take from their mouths the fat cigars and warble. Sometimes one of them at the conclusion of a hymn or even, prematurely, of a verse, will have financial doubts as to the railways. He will ask a question and he will be satisfactorily answered. Then the singing is resumed.[33]

After construction of the KCMO began, private trains often moved over the railway so that investors could see the progress being made. Generally these tours included Mexico City, so that government officials could show their interest, and Chihuahua, where Enrique Creel entertained the travelers. The combination of high-pressure salesmanship, sightseeing, good food and drink, and hymns proved extremely effective. Stilwell raised substantial sums for the KCMO and recruited men of position and wealth as officials and directors of the railway.[34]

In what must be considered an administrative and public relations coup, Stilwell brought into the KCMO organization a number of well-known and successful railroadmen. Edward Dickinson, who served as vice president and general manager, had been general manager of the Union Pacific for thirteen years. The directors included Jabez T. Odell, who built the Bessemer & Lake Erie Railroad for Andrew Carnegie; John F. Wallace, who had been the general manager of the Illinois Central; Warren Purdy, formerly president of the Chicago, Rock Island and Pacific; and George J. Gould, president of the Missouri Pacific. Creel acted as a vice-president, and the Senors Pablo Macedo, Isodro Diaz Lombardo, and Manuel Calero served as directors. Representing English investors was Vice-president Sidney Braithwaite. Other directors included Robert C. Clowry, president of the Western Union Telegraph Company; W. C. Proctor of Proctor and Gamble; and several Missouri and Kansas bankers: Woods, Rule, David Mulvane, James H. Arnold, and Rolla Wells.[35] The inclusion of these well-known business leaders and railroad executives gave the project the appearance of stability and genuineness which the flamboyant promoter often lacked. It demonstrates not only his shrewd approach to the project but also some recognition of his own weaknesses.

---

33. Henry Baerlein, *Mexico: The Land of Unrest* (London: Herbert and Daniel, 1913), 84.

34. Stilwell, "I Had a Hunch," February 4, 1928, 46; the Kansas City *Star*, February 2, 1902; Chicago *Record-Herald*, March 23, 1907.

35. Pamphlet, 1906, Corporate Records Division, Baker Library.

Slowly Stilwell gathered the capital necessary to initiate construction. He had difficulty persuading stockholders of the Trust company to pay in their subscriptions, and until they were paid the English investors refused to participate. Despite the failure to merge the Guardian Trust with the United States and Mexican Trust, the latter proved profitable, paying a 6 percent dividend by August of 1902. The promoter reduced the capitalization of the Trust to $1,000,000 and instituted quarterly dividends of 1 ½ percent. The Trust opened branches in London and Mexico City, and the same address in the latter location housed the offices of the KCMO and the Mexican and Orient Navigation Company. The shipping company operated two coastal steamers from Guaymas, Sonora, to Port Stilwell, where the KCMO had, by 1902, spent more than $66,000 for improvements. The construction companies also sold securities, but while the International stock could be sold only at par, the Union shares of $100 par value sold at $110, and by December of 1902 most of the initial offering had been subscribed. English investors took nearly $5,000,000 in stocks and bonds, and several Bostonians made large purchases. Stilwell managed to keep the debt per mile and the fixed charges low, but the question remained, would the road be profitable even without heavy annual obligations?[36]

While Stilwell raised funds, his engineer, M. P. Paret, and operating vice-president, W. W. Sylvester, worked in the KCMO office in Kansas City drafting engineering plans, obtaining right of way, and purchasing construction materials, locomotives, and rolling stock. The offices contained engineering facilities, a director's room, and two large roll-top desks: one for Sylvester, the other for Stilwell. The comfortable surroundings included potted plants and a false fireplace over which hung a photograph of Queen Wilhelmina of Holland.[37] All the various firms connected with the KCMO and the Trust were housed in the same quarters. Paret's

36. Stilwell to Crary and Stilwell to Craig, May 2, 1902; Stilwell to Stockholders of the United States and Mexican Trust Company, October 20, 1902; Stilwell to Craig, December 31, 1902; all Craig Collection; New York *Times*, September 12, 1902; Andrew D. Barlow, "American Enterprises in Mexico," *A Monthly Summary of Commerce and Labor* (February 1905), Department of Commerce and Labor, Bureau of Statistics, 2822, 2840; *Commercial and Financial Chronicle*, December 6, 1902; *Boston Evening Transcript*, June 16, 1928; the Kansas City *Star*, February 2, 1902.

37. Kerr, *Destination Topolobampo*, 76–77.

engineering work was warmly praised in the first issue of *The Kansas City Gateway,* a puff piece created to boom the KCMO and its townsites. The magazine announced that on January 1, 1903, seven thousand tons of English rails would arrive at Port Stilwell, initiating construction in Mexico, and with subsidies totaling $345,500 being received from counties in Kansas, work on that end of the line had commenced.[38]

The location and date that the first spike was driven on the "Port Stilwell Route" is subject to some dispute. On July 4, 1901, with elaborate ceremonies, Arthur Stilwell drove the "first spike" at Emporia, Kansas. He had spoken to a large audience at the Whitley Opera House there the previous December, telling them that the KCPG "is nothing but a trolley line compared with this new road"; hearty applause greeted his declaration that, "The merits of the road will build it."[39] The town responded by voting a subsidy for the KCMO, and Stilwell rewarded their enthusiasm by holding the "first spike" ceremony there. Ironically, the KCMO only graded a few miles at Emporia, then its crews departed. Not until May 9, 1902, did the railway begin to lay track, and then at Anthony, Kansas, south of Wichita and many miles from Emporia. The latter town would never see a KCMO train pass through.[40]

Even before construction began in Kansas, the KCMO became operative in Texas and in Mexico. On March 3, 1900, Stilwell purchased the Panhandle and Gulf Railway Company which owned eight miles of track and twenty miles of graded right of way south of Sweetwater, Texas. Originally incorporated as the Colorado Valley Railway, the company proposed to build from Sweetwater to San Angelo. The struggling railroad was about to go under when Stilwell announced the projected KCMO. One of the stockholders knew W. S. Woods and through him contacted the promoter who agreed to purchase the railway. Stilwell had its charter amended to authorize extending the line north to the Red River and south to the Rio Grande, and changed the name to the Kansas City, Mexico and Orient Railway Company of Texas. Construction proceeded in both directions from Sweetwater.[41]

38. *The Kansas City Gateway,* December, 1902.
39. The Emporia *Republican,* December 3, 1900; *Commercial and Financial Chronicle,* July 13, 1901.
40. *Ibid.,* May 17, 1902.
41. Carnahan, "Kansas City, Mexico and Orient Railroad Company of Texas,"

Even before the KCMO obtained trackage rights over the Chihuahua and Pacific in 1902, it had began construction at Port Stilwell. The engineers were dispatched to Topolobampo where some grading took place, and a small wharf and other facilities were built to accommodate the rails and equipment which began to arrive. John Case, an engineer from Kansas City, moved to the port and with a crew of native labor started laying rails into the Fuerte River valley. Another work force operating out of Chihuahua began construction east toward Trancas, and yet a third party began to extend the Chihuahua and Pacific track west from Minaca.[42] Work commenced simultaneously in Kansas and Texas.

Stilwell planned to terminate the KCMO in Kansas City and using the same methods he had employed before organized a terminal company to gain entrance to the city. In 1902 he formed the Kansas City, Outer Belt and Electric, capitalized at $1,500,000 with authorization to build 6 miles of track in Kansas and 2¾ miles in Missouri. The KCOBE would also do industrial switching, and own extensive yards in Kansas City, Kansas, and North Kansas City, Missouri. Leases on several large properties were purchased, and some grading and bridging work was undertaken. The KCOBE would, however, receive little attention for several years.[43]

In 1903 and 1904 construction proceeded at a moderate pace at several points along the projected KCMO. Construction in Kansas began south of Wichita, and by April 1, 1903, the KCMO extended to Carmen, Oklahoma Territory, a distance of 75 miles. During the following September an additional 21 miles from Carmen to Fairview opened. John Case and his track gangs completed 60 miles of line from Topolobampo to El Fuerte in April, and the next month 34 miles of track became opera-

---

490–492; R. C. Crane, "Railroads and Community Rivalries: Chapters from the Inside Story of the Orient and Santa Fe in West Texas," *West Texas Historical Association Year Book*, XIX (October 1943), 3–5, 17; S. G. Reed, *A History of the Texas Railroads and of Transportation Conditions under Spain and Mexico and the Republic and the State* (Houston: The St. Clair Publishing Company, 1941), 307.

42. Powell, *The Railroads of Mexico*, 158–159; New York *Times*, September 10, 1900; Draper, "Promoting the Orient," 110–111; *Memoria de la Construccion*, 23–24.

43. *The Railroad Gazette*, August 8, 1902; E. Dickinson, "Report on the Kansas City, Mexico & Orient Railway Company and the Kansas City, Outer Belt & Electric Railroad Company," June 18, 1912, Manuscript Division, Baker Library.

tive east from Chihuahua. Grading work south of Wichita, north of Sweet-water, and west from Minaca continued.[44]

While construction across the Great Plains was relatively easy, serious obstacles began to delay the work in Mexico. Chief Engineer Paret located the line on ridges across Oklahoma and Texas, avoiding bridge work where possible, and maintaining low grades. Large bridges were necessary, however, over the Canadian River in Oklahoma, across the Red River between Oklahoma and Texas, and over the Rio Conchos and Rio Fuerte in Mexico. Stilwell employed the engineering firm of Waddell and Hedrick of Kansas City to design bridges for the KCMO. Bridging and tunnel work in the Sierra Madre would be extensive and expensive, and this section received the least attention of the promoter and his engineers. Yet, hundreds of men and teams were at work in seven different locations in 1903 and 1904.[45]

Port Stilwell grew slowly as ships from Europe began arriving loaded with rails and other supplies. Vessels as large as 6,100 tons and 360 feet long were accommodated in the harbor. Stilwell signed a contract with the Hamburg-American Steamship Line for service from Port Stilwell to the Orient, but the service would begin only after the KCMO was completed. The growth of the port received widespread newspaper and magazine coverage, most of which appears planted by Stilwell.[46]

When the line from Wichita to Carmen opened, the Kansas City Commercial Club toured the railway at Stilwell's invitation. At Carmen a gold-spike ceremony was held celebrating the opening of the first 115 miles of the KCMO. Stilwell probably shuddered when the first hammar blow missed the spike, but the club members returned to Kansas City with enthusiasm. Passenger service between Kansas City and Carmen began, with the cars of the KCMO attached to a Missouri Pacific train from Kansas City to Wichita. The track lacked ballast and had been only slightly elevated above the prairie, but it was operative.[47]

---

44. *The Railway Age*, March 20, 1903; Kerr, *Destination Topolobampo*, 68.
45. *The Railway Age*, March 20, 1903.
46. *El Gazatero* [Topolobampo], quoted in *The New Empire*, May 1903; *The New Empire*, February, 1903; Charles Edward Russell, "The Seven Kings in Mexico," *Cosmopolitan*, XLIII (July 1907), 277; E. P. Lyle, Jr., "American Influence In Mexico," *World's Work*, VI (September 1903), 3854.
47. *The Kansas City Gateway*, March and April, 1903.

The track constructed in Mexico appears to have been more carefully designed and built. Perhaps more care was taken because of the cheap labor, because better engineers were employed, or possibly because of the hazards of mountain railway operations.[48] An American resident of northern Mexico described the operations of track gangs in the area:

I used to see five hundred workmen with perhaps a hundred women and children break camp every few days and move on, as the railroad was built down into the wilderness. . . . We used to expect, when the railroad camp moved, a gamecock to every man, cock fights being more popular by far than bull fights, and the last thing the long line of flat cars that moved the workmen and their families waited for was the capture of the runaway cocks.[49]

Progress on the KCMO was being made, but the operation of four disjointed sections of track failed to produce profits.

Stilwell always tried to present the most favorable view of the physical and fiscal progress of the "Port Stilwell Route" but could report net earnings of only $22,742 in 1903 and $39,093 in 1904. Not only did the four disconnected sections prevent operation of through trains, they also failed to generate much traffic individually. By 1904 the KCMO had issued $3,705,000 in stock, $2,307,000 in bonds, and an equipment trust of $448,655. With a debt of $55,385 per mile, the net earnings were only $180,443.50. This level of operation would continue for six or seven years.[50]

While his railway failed to prosper markedly in its first four years of existence, some of Stilwell's subsidiaries profited, particularly the townsite schemes. As construction proceeded in Oklahoma Territory and Texas, Stilwell established numerous townsites, following the pattern used on the Kansas City, Pittsburg and Gulf. In Oklahoma Territory he created Fairview, Carmen (named for the wife of President Diaz), Ingersoll (for C. E. Ingersoll, a Philadelphia investor), Amorita (the wife of Ingersoll), Orienta, Blair, and Elmer (the latter two towns named for KCMO officials). In Texas, Stilwell located Diaz, Rochester, Hamlin, and

48. *Ibid.*, August 1903, and quoting *The Chihuahua Enterprise*, July 1903.

49. Mary B. Ramsey, "Life In Chihuahua," *New England Magazine*, LI (May 1914), 119, 120.

50. *The Railway Age*, July 14, 1923; Crane, "Railroads and Community Rivalries," 7; United States, Interstate Commerce Commission, *Seventeenth Annual Report of the Statistics of Railways in the United States* (Washington: Government Printing Office, 1905), 250–251, 340–341, 394–395.

the towns of Odell, Sylvester, and Rule which he named for his associates.[51] Various devices were used to boom the towns, including two monthly magazines, *The New Empire* and *The Kansas City Gateway*.

The New Empire, "dedicated to bring up the area served by the KCM&O," sold for 5 cents a copy and featured large advertisements for the towns, testimonials from their residents, and enthusiastic "news" articles on their resources and potential. Carmen received considerable attention, with appeals for both residents and speculators. The town was described as "The Greatest Opportunity for a Cash Investment Ever Offered in All the History of Town Building in the Southwest." Fortunes could be made there as Carmen was destined to be "one of the great commercial centers of the Southwest." By March of 1903, more than 300 people lived there, including Perry Carpenter, a "Baptist minister," who testified that he had borrowed money to buy a farm and had so prospered that he moved from a dugout, to a sod house, and then to a two-story frame home. His health had been poor before he moved to Carmen, but now, said "Brother" Carpenter, he felt "great." A cyclone hit the town the following July, reported *The New Empire,* but it would be rebuilt and would become even more prosperous. By 1960 Carmen had 533 residents.[52]

Fairview, not far from Carmen became a division point on the KCMO, and although not destined to become a metropolitan center, the town proved more successful than the other sites in Oklahoma Territory. The Land Department of the United States and Mexican Trust Company described the area around Fairview as excellent farming country, which it was, and praised the beauty of the valley of the Cimarron River. By the fall of 1903, through passenger service between Wichita and Fairview began, and the little village grew into a sizable community. *The Kansas City Gateway* claimed that, "One result of the building of the Kansas City, Mexico & Orient railway is the establishment of a large number of new towns along the route of the road" which was true, but none of the new communities would become more than small farming centers.[53]

51. George H. Shirk, *Oklahoma Place Names* (Norman: University of Oklahoma Press, 1965), 8, 109, 38, 157, 24, and 72; *The Railway Age,* March 20, 1903.
52. *The New Empire,* March 1903; See *The Kansas City Gateway* throughout 1903 and 1904.
53. *The Kansas City Gateway,* March, June, and September, 1903.

Along the KCMO in Texas, Stilwell added substantially to the size of several established communities. Sweetwater, a junction city on the KCMO and the Texas and Pacific, received his attention after the townsite department acquired 450 acres on the north side of the town which became the "Orient Addition." The Land Department described Sweetwater as healthful, a great place for farming and ranching, and possessed of a "magnificent and up-to-date" school. The opportunities for capital investment were excellent for "The progress of Mr. Stilwell in this great enterprise has been marvelous." The little town invested in the Orient of Texas and the railway established its general offices and shops there. In 1910, however, the facilities were moved to San Angelo, and a suit by Sweetwater failed to prevent the transfer.[54]

The various townsites were financed by the Mexico & Orient Townsite Company which sold seven-year, 4 percent gold bonds in $100 denominations. Many of the bond holders were Englishmen, members of the London Finance Committee. The KCMO issued its own gold bonds as security for the townsite company bonds, but the statement was often made by the officers of the KCMO that the construction companies owned the townsites. The creation of many companies, each owning a part of the other, led to a chaotic situation.[55] One of the men in the townsite operation wrote,

I was not familar with the inside workings of the Orient corporation nor with the numerous subsidiary companies Stilwell organized to bolster his promotion work. But I know the vaults of the United States & Mexican Trust Company, fiscal agents for the railroad, were well filled with corporation seals and charters pertaining to irrigation, townsite, land and other concerns, all of which paid some financial tribute to the railroad.[56]

The same source claimed that some "insiders" were allowed to buy land from the railway at low prices, and when surrounding property, still owned by the railroad, was sold at a higher figure, the insider was carried in on

54. Crane, "Railroads and Community Rivalries," 6–7; *The Kansas City Gateway*, February and April, 1903; Robert L. Martin, *The City Moves West* (Austin: University of Texas Press, 1969), 80.

55. The Kansas City *Star*, January 24, 1904; Pamphlet, "Mexico & Orient Townsite Company Gold Bonds," 1904, Wright Scrapbooks; J. T. Odell to J. F. Stone, December 20, 1904, in a pamphlet (Bureau of Railway Economics Library, Association of American Railroads, Washington, D. C.).

56. Draper, "Promoting the Orient," 112.

the deal at the new price. Stilwell later admitted that sales of town lots had been both extensive and profitable.[57] The promoter brought into the Orient's Land Department many of the men who had worked in a similar capacity on the old KCPG, but one of these men stated,

I knew Mr. Stilwell well, was under his direct orders for several years. We made the company a number of millions of dollars from the sale of land and townsites, but little of the money stuck to Stilwell's fingers.[58]

If, as is claimed, Stilwell failed to profit personally from the opportunistic town and land schemes, the area through which the KCMO passed did make developmental gains in its urban population, for Sweetwater, San Angelo, Fort Stockton, Fairview, and other communities grew quite rapidly. Between 1900 and 1910 the population along the Orient increased by 50 percent compared with a national increase of 20 percent. Even Chihuahua witnessed considerable growth, some of which was attributable to the activity of the KCMO.[59]

The established towns along the KCMO also contributed to the financial progress of the railway; once again Stilwell proved very adept in winning subsidies from towns and counties. By 1903 the construction companies or the railroad were thought to have received $468,500 in Kansas, $125,000 in Texas, $30,000 in Oklahoma Territory, and approximately $3,550,000 in Mexico. Much of the right of way was donated by farmers, and land for stations, yards, and other facilities was donated by the towns. San Angelo subscribed $250,000 in city bonds in order to attract the general offices and shops away from Sweetwater, and Wichita spent considerable sums to obtain the main shops and yards.[60] While not absolutely crucial to the "Orient," these subsidies were helpful for a line always short of cash.

In three years Arthur Stilwell had formed a multitudinous number of companies to carry out a scheme to build almost 1,600 miles of railroad

57. *Ibid.*, 112–113; Stilwell, *Cannibals of Finance*, 121–122; L. H. Davison to George M. Crary, December 26, 1902, Craig Collection.
58. W. R. Draper to R. H. Johnston, September 9, 1946, Bureau of Railway Economics Library.
59. Stilwell, *Cannibals of Finance*, 123–124; Ira G. Clark, *Then Came the Railroads*, (Norman: University of Oklahoma Press, 1958), 258; B. O. Flower, "Chihuahua: Bit of Old Mexico," *Arena*, XXVII (June 1902), 624–629.
60. *The Railway Age*, March 20, 1903; Reed, *A History of the Texas Railroads*, 307.

across the virtually empty plains of Oklahoma and Texas, the desert and mountains of northern Mexico to a bay on the Gulf of California blocked by a sand bar. Millions of dollars and pounds sterling were invested by Americans and Englishmen based on dreams of Mexican wealth and trade with the Orient. That the scheme was becoming a reality demonstrates Stilwell's enormous ability as a salesman. No wonder newspapers and magazines on both sides of the Atlantic were filled with stories about this remarkably talented promoter "with a hunch."

IX

THE PORT STILWELL ROUTE

ARTHUR AND JENNIE STILWELL lived at 720 Armour Boulevard, in a handsome, three-story home. Neither a modest cottage nor a substantial mansion, the home served as a refuge from the vagaries of business and a place to rest between expeditions to London and Mexico City. The home was described as "beautiful," and a feature of the interior always caught the eye of reporters; the parlor contained a splendid pipe organ. Stilwell loved music and composed several hymns, including "Bethlehem Babe," and his passion for music and public attention led him to bring the Theodore Thomas orchestra from Chicago to play at Convention Hall. Stilwell declared,

Kansas City is a great railroad centre, a city of great packing houses, a great manufacturing city, a city of the most handsome boulevards in the United States and a city of fine homes. It has been the dream of my life to make it a great musical centre.[1]

When the Thomas orchestra played two free concerts in 1903, more than 30,000 people attended, extending lengthy applause when Stilwell entered the Hall.[2] Stilwell did not confine his song writing to religious themes, nor did he limit his compositions to music. According to one report he also wrote plays, novels, and even, as has been seen, political speeches. It would be several years, however, before his literary efforts were published.[3]

1. New York *Herald*, September 27, 1908.
2. *The Kansas City Gateway*, June 1903.
3. New York *Herald*, September 27, 1908.

195

Undaunted by adversity, thriving on criticism, buttressed by faith in himself and the future, Stilwell never lost sight of his goal of empire. Part of his optimism and strength came from the security of Christian Science:

This man, Arthur Edward Stilwell, president of the Kansas City, Mexico and Orient Railway, believes he has made a success, not in spite of taking religion into his business, but because of it, it goes with him to his office. When his motor car takes him to his beautiful home in the evening it is there also. . . . There is no cheerier, happy man than Arthur Edward Stilwell.[4]

Another source of his continual exuberance was his confidence in a future of limitless prosperity and his refusal to brood over past misfortunes. He said, and believed, "I regard it as the providence of God that I built and lost the Kansas City Southern so that I might learn how to build and retain the Kansas City, Mexico and Orient. I know how to avoid the rocks."[5] That the latter assertion proved untrue will soon be seen, but eternal optimism remained one of Stilwell's most distinguishing traits.

His epochal vision included his adopted city. "From my point of view," he said, "Kansas City is about to enter upon an era of unprecedented commercial and industrial activity."[6] He labored to attract industry to the area, and several large concerns came as a result of his efforts. The Proctor and Gamble Company built a plant employing between 700 and 1,000 workers, partially because of Stilwell's friendship with William Proctor. Proctor had been a "heavy" investor in the Kansas City, Pittsburg and Gulf and served as a director of the Orient.[7] Stilwell's community service, however, nearly always related to his own business activities.

One of the organizations to which he belonged was the Railroad Club of Kansas City, and it became a forum for public pronouncements about the line to Mexico. He often held dinners which the members attended, and the evenings became paid testimonials and occasions for stock-subscription sales. One such meeting, at the Midland Hotel in January of 1903, attracted 350 men. The decorations included various KCMO symbols and flags of the United States and Mexico. Stilwell spoke at length, relating the progress of the line and introducing its directors. Lumberman R. A. Long, a major investor in the KCMO, encouraged other

4. *Ibid.*
5. *Ibid.*
6. *The Kansas City Gateway,* June 1903.
7. *Ibid.*

guests to purchase securities, and subscription blanks were prominently displayed.[8]

The promoter nearly always followed up his trips to Mexico with a banquet in Kansas City. Those who had been guests on the trip would testify to the railway's economic potential; an audience with President Porfirio Diaz was a part of the excursion, so one of the guests would describe the friendship between the President and Stilwell. Other speakers would relate that they had doubled or tripled their investment as a consequence of the trip. The men who spoke were not unsubstantial citizens, but bankers, businessmen, and railway figures.[9] Neither chicanery nor fraud had been used; Stilwell simply described what he envisioned; his enthusiasm became reality to his listeners, and the KCMO became the proverbial "good thing to get in on." At one of these dinners, on February 19, 1904, the menu included large portions of "Orient Punch," and dessert of "Ice Cream a la Diaz." Former Governor James S. Hogg of Texas offered an "eloquent tribute" to Stilwell; financier-director George Gould sent a congratulatory telegram, and the audience signed subscription blanks for stock in amounts ranging from $1,000 to $170,000. The total of the evening was $1,100,000.[10] The trips and dinners would continue until 1910, with the same format and similar results. On January 2, 1907, the sum raised was $370,000, and on September 3 of the same year a $300,000 sale resulted. Stilwell also gave a public lecture at Convention Hall that September, illustrated with stereopticon views. To 3,500 people he extolled the virtues of the "Orient" and offered subscription blanks for investors.[11] But there was a limited market in Kansas City, and many of the guests on the tours were from the East or Europe.

In Mexico City the "tourists" dined in a private room at the Chapultepec Cafe. The rich food, abundant wine, and good black Mexican cigars prepared the guests for the sales pitch. Dignitaries abounded at these

8. *Ibid.*, January 1903.

9. *Ibid.*, May 1903, and *The Mexican Investor*, quoted in June 1903; Kansas City *Journal*, January 8, 1904.

10. Kansas City *Times*, February 20, 1904.

11. Pamphlet, "Trip to Mexico City and over the line of the Kansas City Mexico & Orient," March 10–24, 1906, H. P. Wright Scrapbooks (University of Missouri-Kansas City Library, Kansas City, Missouri); *Commercial and Financial Chronicle*, January 12, 1907; the Port Arthur *Evening News*, September 4, 1907; Kansas City *Journal*, September 15, 1907.

dinners. On one such evening the American Ambassador, the Governor of the State of Mexico, the Mayor of Mexico City, and the Ministers of Education and Justice were present. President Diaz received Stilwell's party at his home, and the promoter took a large delegation to the President's inaugural in 1904.[12] One of Stilwell's press agents described these gastronomical invasions:

> All of Stilwell's 'prospects' were rich men, accustomed to high-class social entertainment, and . . . they were not let down. I ran my legs off . . . but the biggest part of the job was palaver. . . . The presence of Diaz and his clique established the belief that Stilwell could get whatever he wanted in a land of such untold riches. The wealthy visitors shelled out their money. Looking back, I think how easily it was accomplished: a little display and we collected the money we needed.[13]

Some of the tour trains were of considerable size with as many as six Pullman cars, a diner, and Car 100 involved. The dinners on the train often had five courses, and the promoter entertained in a royal style.[14]

Some members of the tours were English, French, or German, but most of the money from those sources resulted from Stilwell's trips to Europe. "A man of perpetual motion," he hardly shook hands with his guests upon their arrival in Kansas City before he was off to London, Amsterdam, and Berlin. Often taking Edward Dickinson with him to provide factual information and railway expertise, Stilwell had monumental successes in England and Holland; during one trip in 1903, more than $3,000,000 in securities were sold.[15] Without this influx of capital the KCMO would never have been built.

Another aspect of the promotional campaign was the use of newspapers and magazines to disseminate information and propaganda about the KCMO. Respected railway journals proved highly susceptible to Stilwell's statements and press releases, often publishing his most colorful remarks without exercising any editorial restraints. *The Railway Age* printed the most grandiose assertions about the natural resources of

12. *The Mexican Herald* quoted in *The Kansas City Gateway*, June 1903; Kansas City *Journal*, November 26, 1904.

13. W. R. Draper, "Promoting the Orient," *Railroad Magazine*, L (November 1949), 111–112.

14. *Mexican Herald*, March 2, 1905; the Chicago *Record-Herald*, March 23, 1906.

15. Kansas City *Post*, July 20, 1907; *The Kansas City Gateway*, August 1903; *Commercial and Financial Chronicle*, August 22 and December 19, 1903.

northern Mexico, the trade with the Orient, and the attributes of Port Stilwell. *The Manufacturers Record* of Baltimore claimed that the KCMO would be a new route for shipping southern cotton to Japan. Small-town newspaper editors, thirsty for anything spectacular, reprinted the pamphlets and brochures Stilwell and Fred Hornbeck wrote as "news." Even Kansas City newspapers proved susceptible to "Orient" propaganda, publishing some "manufactured" news on their editorial pages. The always-intriguing mileage figures were quoted in many places. *The Railway News* of London published the comparable distances from Kansas City to the West Coast over the established railways and the proposed route of the KCMO. The new "shortline" reduced distances and shipping costs, according to the *News,* but *The Railroad Gazette* noted that the sea voyage from Topolobampo to Japan would be longer than from San Francisco and that the great circle route from Seattle was much shorter; "it must frankly be said that the prospects of the line appear more interesting than inspiring."[16] To offset such negative reactions, Stilwell employed several countermeasures.

The "solicited" testimonial and the "friendly" correspondent were devices used by the promoter again and again. The officers and directors of the KCMO issued statements and published reports on the railway, and, as they were respected men in the business, these were effective in meeting criticism. J. T. Odell wrote to an Ohio banker on the prospects of the "Orient" saying, "I am not employed to promote this enterprise" but concluded, "I am perfectly satisfied that this enterprise has a legitimate right to exist."[17] In the letter, reprinted in pamphlet form, Odell refused to comment on the value of KCMO securities, even though he owned stock in the railway, but one can surmise that his report encouraged potential investors. Numerous reports were also found in the daily press. Usually the correspondent had traveled over the line on one of Stilwell's tours, and some of the romance rubbed off. Descriptions of the KCMO usually contained statements such as "it promises to become one of the most important

16. *The Railway Age*, March 20, 1903; *The Manufacturers Record*, quoted in *The Kansas City Gateway*, March, 1903, and *The Oklahoma State Register* quoted in June 1903; Kansas City *Journal*, January 3, 1907; *The Railway News* (London), July 7, 1906; *The Railroad Gazette*, January 19, 1906.

17. "J. T. Odell to J. F. Stone Regarding the Kansas City, Mexico & Orient Railway, December 20, 1904," pamphlet (Bureau of Railway Economics Library, Association of American Railroads, Washington, D. C.).

transcontinental railway lines in this country." Financing of the KCMO without the benefit of Wall Street led to use of the term "People's railroad," and Stilwell was called the "Ajax of Telamon." Yet one reporter declared, "financial aid to the fullest extent has been forthcoming from the most reputable banking and commercial houses, both of the United States, Great Britain and Holland."[18] Puff pieces appeared in pamphlets, magazines and newspapers. One pamphleteer, who had been impressed by Stilwell's frankness, wrote that the promoter was creating a railroad system by his "wit."[19] A magazine article on Topolobampo proclaimed, "It is a strategic point in international commerce," when the only steamer service was down the coast to Mazatlan.[20] Reporters always found Stilwell good copy, and many articles were published about him and the KCMO.[21] One of the promoter's most considerable talents was the manipulation of the media.

Construction progress received constant attention in newspapers and railway journals. The KCMO slowly began to approach operational status as track gangs continued to lay rails in six locations. In Mexico, the line from Topolobampo to El Fuerte went into operation, but construction west of the Sierra Madre ceased shortly thereafter. When the line west of Chihuahua reached Sanchez the gangs were discharged leaving the section across the Sierra Madre from El Fuerte to Sanchez uncompleted. The KCMO asked for an additional subsidy from the Mexican government for the mountain work, and while $1,200,000 was granted, the sum appears small in relation to the estimated costs. Stilwell directed his track gangs to lay rail east from Chihuahua across a semidesert to the town of Falomir, short of the Rio Grande. The two sections of track in Mexico were operated as distinct divisions.

In the United States, construction from Wichita south through Oklahoma Territory proceeded. When the KCMO reached Fairview, the Union Construction Company issued the first of many short-term notes to finance construction south to Sweetwater, Texas. Although grading had been

18. *The Railway News* (London), July 7, 1906.

19. *Building a Great Transcontinental Railroad* (New York: [Articles published in the *Financial World*], 1906), 6–7, 20–21, 25–26.

20. Courtenay DeKalb, "Topolobampo and the Fuerte Valley," *The Nation*, LXXXII (May 31, 1906), 446–447.

21. See, for example, the Kansas City *Post*, July 20, 1907.

completed on some sections of the line from Wichita to Kansas City, nothing further was done in the area and this portion of the KCMO languished. With track gangs working rapidly, the KCMO pushed south across the plains of Oklahoma reaching Foley, where a connection was made with the Saint Louis and San Francisco railway. Trackage rights over that railway for twelve miles and construction of a few miles of new track gave the KCMO a line from Wichita to the agricultural community of Clinton. The large and costly steel bridge over the Canadian River opened in September 1906, eliminating one major obstacle.[22]

In Texas, work proceeded slowly both north and south from Sweetwater. Grading north toward the Red River was completed, and in 1907 rails were laid to the town of Benjamin, a distance of ninety miles. A contract for the line south from Sweetwater to San Angelo was signed in June 1905, but the railway did not open until December 1907. Shortly after the KCMO reached San Angelo, the shops and headquarters were moved there from Sweetwater. The construction north to the Red River stopped to await the opening of the lengthy bridge. There remained to be built the significant gap between the Red River and Clinton.[23]

The quality of construction, according to Stilwell and KCMO engineers, ranged from good to excellent. They reported that the grades from Wichita to San Angelo were low, curvature was limited to 4 degrees, and all bridges were designed to carry two 2-8-0 locomotives and a load of 4,000 pounds per lineal foot. The roadbed embankments had a width of 15 feet at the crown, slopes of 1½ to 1, and excavations were 20 feet wide at the base with slopes of 1 to 1. All rail was 70 pound, connected by angle bars with staggered bolts.[24] Ties were of redwood and laid closely together, it was reported, and "only the best of materials were employed.[25] Actually, the track lacked ballast; in many places the roadbed scarcely

22. *Memoria De La Construccion Del Ferrocarril Chihuahua al Pacifico* (Mexico City: Secretaria De Obras Publicas, 1963), 24–25; *The Railroad Gazette*, September 8 and 22, 1905, and September 14, 1906.

23. *The Railroad Gazette*, June 23 and July 21, 1905; Arthur L. Carnahan, "Kansas City, Mexico and Orient Railroad Company of Texas and Its Predecessors," *Southwestern Historical Quarterly*, LIV (April 1951), 492–493; R. C. Crane, "Railroads and Community Rivalries; Chapters from The Inside Story of the Orient and Santa Fe In West Texas," *West Texas Historical Association Yearbook*, XIX (October 1943), 8–9.

24. *The Railroad Gazette*, December 21, 1906.

25. *The Railway News* (London), July 7, 1906.

rose above the terrain, and grades exceeded estimates.[26] It should be noted, however, that the area traversed by the railway lacked population and potential traffic of a dense variety. Stilwell and his engineers envisioned short, light trains, operated on frequent schedules, thus eliminating the need for heavy construction.

The same concept prevailed regarding purchases of locomotives and rolling stock. The first thirteen locomotives acquired included both new and used engines, either 4-4-0s, or 2-6-0s, (with one exception, number 12, a 4-6-0), manufactured by Dickson, Rhode Island, Rogers, and the Baldwin locomotive companies. Many of the early locomotives remain unidentified, but others were highly personalized by their crews. Locomotive number 2, a Dickson 2-6-0 built in 1875, had a large pair of antlers mounted over the leadlight, with "ORIENTE" in large letters on the tender. The construction trains south of Wichita were pulled by this locomotive, or by number 7, a Rogers 4-4-0 built in 1880. It had a wooden cab, and its spindly lines made it appear even lighter than it was. Some locomotives were purchased used, such as number 4, a Baldwin 2-6-0 built in 1885, obtained from the Gulf, Colorado and Santa Fe. Other locomotives were wood-burners used at Chihuahua or Topolobampo; number 8, a 2-6-0 built by Baldwin operated out of Chihuahua.[27] After these initial acquisitions, the bulk of the motive power came from the American Locomotive Company or its subsidiaries.

Beginning in 1903, the Orient purchased a considerable number of locomotives. That year, two 2-6-0s (numbers 101 and 102) were bought from the Cooke Works; these two engines were well proportioned and of a larger capacity than engines previously on the roster. Ten additional locomotives were ordered from American in January 1906. For its Mexican lines, the KCMO bought four 2-8-0 wood burners from Cooke (251–252 and 301–302); these locomotives, however, were later converted to oil-burners and used in the United States. The same company built four 4-4-0 passenger locomotives (501–505) which were of fairly substantial size,

26. J. Wallace Higgins, III, "The Orient Road: A History of the Kansas City, Mexico, and Orient Railroad," *Railway and Locomotive Historical Society Bulletin*, VC (October 1956), 16.

27. John Leeds Kerr with Frank Donovan, *Destination Topolobampo: The Kansas City, Mexico & Orient Railway* (San Marino, California: Golden West Books, 1968), 258; George Abdill, *Rails West* (New York: Bonanza Books, 1960), 117.

clean of lines, and capable of moving mainline varnish at a high rate of speed. The first substantial locomotive purchase, however, did not occur until 1907, when the KCMO bought thirty 2-6-0s from American Locomotive's Cooke subsidiary. Numbers 126–156 were used in both the United States and Mexico in dual service as passenger and freight locomotives. They were squatty coal-burners with large diamond smokestacks and were paid for with an equipment trust of $1,000,000.[28]

A similar trust was issued in order to purchase freight and passenger cars. By 1903 the KCMO owned only seven passenger and 112 freight cars, and these were divided between the divisions in Mexico and the United States. Orders were placed with the American Car and Foundry Company in 1904 and 1905 for eleven passenger and 654 freight cars. Much of the freight equipment consisted of flat or ballast cars used in construction. Some box and stock cars were also acquired. The passenger cars were of high quality with Pintsch gas lights and cast steel trucks and platforms. By 1906 the KCMO equipment roster included 655 freight and 14 passenger cars. Financing for more purchases in 1908 came from the issuance of a $2,000,000 equipment trust.[29] The KCMO lacked necessary locomotives and rolling stock, partially as a result of the line's being divided into three or more disconnected sections. Always short of cash, the "Orient" could ill afford to invest large sums in equipment.

The agency responsible for selling the securities of the railway and the allied construction companies was the United States and Mexican Trust Company. From its founding in 1901 the Trust made money and within two years had profits and an undivided surplus of $156,033.07 while paying quarterly dividends of 1½ percent. The resources grew to $1,325,728.50, but hopes that the assets of the Guardian Trust could be acquired through merger were dashed by an adverse court ruling. Nevertheless, the Trust continued to profit through commissions it received selling the securities of the Stilwell concerns. The offices of the Trust at Tenth and Baltimore in Kansas City were plush, and the staff had orders to wear

28. Kerr, *Destination Topolobampo*, 258–263; *The Railway Age*, January 5, 1906; Abdill, *Rails West*, 119; *Moody's Manual of Railroad and Corporation Securities*, 1908, 409. Cited hereafter as *Moody's Manual*, date and page.

29. *The Railway Age*, March 20, 1903, August 14, 1904, May 12, June 9 and 16, 1905; *Moody's Manual*, 1908, 409; Henry V. Poor, *Manual of the Railroads of the United States* (New York: Poor's Publishing Company, 1906), 483–485, and 1907, 665–668. Cited hereafter as Poor, *Manual*, date and page.

stylish clothing and to present an appearance of prosperity. At least one
of the staff felt that this requirement was not Stilwell's but the fastidious
Fred Hornbeck's.[30]

Another Stilwell creation, the Mexican and Orient Townsite Company, also enjoyed spectacular profits. The promoter hired Fred Hornbeck
away from the Kansas City Southern, and the two began to advertise
KCMO towns as they had boomed the sites on the old Kansas City, Pittsburg and Gulf. Even respected railroader J. T. Odell wrote letters and
pamphlets extolling the virtues of the proposed villages: "One of the best
assets of the Construction Companies are the townsites; there is no telling
just what the final outcome will be, but beyond any estimate now placed
on their value."[31] Not only did the townsite company create new towns, it
also bought land in or near established communities, creating new subdivisions. To finance its operations the company sold $850,000 in 7 percent collateral trust bonds secured by an equal amount in KCMO bonds.
W. R. Draper, employed by Hornbeck to write advertising copy and sell
real estate, claimed that "insiders" made substantial profits on the sites
and subdivisions. He reported that Hornbeck sold $350,000 worth of
lots for investors at Fort Stockton, Texas, yielding an immense return.[32]
This operation acted as a lure to attract stock and bond purchasers for the
railway and the construction companies.

Stilwell sold the securities of the KCMO at a slow pace from 1903 to
1910. The bonded indebtedness rose from $2,805,000 to $18,199,000,
while common stock issued increased from $1,705,600 to $12,264,135.
Net earnings, however, climbed not at all, and the railroad began to operate at a loss. The gross income in 1904 was $180,443, yielding a profit of
$8,360, but by 1910 the KCMO gross of $1,747,940 produced a loss of

30. *The Kansas City Gateway*, January 1903; "Financial Report of the United
States and Mexican Trust Company, July 1, 1903," Wright Scrapbooks; "Proxy
slip" for Guardian Trust Company meeting of October 28, 1903, John A. Prescott
Scrapbooks (University of Missouri–Kansas City Library); Draper, "Promoting
the Orient," 114.

31. J. T. Odell to Charles Babcock, December 15, 1906, reprinted in pamphlet
form (Corporate Records Division, Baker Library, Harvard University Graduate
School of Business Administration, Boston, Massachusetts).

32. *The Railway News* (London), July 7, 1906; *Commercial and Financial
Chronicle* August 10, 1907; "Townsite Pamphlet," Corporate Records Division,
Baker Library; W. R. Draper, "Kansas City Southern," *Railroad Magazine*, XLIV
(October 1947), 22.

$145,118. Only in 1904, 1905, and 1907 did the railway have a surplus. The indebtedness also included larger and larger equipment and locomotive trust payments. Compounding the distressing financial picture, the net earnings per mile fell from $486 in 1905 to $159 in 1908. A Moody analysis of the railway's securities in 1910 rated the KCMO bonds as "Baa" (speculative, second grade), the preferred stock as "B," and common stock only as "Ca."[33] As losses continued, Stilwell and his associates increased the tempo of their sales pitch.

Optimism abounded whenever the promoter issued a statement or was interviewed. In 1905 he proclaimed,

This will be the greatest year in the history of the Orient Railroad. We expect to have 1,100 miles of the system in operation before the end of one year, including the line between Kansas City and Sweetwater, Texas, and all except 180 miles of the system in Mexico will be in operation.[34]

Other officials issued similar statements, each announcing that completion and prosperity were only a few months away. Misleading mileage estimates for the KCMO were issued, as Stilwell often included miles of graded line or track under construction as being in operation. The representations to bond purchasers were accurate, as far as can be ascertained, but when Stilwell went to England in the summer of 1906 to sell $15,000,000 in bonds, he undoubtedly placed the operation in the most positive light.[35]

The bonds which Stilwell issued in 1906 and 1907 were intended for specific markets. The $2,000,000 issue of first-mortgage, 50-year, 4 percent bonds of September 19, 1906, were directed at English investors. The London office of the Trust issued a prospectus which emphasized that five of the ten trustees of the KCMO were English, and the importance of the support of the government of Mexico. The various Mexican subsidies were enumerated, and the four pages of text described northern Mexico as an investor's paradise. The bonds, sold in $1,000 denominations, in-

33. Clarence O. Senior, "The Kansas City, Mexico and Orient Railroad," (Unpublished Masters Thesis, University of Kansas City, 1942), 82, 84, 121–122; Poor, *Manual*, 1904, 542–543.
34. *The Railway Age*, March 24, 1905.
35. Odell to Babcock, December 15, 1906; Senior, "The Kansas City, Mexico and Orient Railroad," 82; *The Railroad Gazette*, July 27 and November 2, 1906; *The Railway Age*, August 3 and October 5, 1906.

cluded bonuses of $400 in preferred stock and $400 in common. When sales reached only $370,000 by January of 1907, Stilwell shifted the emphasis of his campaign and the securities offered.[36]

From the time he formed the KCMO, Stilwell sought and received the support of several leading businessmen in the United States. Midwestern bankers, lumber barons, and flour millers acted as directors of the KCMO as did the president of Western Union and the vice-president of Buffalo General Electric. With these men making contacts for him, Stilwell began to solicit investments from other business figures. Benjamin N. Duke, member of the tobacco trust family, received numerous appeals from Stilwell and eventually became a stockholder. Sometimes the promoter wrote Duke a personal letter; at other times he sent only a "to-the-stockholders" circular, but the appeal was always the same. The personal letters usually contained mile-by-mile reports on construction with the most optimistic projections. Stilwell dropped names throughout his correspondence in an attempt to lend an impression of stability to his scheme. He told Duke that the townsites produced $260,000 in profits in 1906, that English investors were eagerly buying his securities, and that he was now asking the stockholders and directors to subscribe to an additional $1,500,000 in bonds. He personally purchased $50,000, he related, as did Dickinson and Sylvester, and Long bought $25,000. Stilwell told Duke that he could definitely sell all the bonds if he had time to call on each stockholder personally, but the press of business kept him in Kansas City. Five months later the promoter confessed that the solicitation by mail had failed. Now, he asked that seventy-five stockholders, including Duke, each buy one bond of $1,000 to keep all work on the railway from coming to a halt; needs were so urgent that he asked Duke to wire his acceptance. The next month he dispatched a general request for funds, as money was needed to buy rails to connect the lines in Oklahoma Territory and Texas; through-business would increase earnings. Stilwell then offered $150,000 in 8

36. "Kansas City, Mexico & Orient Railway Company First Mortgage 50 year 4 percent Gold Bonds," September 19, 1906, Pliny Fisk Collection (Pliny Fisk Library, Princeton University, Princeton, New Jersey); Prospectus, "Kansas City, Mexico & Orient Railway Company . . . January 1, 1907," Corporate Records Division, Baker Library; David M. Pletcher, *Rails, Mines, and Progress: Seven American Promoters in Mexico, 1867–1911* (Ithaca: Cornell University Press, 1958), 283–284.

percent, one year notes.[37] The financial situation was, obviously, becoming worse for the promoter was reduced to short-term borrowing as all else had failed.

With money trickling in, construction proceeded slowly. All work in Mexico had terminated, leaving a disconnected section on each side of the Sierra Madre. Stilwell put all of the resources of the KCMO into the completion of the line from Clinton, Oklahoma, to Benjamin, Texas. Work on this section and the 3,000-foot bridge over the Red River continued sporadically throughout 1908. In early 1909 the KCMO completed trackage from Wichita to Sweetwater, 432 miles, and in September, the 77-mile line from Sweetwater to San Angelo opened. During the next two years, work on the KCMO moved slowly, and 132 miles of track from San Angelo to Girvin was completed. Not until 1913 did the railway reach Alpine and make a connection with the Southern Pacific's "Sunset Route" between Los Angeles and New Orleans.[38]

The opening of several hundred miles of new track taxed unmercifully the motive power and rolling stock of the KCMO. Operations in the Wichita terminal required switching locomotives and four 0-6-0s (17–20) with slope-back tenders were purchased from the Pittsburgh Locomotive Works. The same year Pittsburgh delivered numbers 201–205, heavier 2-8-0 locomotives, and in 1910, ten more 2-8-0s (206–215) were purchased. By 1912 the KCMO owned 75 locomotives of which 64 had been purchased new and 11 used. Most of the second-hand motive power operated over the Mexican mileage.[39] The "Orient" owned 39 passenger cars, of which 14 were in Mexico, and a total of 2,126 freight cars. All major repair facilities were located in Wichita, Kansas. That city voted a subsidy for the KCMO several times before actual construction of the facility began in May 1910. Large car shops and a 10-stall roundhouse with an 80-foot turntable were designed by Westinghouse, Church, Kerr and Com-

37. Stilwell to B. N. Duke, June 17 and November 22, 1907, and "To the Stockholders," December 18, 1907, Benjamin Newton Duke Collection (William R. Perkins Library, Duke University, Durham, North Carolina).

38. *Memoria De La Construccion*, 9; *The Railway Age*, May 29, 1908; *The Railroad Gazette*, January 24, 1908; Stilwell to "The Stockholders," April 12, 1909, Duke Collection; Kerr, *Destination Topolobampo*, 85.

39. Kerr, *Destination Topolobampo*, 258–264; E. Dickinson, "Report on the Kansas City, Mexico & Orient Railway Company. . . ." June 18, 1912, Manuscript Division, Baker Library.

pany.[40] The facilities were one of the most productive assets of the railway, and the men who worked there would become adroit at rebuilding and repairing equipment most railroads would have scrapped years before.

While construction on the Mexican portion of the KCMO had halted, and equipment there was marginal at best, the KCMO did not suffer the fate of some foreign-owned railways in that country. In 1909 a plan to nationalize the railroads was drafted, and the next year the National Railways of Mexico came into existence. The new system excluded the KCMO and the Chihuahua and Pacific. The latter railroad, which had leased its line from Chihuahua to Minaca to the KCMO, became part of the independent Mexico North-Western Railway. The lease remained in effect, and the KCMO retained all rights to construct across the Sierra Madre, although the option was not exercised. The KCMO operated 480 kilometers of track in Mexico, but it was one of the least significant railways in the country.[41] Stilwell had shifted his concern to the more profitable operation from Wichita to San Angelo.

From 1907 until the spring of 1909, Stilwell devoted most of his energy to raising funds for the KCMO. The recession of 1907 and a growing national awareness of the financial plight of some railways made the sale of such securities quite difficult. Stilwell persisted, however, using the same methods he had employed since 1886. His letters of solicitation always prophesied abundant profits, rising traffic, and Mexican mineral wealth. Zinc, gold, copper, and oil were being found along the KCMO east of Chihuahua, he reported, and would yield immense carloadings if the line could be opened. He enclosed postal cards with his letters, and subscribers needed only to fill in an amount and sign the card. Simultaneously, he sold bonds of the railway and stock of the construction companies, sweetening each offering with a multiplicity of bonuses. Although he nearly always reported successful drives for funds, it was becoming increasingly difficult to attract investors.[42]

One of Stilwell's investors, Edward F. Goltra, received a constant

40. *Ibid.*; *Railway Age Gazette*, June 2, 1911; *The Railway and Engineering Review*, June 24, 1911.

41. Fred Wilbur Powell, *The Railroads of Mexico* (Boston: The Stratford Co., Publishers, 1921), 4–6, 8; Osgood Hardy, "The Revolution and the Railroads of Mexico," *Pacific Historical Review*, III (September 1934), 250–251.

42. Stilwell to "The Stockholders," February 10, 1908, and Postal Card and

stream of correspondence urging that he increase the size of his holdings. Goltra, a Saint Louis iron and railroad company executive, was asked to purchase twenty-year bonds, or eighteen-month notes, or common or preferred stocks, but to put money into the enterprise. The promoter also asked Goltra to use his contacts in the steel industry in an effort to obtain rails at a lower price, and the Saint Louis businessman complied with the request.[43]

When men such as Benjamin Duke or Edward Goltra failed to respond, Stilwell went to Europe, particularly England, to obtain additional funds from either the London Finance Committee or his Dutch and German supporters. Even the promoter admitted that the failure to complete any section of the railway and the depressed market for securities was hurting the project. Investors were asked to pass on to their friends information about the KCMO and to be positive in their assessment of the project. In order to build from Sweetwater to San Angelo, Stilwell issued two-year collateral trust notes secured by first-mortgage bonds of the KCMO. These bonds were selling at 73 to 75 in London, indicating continued confidence in the project in that quarter. During 1908 Stilwell sold additional bonds in London, enabling the KCMO to open the line to San Angelo.[44]

In order to obtain English and Dutch capital, Stilwell sought to sell $300,000 in bonds in the United States to demonstrate faith in the project in this country. He announced a personal purchase of $15,000 and urged previous investors to show their confidence by additional acquisitions. One characteristic of an entrepreneurial error was constantly present—the need for investors to put more funds into the scheme to save that which they had already committed. The London Finance Committee supported an issue of Convertible Sterling Notes and used their influence to provide

---

Subscription Blank, Duke Collection; *The Railroad Gazette*, February 21, and April 17, 1908.

43. John W. Leonard (ed.), *The Book of St. Louisans* (St. Louis: The St. Louis Republic, 1906), 227; Stilwell to Edward F. Goltra, February 15, 1908; Stilwell "To the Stockholders," February 15, 1908; Goltra to Stilwell February 18, 1908; all Edward F. Goltra Papers (Missouri Historical Society, Saint Louis, Missouri).

44. Stilwell "To the Stockholders," April 2, 1908, Goltra Papers; Stilwell to Duke, April 2, 1908; Prospectus for KCMO collateral notes 1908; Stilwell to Duke, May 20, 1908, all Duke Collection.

the promoter with publicity and a public platform.[45] He spoke at the Crystal Palace in London, for example, indicating the importance of his relationship with President Diaz and the Mexican subsidy. Paraphrasing an earlier statement by his old adversary Elihu Root, Stilwell declared of the Mexican President,

> If I were a [sculptor], I would spend my days in carving his likeness out of solid granite; were I an historian, I would give my time to writing of the man as I know him; were I a poet, I would forever sing his praises, all I can do is to rest in the satisfaction that he is my friend and the friend of this railroad.[46]

The endorsements by leading American businessmen, London financiers, and the Mexican government aided Stilwell, but were tempered by less favorable reports in financial journals.

The *Anglo-American and Mexican Mining Guide* noted that "This railway. . . is always doing wonderful things for everybody but the majority of the share and stockholders . . . who are waiting with what patience they may to see some return on their investment," while *Moody's Manual* called the KCMO securities, "good, but second-grade issues." And the *Wall Street Journal*, never very positive about the KCMO, called its stock "a gamble," and said it should "be bought for a long pull."[47] Not even these market analysts could foresee just how long the "long pull" would be.

Nevertheless, English investors pumped money into the "Orient." British investments in Latin America grew between 1904 and 1911, with 50 percent of the total commitment in Mexico being in railways. By 1911, the KCMO had placed £ 308,642 in securities in England but, like most Mexican railways, failed to pay any dividends and often deferred interest. A number of leading London brokerage firms sold Stilwell's bonds and notes, and the prestige of these houses and the low denominations of the notes attracted small investors.[48] Stilwell returned to Kansas City from England, enthusiastically reporting the success of his mission. But to Goltra he confided that the stock of the construction companies could not be sold

45. Identical letters from Stilwell to Goltra and Duke, July 1 and 2, 1908, Goltra Papers and Duke Collection; Prospectus for Sterling Notes, Duke Collection.

46. *Anglo-American and Mexican Mining Guide*, XI (July 29, 1908), 104, quoted in Pletcher, *Rails, Mines, and Progress*, 277.

47. *Ibid.*, 285.

48. Mabel G. Coolsen, "British Interest in Mexico, 1900–1926," (Unpublished Doctoral Dissertation, University of Illinois, 1943), 2–4, 64; William Rodney Long, *Railways of Mexico* (Washington: Government Printing Office, 1925), 134.

at all and published reports indicated a net loss of $210,743 in 1908.[49]

Operating conditions on the KCMO improved markedly in 1909, for the opening of the Red River bridge gave the railway a long haul from Wichita to Sweetwater causing revenues to triple. As the situation improved, Goltra and KCMO vice-president Dickinson discussed possible mergers with other railways, but when they confronted the promoter with the proposal, he vetoed the idea. Continuing his almost frantic efforts to attract capital, Stilwell issued almost daily reviews of the mileage constructed and the earnings. Short-term loans continued to be sought, and the promoter commuted from Kansas City to his office in the Singer Building in New York City. When the track from Sweetwater to San Angelo was completed in September, Stilwell issued letters of self-congratulation, but the line again lost money.[50]

To counter the criticism that mounted yearly, Stilwell published numerous reports on the KCMO written by executives of the railway or by its supporters. In 1908, J. Crosland Taylor, secretary of the London Finance Committee, published a sixteen-page pamphlet praising the KCMO. Taylor emphasized the low per mile bonded indebtedness, the support of the Diaz regime and the importance of the "Voting Trust," which was designed to protect the KCMO from "raiding." The next year Edward Dickinson and J. T. Odell reported on the KCMO. They claimed theirs was an independent report, free from instruction, and that they acted as stockholders, not as officers. Dutifully they praised the road, its conception, and its economic future. *The Railway Age Gazette* ridiculed the report, but John Wallace, a former Illinois Central executive, found it to be "more than conservative." Wallace also prepared an analysis, although he too had become an officer of the firm, and his report contained information equally positive and optimistic.[51]

49. Stilwell to Goltra, December 1, 1908, Goltra Papers; United States, Interstate Commerce Commission, *Twenty-first Annual Report of the Statistics of Railways in the United States* (Washington: Government Printing Office, 1909), 506–507. Cited hereafter by title only.

50. Dickinson to Goltra, March 24, 1909; Goltra to Dickinson, March 25, 1909, and July 20, 1909; Stilwell to Goltra, August 26, 1909; Goltra to Stilwell, August 28, 1909; and Stilwell "To the Stockholders," September 21, 1909, all Goltra Papers; Stilwell "To the Stockholders," July 17, 1909, Duke Collection; *Twenty-second Annual Report of the Statistics of Railways In the United States*, 500–501.

51. J. Crosland Taylor, "Kansas City, Mexico & Orient Railway," November

Stillwell felt compelled to respond to negative statements personally, and in 1910 he had published *Confidence or National Suicide?*, a book which contended that naysayers were destroying the securities market and that overregulation of railroads would terminate their expansion. When the Kansas City *Star* suggested he had "watered" the stocks of his various railroads, Stilwell protested and noted that while authorized securities per mile were sizable, only a small amount had actually been issued. He also opposed the "progressive" idea of physical examination of railroads by the Interstate Commerce Commission in order to establish true value of the property and their securities. He contended that the trading value of stocks and bonds, not the property, created their worth; the stock markets have already established value, he said, and low property valuations would lead to lower rates and depression. The public must have confidence, he maintained.[52]

Stilwell had confidence in the KCMO, and rising revenues were used to tempt the English investors who also exhibited new enthusiasm for the "Orient." In the summer of 1910 the promoter went to England offering a large issue of collateral trust bonds. On July 1, he cabled Kansas City that $5,000,000 of first-mortgage, 50-year, 4 percent bonds had been sold to a syndicate of English brokers, allowing construction to begin again east of Chihuahua. This syndicate had been in operation since February and had held the price of KCMO bonds on the London market at 86; the syndicate refused to handle the securities at less than that figure. The promoter returned to the United States in triumph but announced that further sales of American securities in Europe would be difficult because of the "condition of unrest" and "constant agitation" in this country for federal regulation of business and industry.[53]

20, 1908; E. Dickinson and J. T. Odell, "Report on the Kansas City, Mexico and Orient Railway Company," November 22, 1909; John F. Wallace, "Report on the Kansas City, Mexico and Orient Railway Company," December 31, 1909, all Corporate Records Division, Baker Library; *Railway Age Gazette*, January 21, 1910.

52. Arthur E. Stilwell, *Confidence or National Suicide?* (New York: Bankers Publishing Company, 1910), further analysis of this book will be found in the next chapter; the Kansas City *Star*, September 18, 1910; *The Railway and Engineering Review*, November 12, 1910.

53. William Z. Ripley, *Railroads: Finance & Organization* (New York: Longmans, Green and Co., 1915), 155–156; Stilwell to Goltra, February 23, 1910, Goltra Papers; *Wall Street Journal*, July 1, and August 2, 1910.

While Stilwell's concern had some validity, that is, European investors were becoming wary of American securities in general, his problems in London and Paris were also the result of questions raised about the future of the KCMO. Another serious question was that of the variety of financial reports issued by the railroad. Regarding operations in 1910, at least three sets of figures are available. The Interstate Commerce Commission reported a net corporation income loss of $61,514. H. V. Poor's *Manual* showed an operating deficit of $390,666.09, while another audit indicated a loss of $454,851.59.[54] One would suspect that discerning investors might have reasonable doubts when confronted with these conflicting figures.

Their concern might have been assuaged by the massive outpouring of favorable reports about the "Orient" and Stilwell. Always the master of media techniques, the promoter made sure that a positive image existed to counter unfriendly publicity. One of the most favorable financial analyses came from *Moody's Magazine* in February of 1910. That journal noted a rising prosperity of the area through which the KCMO passed and the rapid rate of urbanization along the line. Further, the KCMO had an unusually low capitalization with a fixed-charge obligation of less than $1,500 per mile. Moody concluded that the stocks and bonds of the KCMO were an "exceptionally good opportunity for the investor who is willing to stake his money a little into the future." An additional story the following August reported on Stilwell's successful sale of securities in England and praised the promoter's "indefatigable"' efforts to raise money without the aid of any "great banking interests." "The completed system," Moody proclaimed, "will be Mr. Stilwell's monument, to which his posterity may well point with pride."[55] Similar articles appeared in the *Financial World,* and so generous was this account that Stilwell had it reprinted in pamphlet form as *Building a Great Transcontinental Railroad.* Yet another reputable financial journal, *Banker's Magazine,* featured a sixteen-page article by Landon Gates praising Stilwell as a minor "Empire

54. *Twenty-third Annual Report of the Statistics of Railways in the United States,* 310–311, 462–463; Poor, *Manual,* 1910, 1024–1027; E. W. McKenna, "Report of An Examination of the Kansas City, Mexico & Orient Railroad," September 15, 1916, Bureau of Railway Economics Library.

55. John Moody, "The Kansas City, Mexico and Orient Railway," *Moody's Magazine,* IX (February 1910), 118–124, and (August 1910), 87–88.

Builder." Reprinted by the promoter, the Gates piece concluded that the fiscal arrangements of the KCMO were impeccable.[56] Regional publications and newspapers proved highly susceptible to Stilwell's flamboyancy, and reporters and feature writers found him to be great copy. William E. Curtis in *The Texas Magazine* alternated glowing accounts of the Texas countryside with extravagant descriptions of Topolobampo and KCMO construction methods. The agricultural and mineral wealth, Curtis exclaimed, was potentially greater than that passed through by any other railroad.[57] Newspapers in Kansas City, Saint Louis, Chicago, New York, and elsewhere published accounts of Stilwell, but few could match the pitch reached by the Saint Louis *Globe-Democrat*:

> His is the mind that has projected this road, and to him be the honor. He has the true vision of the empire builder who sees lasting good to the country in the extension of the steel lines of prosperity and hears the epic song of America in the thunderous beats of the driving wheels on the rails. If he acquires a great personal fortune in the process it is only a small percentage of the wealth which he adds to the nation's resorces.[58]

These stories had a seductive impact on investors and tended to mask the rapid deterioration of the KCMO fiscally and, in Mexico, its physical well being.

After 1910, the superficial tranquility that the Diaz regime had maintained through repression and terror ended in violent revolution. Radical syndicalists, liberal intellectuals, and moderate, middle-class progressives acted, without union or concert, to end the reign of Diaz and his *científico* advisors. Lulled into dreams of economic and political stability in Mexico, foreign investors tended to discount the early rumblings of revolt as only a temporary dislocation of political power; they were wholly unprepared for the years of bloody revolution that followed. The foreign investors not only took a calloused view of the revolution because of the property losses involved but also because of an open disdain for the "lesser" race and its lack of understanding that "order" meant "prosperity." As the revolution spread, armies were formed, bands of brigands

56. *Building a Great Transcontinental Railroad*, 1–10; Landon Gates, "The Stilwell International Trans-continental Railroad," *Banker's Magazine,* LXXX (April 1910), 608–623.

57. William E. Curtis, "The Orient—The Rise of a Railroad," *The Texas Magazine*, II (July 1910), 11–17.

58. Saint Louis *Globe-Democrat*, December 18, 1910.

began to pillage, and dreams of the "Treasure Chest" of Mexico evaporated. The KCMO became one of the victims of the revolution.

When the revolution began, its impact on the "Orient" was largely disruptive rather than destructive. The attempt to defeat Diaz in the presidential election of 1910 ended with the President arresting his opponent, Francesco Madero. By the late spring of 1911, however, the peasant leaders Pascual Orozco and Poroteo Arango (Pancho Villa) fomented revolution in the state of Chihuahua, and Madero escaped from jail and joined them. In the years from 1911 to 1917 the peasants under leaders such as Villa or Emiliano Zapata or "armies" led by Victoriano Huerta, Alvaro Obregon, and others pillaged the countryside, and, as many of the revolutionists and the generals were "Men of the North," northern Mexico suffered greatly. Exposed to their depredations were the two divisions of the Kansas City, Mexico and Orient.

When fighting broke out in Chihuahua in 1911, Stilwell maintained that the KCMO was not in danger and that the revolutionaries were not unhappy about the concession the railroad had obtained from the Diaz regime. He agreed that the insurrection had terminated construction work but denied that contractors were not paying their workers at the construction site east of Chihuahua. Business leaders in the city of Chihuahua and the town of Ojinaga asked for support from Mexico City to open the line to the Rio Grande, but turbulence in the government prevented any positive action. The KCMO loomed large in the plans of revolutionists such as Villa, for the railway was the only means to move men and material quickly across northern Mexico. One of Stilwell's associates later wrote that Villa had a grudge to settle with the promoter. The revolutionary had once been a contractor on the KCMO, but Stilwell snubbed and insulted this "roughneck" who smelled of hair oil. According to this account, Villa retaliated during the revolution by ripping up KCMO track and blowing up bridges. The situation deteriorated after 1913, and the track between Marquez and San Sostenes was virtually destroyed. The rather significant improvements at Topolobampo fell into disrepair, and on those portions of the line remaining operative normal maintenance terminated, causing the line to fall apart literally. By 1915, many bridges and stations and much equipment had been destroyed or rendered useless, and service, where available, was irregular at best. It should be noted however, that nearly all of the property loss on the KCMO occurred after

1911 and that even before the revolution the Mexican lines consistently lost money.[59]

Had Pancho Villa been Stilwell's only problem it would have been a serious one indeed, but other developments were pressing. Stilwell tried to create a $3,000,000 syndicate to complete the KCMO from San Angelo to Alpine, Texas, and failed when subscribers refused to pay their assessments. He tried to sweeten the sale of securities by giving purchasers shares in a new telephone device he had discovered, but still there were few takers. Unable to find money in the United States or England, Stilwell went to Paris and tried to arrange for an offering of securities there, but he failed again. Complicating his efforts was a lawsuit filed by Marie L. H. Owen, wife of Albert Owen, in which she alleged that Stilwell had never paid her or her husband the $200,000 he promised when he purchased their concession. The promoter nevertheless displayed a public attitude of confidence as late as November of 1911, when he organized the First American Land and Irrigation Exposition in New York City. Several state governments and railroads exhibited at the show which was designed to lure men "back to the land." The promoter undoubtedly presented to those who attended the show opportunities to purchase property along the "Orient."[60]

The "Orient" needed more than additional land sales to save the railway. While the total sum of stocks and bonds sold remained low, operations resulted in consistent losses. The KCMO had issued $12,500,000 in cumulative preferred stock, $12,264,135 in common stock, $18,199,000 of first-mortgage bonds, £ 200,000 in 6 percent, five-year notes due in 1913, and owed $1,618,885 in equipment trusts. Only $6,000,000 in bonds had been sold, while $3,489,000 remained in the treasury, and the rest were held by the construction companies. While Stilwell rightly contended that the per mile indebtedness was low, the KCMO could not pay its fixed charges. Operating losses in 1911 were variously reported as ranging from $229,324.97 to $454,851.59. Why had the "Orient" failed

59. *Commercial and Financial Chronicle*, October 21, 1911; Senior, "The Kansas City, Mexico and Orient Railroad," 72–73, 78, 101, 118; Draper, "Promoting the Orient," 104–109, 116; Powell, *The Railroads of Mexico*, 13–14; "The Condition of Mexican Railways," *Pan American Magazine*, XXVIII (November 1918), 46–48.

60. Stilwell to Goltra, May 10, 1911, Goltra Papers; Stilwell to "The Stockholders," September 22, 1911, Duke Collection; *Railway Age Gazette*, October 6, 1911; Pletcher, *Rails, Mines, and Progress*, 286–288; the Chicago *Record–Herald*, January 14, 1911; "Portrait," *The World's Work*, XXIII (November 1911), 4, 15.

to produce profits and why did it remain uncompleted? The answer, said Stilwell, was the opposition of the "Money Trust."[61]

From the very start of the KCMO project, Stilwell and other officers of the railway contended that "Wall Street," the "Money Trust," and other railroads were fighting them. Statements such as "it [KCMO] is a marvel all over the middle west from Kansas City clear through the Atlantic ocean, and this has been accomplished in the face of every big railroad in the west and Wall Street in the east fighting against us," were commonly made by "Orient" officials. By February of 1912, Stilwell contended that "artificial barriers" were the result of bitter opposition; detectives followed him and his agents, friendly bankers were threatened with ruin by the "Money Trust," the Mexican government had been encouraged to cancel the concession, and stockholders received anonymous telephone calls urging them to sell their securities quickly and cheaply. He proclaimed, "I have started out in a campaign to help free American business from the inquisition of the money power," after having suffered, "sixteen years of unrelenting persecution." He praised the members of the stock exchanges and urged them to act as financial censors. His chief enemies, he reported, were his old adversaries Ernest Thalmann, E. H. Harriman, Herman Sielcken, and the "Rockefeller" interests. On March 8, 1912, Stilwell addressed a large audience at Carnegie Hall on the evils of "Wall Street." The day before, the "Orient" had gone into receivership.[62]

Representatives of the United States and Mexican Trust Company, the construction companies, and the Western Tie and Timber Company appeared before federal Judge John C. Pollock on March 7, and asked for a receivership. They feared that if the railroad collapsed the Mexican government would cancel the concession in that country and the property there would be forfeited. Edward Dickinson and bankers M. L. Turner and

61. Pletcher, *Rails, Mines, and Progress,* 284; Poor, *Manual,* 1911, 1032–1036; *Twenty-fourth Annual Report of the Statistics of Railways in the United States,* 304–305; McKenna, "Report of an Examination of the Kansas City, Mexico & Orient Railroad."

62. The Kansas City *Star,* September 17, 1900; the El Reno (Oklahoma) *American News,* September 26, 1901; Stilwell to "The Stockholders," February 1, 1912, Corporate Records Division, Baker Library; Charles W. Gerstenberg, *Materials of Corporation Finance* (New York: Prentice-Hall, Inc., 1915), 412–424; Stilwell "To the Stockholders," March 2, 1912, Duke Collection; Arthur Stilwell, *Cannibals of Finance* (Chicago: Farnum Publishing Company, 1912), 124–125; Arthur E. Stilwell, *Forty Years of Business Life* (New York: n.p., 1926 [?]), 21–23.

J. O. Davidson were named receivers the next day. Impetus for the receivership came from the English bondholders who established a Bondholders Protective Committee with Lord Monson as chairman. Like the Kansas City, Pittsburg and Gulf, Stilwell controlled the KCMO by the force of his personality, and when the investors lost confidence they turned to a receivership. At first the promoter maintained that the receivership was friendly and that he would not resign as president of the railway. He resigned as president of the Union and International Construction Companies and shortly was ousted as president of the Trust company.[63] The receivers began to untangle the financial chaos and finished the line to Alpine.

At the request of Lord Monson, Edward Dickinson prepared a report on the KCMO which was far more objective than his earlier study written with Odell. Although Dickinson expressed faith in the future of the railway, he acknowledged that cars and locomotives were inadequate and that construction had been less than first class: standards, he said, were based on construction costs and revenue. The track lacked ballast, ties were untreated, the line in Mexico was poorly maintained, and rental of facilities in Chihuahua was very expensive. Shops, stations, and repair facilities in the United States were only adequate. The line had lost money, he agreed, but his solution, like Stilwell's, was expansion; the railway must be completed to Alpine immediately, and work should begin in Mexico, both east and west of Chihuahua. Traffic was increasing, and extension would produce a profit. Critics disagreed, saying that Dickinson had been around Stilwell too long and suffered from the same rosy optimism. Other experts reported the line was in far worse shape than Dickinson admitted and that financial conditions were "unfathomable." Long-time critics such as *The Economist* and *The Statist* chorused their "I-told-you-sos," and announced that the receivership came as "no surprise." Their analysis suggested that Stilwell was a great money getter, but a poor money spender.[64]

Arthur Stilwell explained the receivership in many ways. He always

63. The Chicago *Record-Herald*, March 8, 1912; New York *Times*, March 8, 1912; Poor, *Manual*, 1912, 1084–1088, and 3026–3027; *Railway Age Gazette*, March 15, 1912; Kansas City *Post*, March 19 and 29, 1912; *Commercial and Financial Chronicle*, October 26, 1912.

64. E. Dickinson, "Report on the Kansas City, Mexico & Orient Railway Company. . . ." June 18, 1912, Corporate Records Division, Baker Library; Kansas City *Post*, April 6, 1912; *The Economist*, March 23, 1912; *The Statist*, March 23, 1912.

blamed the revolution in Mexico for disrupting construction and destroying the track, but very little construction was under way in 1911, and the Mexican portion of the KCMO had never made a profit. "The receivership is hard luck," he maintained, "but it's just one of those things apt to happen to anybody." That sad lament failed to satisfy even the promoter, who later elaborated on the causes. The revolution, the "Money Trust," Pancho Villa, and his old enemies from "Wall Street" became the arch villains.[65]

The receivership actually resulted from many factors including the disruptions in Mexico and the opposition of major financial houses who felt the KCMO was not a desirable investment. Even John Moody, one of the most optimistic analysts concluded that "Orient" bonds were "a pure speculation." Also, there were numerous railroad failures in the midwest and southwest between 1907 and 1917. The mileage of railroads in receivership jumped from 4,593 in 1911 to 16,286 in 1913. A loss of confidence by investors, declining revenues, and a recession in agriculture led to foreclosures. The "Orient" had special problems too: it was not completed, its three sections of track went from nowhere to nowhere, and new securities had been sold when the road could not pay its existing fixed charges. Most of the construction of the KCMO far exceeded original estimates, and Stilwell never acknowledged the astronomical cost of crossing the Sierra Madre or opening the harbor at Topolobampo to deep-draft vessels. Like other promoters, Stilwell assumed the existence of a peaceful Mexico, governed by a friendly administration, would allow for a bountiful return. Indeed, massive entrepreneurial errors had been made, and the original investors refused to put more funds into the scheme. One report later maintained that the English were so embittered that Stilwell would have been jailed had he returned to that country, but this appears untrue. The promoter had made the mistake of starting a gigantic project in an era of waning faith in American railroads and their securities.[66]

65. *Commercial and Financial Chronicle*, March 9, 1912; Stilwell, *Forty Years of Business Life*, 3, 29–30; Arthur E. Stilwell and James R. Crowell, "I Had a Hunch," *The Saturday Evening Post*, CC (February 4, 1928), 46.

66. John Moody, *Moody's Analysis of Railroad Investments* (New York: Analysis Publishing Co., 1912), 591; United States, Interstate Commerce Commission, Bureau of Transport Economics and Statistics, *Receiverships and Trusteeships, 1894–1942* (Washington: Government Printing Office, 1943); Stuart Daggett, "Recent Railroad Failures and Reorganizations," *Quarterly Journal of Economics*, XXXII (May 1918), 446–467; John Leeds Kerr, *A Brief Analysis and History of*

Receivers Dickinson, Turner, and Davidson sold $1,000,000 in receiver's certificates and completed the track to Alpine, giving the KCMO a mainline to Wichita of 737 miles. Additional certificates were issued to pay fixed charges with this new indebtedness growing to $2,617,000. Although Lord Monson's committee kept close watch on the receivers, in the words of one regulatory agency, "the receivership of the company proved expensive and disastrous." A reorganization in 1912–13 led to the creation of the *Railroad* Company to replace the *Railway* Company, and the elimination of all preferred and common stock. The bondholders found their equity reduced, receiving in compensation new common stock. At a foreclosure sale on July 6, 1914, William T. Kemper, John B. Niven and Arthur M. Wickwire, representing the bondholders, bought the KCMO for $6,001,000. Edward Dickinson replaced Stilwell as president, but Kansas City banker William Kemper became the decision-maker for the railroad.[67]

The new management failed to produce profits or pay fixed charges, and on April 16, 1917, a second receivership began with Kemper named as sole receiver. The "Orient," like other railroads, was operated by the United States Railroad Administration during World War I, but only after Kemper demanded that the USRA take over the line or he would sell it for salvage. When the USRA returned the KCMO to Kemper at the end of the war, he asked the Interstate Commerce Commisison for a loan. His initial request was refused, but he ultimately obtained some federal support. Unable to operate the line at a profit, Kemper then asked for permission to abandon the entire operation, but a fortuitous event saved the KCMO. In 1923 the Big Lake oil field opened astride the KCMO in West Texas, and revenues increased rapidly. The Mexican government, to repay the KCMO for damages during the revolution, financed the completion of the line from Chihuahua north to the Rio Grande. Interest on the KCMO debt remained unpaid, however, and the Interstate Commerce Commission ordered the line sold.

the *Kansas City, Mexico and Orient Railway* (New York: Railway Research Society Publications, 1928), 4; *The Orient Magazine*, October 1928; Ripley, *Railroads: Finance & Organization*, 48.

67. Senior, "The Kansas City, Mexico and Orient Railroad," 86–88; "Before the Public Utilities Commission for the State of Kansas," July 15, 1914 (Topeka: Kansas Public Laws and Cases, 1914), 2; Daggett, "Recent Railroad Failures and Reorganizations," 472, 473, 484.

On March 27, 1924, Kemper and his attorney Clifford Histed bought the KCMO for $3,000,000. With federal support and oil revenues from Big Lake, Kemper bought more rolling stock and a number of used locomotives. Two more oil fields opened on the KCMO, but prospects remained dim. Kemper and Histed, however, bought up many of the outstanding bonds at prices of $150 to $200 per $1,000 bond. A reorganization in 1927 ended all the original debt, and the equity of the English investors was diluted further. Finally, in 1928, Kemper found a buyer for the "Orient" when the Atchison, Topeka and Santa Fe Railway agreed to purchase the line. Some of the original stockholders sued Kemper, claiming he made more than $6,000,000 from purchasing securities at low prices when he knew that sale of the KCMO was imminent. The charges were not proven. To his credit, Kemper had held the line together for more than ten years.

The Santa Fe acted quickly to put its acquisition into profitable operation. Seventy-three miles of new construction, trackage rights over eleven miles of the Southern Pacific, and a bridge over the Rio Grande brought the KCMO track from Alpine to Presidio and Oijinaga where a connection was made with the line to Chihuahua. In May of 1929, the Santa Fe sold all of the "Orient" mileage in Mexico to B. F. Johnston, an American sugar farmer in Los Mochis, Mexico. Johnston hoped to complete the railway across the Sierra Madre, but died in 1937, before the project could be initiated. Three years later the Mexican government purchased the railroad from Mrs. Johnston and the Santa Fe which still held a mortgage on the property.

The government of Mexico announced plans to build across the mountains, but World War II intervened. From 1940 until 1953, however, large sums were spent to improve the old KCMO. Beginning in 1958, major appropriations initiated construction, and on November 20, 1961, the first train moved from Chihuahua to the sea. Sixty-one years after Stilwell announced his hunch, the route opened. The mountain construction cost the Ferrocarril de Chihuahua al Pacifico, as the old "Orient" is now called, $88,000,000. A fantastic construction project, the line over the Sierra Madre and along the spectacular Barranca del Cobre (Copper Canyon) have become a substantial tourist attraction. Topolobampo does not rival San Francisco as Stilwell hoped, but it has an extensive fishing fleet, and the Mexican government has announced plans for additional development.[68] Although the editor of a leading railroad journal has questioned the spending of such an enormous sum for a "tourist" railway, the explanations seem to be the need for an east-west line of communication and transport between Mexico City and the border with the United States and to open large areas of three Mexican states to development and attract tourists.[69] Ferry service from Topolobampo across the Gulf of California to La Paz in Baja California will provide a new transportation link to that isolated area. One needs only to read magazines such as *Esquire, Travel,* and *Holiday* to see the growing interest in the western coast of Mexico and the impact of numerous rail excursions using the new Chihuahua-Pacific line. Tourism may become the commodity providing the glamor for the Chihuahua-Pacific, but freight traffic has started to grow with shipments of tomatoes and other winter produce from the Fuerte Valley north to Presidio and the connection with the Santa Fe Railway.

Arthur Stilwell committed a series of entrepreneurial errors in creating the "Orient" and did not live to see the completion of the railway by a national government. He always claimed that no one suffered a fiscal loss from the KCMO receiverships, but many did. It is indeed true that these same investors profited from land speculation, the modestly successful town promotions, and from the construction companies. Although no town on the KCMO ever became a metropolitan center, Stilwell claimed that his "Brownies" revealed to him that the massive west Texas oil strikes would save the railroad in the 1920s. The "Orient" line of the Sante Fe Railway from Wichita to Presidio is a significant branch, but not a mainline. Yet, this dream, hunch, or vision became reality, and few in 1900, 1912, or 1928 could have foreseen that Stilwell was right when he wrote, "all I ever planned has remained as I planned it."[70]

Stilwell undoubtedly suffered mentally from the lengthy struggle during the receivership, but he also suffered a serious physical impairment. Shortly after he lost the "Orient," an elevator in which he was a passenger in a New York City office building fell, and as a result of the accident he became an invalid. An active man, a vigorous man, he now knew the lone-

68. Kerr, *Destination Topolobampo*, 131–233.

69. David P. Morgan, review of Kerr, *Destination Topolobampo*, in *Trains*, XXIX (May 1969), 67.

70. Stilwell, *Forty Years of Business Life*, 25, 30; Stilwell, "I Had a Hunch," February 4, 1928, 46.

liness of retirement and convalescence. Most men seek seclusion in retirement, accepting the "golden years" either as a badge of honor or as a burden which cannot be terminated. Arthur Stilwell said that retirement meant something entirely different:

I concentrated my mind on the thought that life is eternal and that youth is a condition we misinterpret, being not merely a state of immaturity, as supposed, but a state of mind and body which gathers increasing freshness and virility as we carry on year by year.[71]

He decided, at the age of fifty-three, to embark on a new career.

71. *Ibid.*

X

DREAMS, FAIRIES, AND BROWNIES

A FORCEFUL, vigorous, active man, Arthur Stilwell found retirement difficult and unsatisfying. In the public eye since the late 1880s, he could not
accept isolation from the reporters and journalists who had been so significant in promoting his financial schemes. He thrived on acclaim and
attention; these were essential for a promoter, but following the elevator
accident he all but disappeared from public view for several years. For a
man with Stilwell's ego and drive, such a condition was intolerable. Seeking an outlet for his energies and a device to recapture headlines and
public interest, he spent the last fifteen years of his life writing books,
poems, and plays.

Stilwell, largely self-educated, lacked formal training as an author,
but this proved to be an asset; he was always a firm advocate of the myth
of the self-made man and its corollary that the best education was in the
school of "hard knocks." During the years he spent as a printer and salesman he became a "word hound," developing an expansive, if oftimes con-
voluted, style. His publications reflected his religious beliefs, his contacts
with businessmen of various levels of morality, and the concerns and
prejudices of his European associates. Before 1910, Stilwell's publications
were limited to several songs, the political pamphlets of the McKinley
campaign, and articles and brochures used to promote his railroads and
townsites. Indeed, his first major works were directly concerned with his
efforts to promote the Kansas City, Mexico and Orient Railway, and his
encounters with "Wall Street."

By 1910 Arthur Stilwell knew that the future of the "Orient" was bleak; funds in this country and Europe were drying up. A primary factor affecting not only his project but the entire stock market was a loss of confidence by the general public. The so-called progressive movement encompassed widespread reforms designed to stop or reduce unfair business practices. Exposés of Standard Oil Company operations, the revelations of Upton Sinclair's *The Jungle,* the neo-Populist attacks on "Wall Street," the public desire to regulate trusts and cartels, and the general political mood reflected in proposals by such diverse figures as Theodore Roosevelt, William Howard Taft, William Jennings Bryan, and Woodrow Wilson to either break up or control monopolies all suggest the deep-seated anxiety or even hostility which had developed toward the financial community. The effect on men seeking capital was, of course, devastating. Stilwell sought to combat this trend by publishing an appeal for "honest business methods and legislative sanity."

Confidence or National Suicide? was Stilwell's first venture into book-length publication, and it proved to be one of his more successful efforts.[1] Stilwell wrote the book as a frank defense of the railroads against the growing demand for stronger public regulation. The author claimed that friends had urged that he publish the book because of the impending crisis among American railroads. He admitted that as a railway president he was prejudiced, but he argued that all sides of the question should be heard. He bluntly defended his own activities:

Is there a more important calling than that of a railroad constructor? Is there any achievement more helpful to the Nation than the building of a railroad; opening up a virgin territory; developing a new country; making farm lands advance in value from five to thirty dollars an acre; forcing new towns to spring up, where happy, healthy school children greet us; witnessing the division into farms of great territories heretofore devoted to ranching? No occupation could be more gratifying than this. . . .[2]

The satisfaction included not only the acquisition of individual wealth on the part of the builder, officials, and investors, but also bringing strength and prosperity to the nation.

Yet, according to Stilwell, the plight of these contributors to the

1. Arthur E. Stilwell, *Confidence or National Suicide?* (New York: Bankers Publishing Company, 1910).
2. *Ibid.,* v-vi.

national economy was desperate. State regulatory agencies were establishing such low rates that operations were unprofitable. Attacks on the management of railways must stop, he wrote, and questioning the valuation of rail properties was detrimental to selling securities to expand and improve the companies. When the railroads asked for an increase in rates, the Interstate Commerce Commission had refused the request, but the companies were being forced to increase wages and to pay higher prices for equipment and maintenance. Shippers wanted lower rates, the public wanted better service, and labor desired higher wages, but who expressed concern for the investor's equity?[3] The turbulence in the economy and the loss of confidence frightened European investors who would no longer place their capital in the United States. Having just failed to raise funds for the KCMO in London and Paris, Stilwell knew from personal experience the impact of this loss of confidence.

But, he also believed that part of the loss of confidence resulted from dishonesty in business and "bear raiders" in the stock market. The "needless" panic of 1907, indicated the financial power of these bears, he maintained, and the raiders were driving away necessary investments.[4] Legislation could help restore confidence by limiting the activities of the bears. There were many honest business leaders, and what the country needed, wrote Stilwell, was a man such as Marshall Field or Andrew Carnegie in the White House.[5] He praised James J. Hill, builder of the Great Northern Railway, Carnegie, and Henry Flagler, developer of Florida's east coast, as examples of noteworthy builders of the national economy. In another passage, however, he also excoriated those who would accumulate wealth for its own sake.[6] At a time when many seriously questioned the cult of the self-made man and the gospel of wealth, Stilwell remained a staunch defender of the myth, although admitting some interlopers were harming the system.

Stilwell attempted to justify business practices which the "progressives" abhored, particularly watered stock. Sure, wrote Stilwell, rail-

---

3. *Ibid.*, vii–viii. For a general survey of the larger ramifications of this question, see K. Austin Kerr, *American Railroad Politics, 1914–1920: Rates, Wages, and Efficiency* (Pittsburgh: University of Pittsburgh Press, 1968).

4. Stilwell, *Confidence or National Suicide?*, 3–6.

5. *Ibid.*, 33.

6. *Ibid.*, 45–52, 63, and 113.

roads and other corporations issued stock in excess of the worth of the business, but "who wants to build railroads for the fun of the thing?"[7] "Do not capitalists who have had the nerve to bring such increased prosperity to [a] territory deserve credit, reward and profit?"[8] Without watered stock most railways could not be built, and the surrounding region would not be developed. "In the United States, however, the promoters and the builders are hounded," for the public refused to admit that "men who take financial risks are entitled to profit!"[9] In this blatantly frank defense of his own operations he made the case for questionable business practices, not for personal service, but in the name of national prosperity and development. It was natural he should take such a position, even though reformers such as Louis Brandeis, Robert La Follette, and "Pitchfork" Ben Tillman would find it repugnant.

To halt unfair business practices, discriminatory railroad rates, and manipulation of the stock market, Stilwell decried the use of state and federal regulatory agencies. He preferred a corporation court where gross offenders such as Standard Oil and the American Tobacco trust could be dealt with; trusts were evil, he agreed, and should be destroyed. The Interstate Commerce Commission should set railroad rates but make them long-term rates, say for fifteen years, to give investors confidence in railway securities.[10] Confidence in businessmen would attract European investors again and thus restore a favorable balance of trade. The English were prospering because of their high standards of integrity in business and their imperialistic trading system, he claimed. Writing at the very moment that the Mexican revolution was reaching the eruptive stage, he praised President Diaz whom he thought had brought stability and order south of the Rio Grande, for "nowhere is foreign money more secure."[11] His defense of certain railway financial practices proved to have more validity than his analysis of the internal affairs of Mexico.

Confidence or National Suicide? met with a variety of responses among reviewers. The New York *Times* referred to the book as a "spirited and earnest plea for fair treatment of railroads by the law-making and law-

7. *Ibid.*, 37.
8. *Ibid.*, 39.
9. *Ibid.*, 42.
10. *Ibid.*, 85, 88–89, 97–99, 103–104.
11. *Ibid.*, 16–17, 21–25, 29.

administering powers of the country," but offered no criticism of the "slim volume." *The American Review of Reviews* noted that "it is a veritable calcium that streams from the pages of Mr. Arthur Stilwell's eloquent appeal for a different sort of 'Wall Street,' " and concluded, "The book is an unusual human document of our weightiest financial problem." *Engineering News,* in a hostile review, contended that Stilwell developed a "splendid" argument for the advocates of the single tax and those who favored nationalization of the railways; his was an "extremist" voice, the review concluded. The book found favorable notice in newspapers such as the *Wall Street Journal* and the Boston *Herald,* less enthusiasm in the daily press edited by "progressive" editors. Portions of the volume were reprinted in several books, and some authors, such as Charles Gerstenberg, used it to illustrate the problems of the financial community.[12]

The following year Stilwell explained that he had written *Confidence or National Suicide?* to expose the money trust, but it appears also to have been the plea of a promoter who had failed to secure funds to complete his project and was seeking to place the blame. The plea fell on receptive ears, for the national temper regarded with disdain the unscrupulous manipulations of securities, even though Stilwell's solution of the railway problem ran against the grain of conventional confidence in governmental regulation. Selling for only $1.50, the book was in its seventh edition by 1912. There is some evidence it was a subsidized publication, for Elmer Youngman, editor of *Banker's Magazine* and publisher of the book, was Stilwell's close friend.[13] The success of his first literary venture caused Stilwell to release other attacks on "Wall Street."

In August of 1910 Stilwell returned from England, and in *Moody's Magazine* deplored the fact that Europeans were afraid to invest in the United States. Investigations of American business by federal and state agencies frightened Europeans and made them wary of our securities;

12. New York *Times,* September 10, 1912; *The American Review of Reviews,* XLII (November 1910), 640; *Engineering News,* October 13, 1910; see excerpts from reviews on an advertisement page in Arthur E. Stilwell, *Universal Peace—War Is Mesmerism* (New York: Bankers Publishing Company, 1911); Charles W. Gerstenberg, *Materials of Corporation Finance* (New York: Prentice-Hall, Inc., 1915), 416–417.

13. Arthur E. Stilwell, *Cannibals of Finance* (Chicago: Farnum Publishing Company, 1912), 141; Timothy W. Warren, editor, Banker's Publishing Company, to the author, January 5, 1970.

besides, it was all "politics" he said. A pamphlet calling railway expenditures "America's greatest Christmas tree," also appeared that month, followed by a fierce attack on property valuation as a gauge for fixing railroad rates. Newspapers and magazines carried his story to their readers as he defended "honest" railway men and called for fair rates as a means to maintain prosperity.[14]

These publications were a prelude to a frontal assault on the financial community. Since 1900 Stilwell had openly excoriated certain business leaders and practices, and the impending loss of the "Orient" simply led to a more extensive delineation of what he considered to be malpractices. Not alone in his condemnation, Stilwell's publications were part of a literary genré attacking the speculators, stock manipulators, and bears of finance. Thomas W. Lawson's *Frenzied Finance,* published in 1904, was an exposé of the machinations of "Wall Street" by a former insider, and is typical of such publications. Neo-Populists in the Congress found Stilwell's revelations useful in their diatribes against the "money trust." Representative Robert L. Henry of Texas, conducting an investigation of federal monetary policy, introduced several letters from Stilwell into the *Congressional Record* midst Henry's own assault on Standard Oil, J. P. Morgan, and others. In the same month the "Orient" went into receivership, Stilwell addressed more than 1,000 people at Carnegie Hall, claiming that eastern capitalists had destroyed his enterprises just as they had seized the properties developed by inventor George Westinghouse and railroad builder David Moffat.[15]

Angry at the loss of his second "hunch" through the receiver's court, Stilwell sat down at his desk and in six days completed the manuscript of his most successful book, *Cannibals of Finance.* This rambling discourse lambasted the "money trust," which he linked by analogy to the Czar of

14. Arthur E. Stilwell, "Europeans Afraid of our Markets," *Moody's Magazine* (August 1910), 87–88; A. E. Stilwell, *Think It Over*, three-page pamphlet, August 1910 (Bureau of Railway Economics Library, Association of American Railroads, Washington, D. C.); "Mr. Stilwell on the Expediency of Valuation," *Railway and Engineering Review*, November 12, 1910; "Railroads and the Nation," *Detroit Free Press*, reprinted in *The Square Deal*, VII (January 1911), 561–562.

15. The Kansas City *Journal*, February 11, 1900; Peter de'A. Jones, *The Robber Barons Revisited* (Boston: D. C. Heath and Company, 1968), 102; *Congressional Record* (62nd Congress, 2nd Session), XLVIII, Part 3, 2382–2386; Kansas City *Post*, March 9, 1912.

Russia with stockholders playing the role of serfs. Claiming he had been "blacklisted" by the financiers, Stilwell contended they opposed him because he tried to use regional capital rather than "Wall Street" and because of the geographical strength of his projects; further, he was used as an example to others who might seek financial independence. Laboriously he related the struggles to finance the "Orient," enumerating nefarious schemes and devices used to undermine the confidence of his stockholders. Spies followed him, supporters were threatened with financial reprisals, President Diaz received anonymous stories about him, and the Standard Oil "crowd" declared that he was to be ruined.[16] He did not oppose concentrated wealth:

My fight is not against wealth, against banks or great business combinations. These are a part of the development of the day; but when wealth strangles competition, ruins men and enterprises, it is time to call a halt. We do not need to count the cost, for in crushing evil nothing is lost, but all is gained.[17]

The book contained an elaborate analysis of the Kansas City, Mexico and Orient Railway and can be viewed as a defense of the scheme and a rationalization for its collapse. Stilwell never accepted any responsibility for the failures of his schemes, and this was no exception; the idea was sound, the financing above board, and the road was potentially a great money maker. It collapsed because of crop failures in the southwest, the insurrection in Mexico, and his inability to sell bond issues in Europe because of the "money trust." Topolobampo would become a great port he prophesied, and the Fuerte Valley was as rich as the Nile. The legends of Mexican mineral wealth and trade with the Orient were repeated, echoing previously published promotional literature. Even the reorganization committee of the United States and Mexican Trust was not his choice, he related, and he withdrew from the firm.[18] Reaching out in several directions he sought to explain away his own entrepreneurial errors as the result of natural calamities, revolutionary damage, and the monetary conspiracy.

Then he made a complete about-face in his political views. He endorsed Woodrow Wilson for president and praised his former adversary

16. Stilwell, *Cannibals of Finance*, 37, 42–43, 130–135.
17. *Ibid.*, 144.
18. *Ibid.*, 126–129, 165–168.

William Jennings Bryan for having the courage to attack business mal-practices at the Democratic National Convention. He expressed hope that the Democratic party would be victorious and enact federal legisla-tion regulating the "money trust." He had been asked by some Republicans to run as William Howard Taft's vice-presidential candidate, Stilwell re-vealed, but the party would not agree to include a plank in the platform calling for an investigation of Wall Street. He trusted Governor Wilson who seemed more aware of the threat to honest businessmen the bears represented. Ironically, Stilwell had stood shoulder-to-shoulder with the leaders of Wall Street in 1896 when they donated vast sums for William McKinley, the protective tariff, and the gold standard. Now, after two reversals of fortune, Stilwell picked up the banner of Bryan, Wilson, and federal regulation.[19]

Was he discouraged or disheartened? Did defeat lead to bitterness? Stilwell still displayed some of his ever-present optimism, if in a bitter-sweet form:

Out West were two men [Stilwell and Edward Dickinson] striving to help their nation, men who did not know the first act in the game of corruption. In that golden West was a great empire needing development. There were thousands of chances for the young men of the West to go into this new territory. There cities would spring up; all would be benefited by this work that gave to all and took from no one.[20]

But he had been thwarted by the *Cannibals of Finance,* and he intended to tell his story without fear.

The book sold widely, and at least seven editions were published. Although no records are extant as to the total number of copies printed or sold, the book is found frequently in libraries and used-book shops. It is a poignant personal statement by a man who discovered that everyone did not play by the same rules. Perhaps Stilwell's naïvete, his faith, and confidence in the future and his strong ambitions had misled him, but his optimism and zest for living did not falter.

In October of 1913, Stilwell fired one last shot at his oppressors, real or imaginary. He contributed a summary of his personal experiences with "Wall Street" to the Senate Banking and Currency Committee, which was considering new currency legislation. Frank A. Vanderlip, however, testi-

19. *Ibid.,* 141, 194–196.
20. *Ibid.,* 30–31.

fying for the New York banking houses, replied that "the Street" withheld funds from the promoter because the "Orient" was unsound, not because of a conspiracy.[21] Stilwell did not respond; following the elevator accident he departed for Europe. He terminated for fifteen years his condemnation of the "money trust" and returned to writing about an earlier concern; peace and international relations.

Between the appearance of *Confidence or National Suicide?* and *Cannibals of Finance*, Stilwell published another volume with Bankers Publishing Company, *Universal Peace—War Is Mesmerism*. This book urged the nations of western Europe and North America to avoid war at all costs. Stilwell denounced war on ethical and economic grounds. Dedicated to Andrew Carnegie and addressed to King George of England, Kaiser Wilhelm of Germany, and Czar Nicholas of Russia, the book pleaded for these "Christian" men to endorse international disarmament. Stilwell lauded Carnegie's bequest establishing an organization dedicated to world peace, and he asked the three rulers to create secretariats of peace in their governments. All international disputes should be resolved by arbitration, he declared, for war did not bring political victories, only economic distress. "Love is the solvent, as it is the fulfilling of the Law," he wrote.[22] Ancient nations which rose by the sword perished in the same manner, and modern nations could not afford the financial losses wars produced. Wars levied heavier taxes on the masses, and, Stilwell warned, this burden hastened countries down the road to socialism. He urged these three sovereigns to declare an official period of peace to prevent war profiteering by the international arms cartel. He refused to buy stocks in arms companies in order to reduce "investments in death or burden-producing machines."[23] He proposed that all nations agree to reduce their armies by one tenth every year for nine years, and in the tenth year donate to the Hague Tribunal the remaining tenth to finance an international peace-keeping force.

Turning his attention to imperialism in general and Latin America in particular, he contended that the Monroe Doctrine was a national fetish and stood in the way of universal peace. The Doctrine prevented British

21. New York *Times*, October 10, 1913.
22. Stilwell, *Universal Peace*, 25.
23. *Ibid.*, 68–69.

involvement in Latin America, when such entrance would have led to stronger, more stable governments. Further, there was often urgent need to intervene in Latin America: "The idea of a strong country taking charge of the government of a weak, unruly country, is not wrong if it gives it a good government."[24] The United States could do well to allow the British to enter Latin America unfettered and could do worse than emulate that country's efforts to bring stability to the world. Shifting his stance only slightly, he praised economic imperialism, United Fruit Company's role in the "Banana Republics," and called for a joint American-Mexican protectorate over all of Central America.[25] Displaying his growing Anglophilism, he praised the impact of the British throughout the world and expressed the hope that the United States could be as successful.

Stilwell did not see the contradiction between his calls for pacifism and imperialism. He did not see the relationship between the arms race and economic rivalry for colonies and overseas markets. Reviewers generally noted Stilwell's lack of comprehension of the peace movement, though most thought it encouraging that a businessman had an interest in preventing war. Several journals simply summarized the contents without comment.[26] Like most things he wrote, it expressed his faith in Christianity, his optimism in the future, and his superficial knowledge of world affairs.

Written in late 1910, *Universal Peace* demonstrates not only Stilwell's concern for world stability but also his appreciation of what war in Europe would do to the sale of securities. The book shows not only growing Anglophilism but also the impact of his English contacts. Some, like Lord Monson, had been in the British Foreign Service, and others were leading political figures and office-holders. Their international views became his, even to the point of criticizing the Monroe Doctrine. Praise of English culture and institutions, imperialism, and efficiently governed colonies also might sell additional securities in London. Mixed motivations no doubt; humanitarian, Christian, economic, and self-serving.

By 1914 Arthur and Jennie were residing in a suburb of Paris. When

24. *Ibid.*, 108.
25. *Ibid.*, 114–117, 124–125.
26. See for example, *The Independent*, LXX (April 27, 1911), 902; *The Literary Digest*, XLII (March 18, 1911), 530; *The American Review of Reviews*, XLIII (April 1911), 510; and the New York *Times*, March 12, 1911.

World War I broke out Arthur sided immediately with the English and the French, blaming the Germans entirely for the conflagration. He took up his pen and castigated the Kaiser with direct, if pretentious, poetry:

God, Allah And Me

I'll build for myself a tower of fame
With the lives of a million or two
And leave more wrecks on the shores of time
Than Napolean or Caesar could do.

On the battle field my Kultur I'll stamp
With the blood of the young and the bold
And march again to the heart of France
As my grandsire did of old.

I'll call on God to bless my cause
Curse all who oppose my aim
To my royal will the world will bow
As I lead to the road to fame.

The compassionate Turk if led by me
Will unite the Mohammedan fold
And Egypt again by the crescent be ruled
As it was in the days of old.

I'll march my men to the Dover Straits
And control the English sea
And the only rulers this world will have
Will be God and Allah and me.[27]

The same journal carried "After-Math," another poem by Stilwell describing the destruction of the war and the faith that would keep men strong, faith in an ultimate and just peace.

The following year Stilwell published *To All the World (Except Germany),* which contained a plan for world peace.[28] This volume Stilwell dedicated to Albert, King of the Belgians, for his heroic stand against the Germans, and to Henry Ford for his effort to "uplift mankind." The Germans were solely at fault for leading the world into this horrible war, he wrote, and this "disease or mesmerism" had to be stopped by Christian ideals and the hope for peace. An international peace-keeping organiza-

27. *The English Herald* (Montreux), November 21, 1914.
28. Arthur E. Stilwell, *To All the World (Except Germany),* (London: George Allen & Unwin, Ltd., 1915).

tion and a tribunal to hear disputes between nations was the only hope for future tranquility. If wars could not be abolished, Stilwell asked, could they not be limited? To help maintain peace, freedom of the seas should be guaranteed and there should be a Jewish kingdom in Palestine. His program, combining Wilsonian foreign policy and traditional English views, rested on the concept of international co-operation. Like Woodrow Wilson, he advocated redrawing the map of Europe, not seeing that this, in and of itself, could lead to future hostility. Enumerating in the most crude kind of illustrations the losses of the war, Stilwell pleaded for support for the Carnegie Endowment for International Peace and the Hague Tribunal. He suggested the United States establish a twenty-year protectorate over Mexico and Central America if the people of those nations approved. Although peace was a dream and visionary, he concluded it was possible.

The volume received mixed reviews, with most praise coming from pacifist and peace organizations. His scheme for compulsory negotiation was not well received by the New York *Times*, which dismissed him as "an idealist."[29] The publishers, George Allen and Unwin, Limited, printed 1,500 copies of the book, and some royalties were paid as late as 1918.[30] *To All the World* did not contain any new peace formula, although in detail it differed from other proposals. The concept demonstrates Stilwell's continuing faith in his fellow man and his hope for the future.

An article Stilwell had published in December of 1915 expanded upon this proposal but exhibited some fear for the future course of mankind. Stilwell urged that the first step toward disarmament be made on Christmas Day, 1916, by sinking all the warships in all navies. Peace would follow, he contended, if an international fund could be created to pay for all the physical damages of the war. Then, on a highly pessimistic note, he said that wars had to be terminated for, "Future wars will probably not be fought with guns or warships, but by some refined method of distributing disease germs."[31] This awesome prediction has not come true,

29. New York *Times*, July 25, 1915.
30. Payne Unwin to the author, January 12, 1970. The exact financial arrangements are unknown as George Allen & Unwin, like most British publishing houses, lost most of their records in the Blitz.
31. Arthur Edward Stilwell, "A Practical Plan for a Warless World," *The Resur-*

but the world has not yet been able to develop either peace-making machinery or restrictions on germ warfare. In a few instances, Stilwell's publications would show some insight into problems neither generally recognized in his own era nor solved in ours.

During the next two years virtually nothing is known about the Stilwells, where they lived or what he was doing. They resided in France or England, and he apparently continued to write, for in 1918 he had published two books on financing the debts created by the war. *The Great Plan: How To Pay for the War* was published in England and went into at least ten editions. It was also published in translation in Paris and Stockholm.[32] This book contained much material from *Universal Peace* and *To All the World*, and the second book published in 1918, *How To Reduce Your Income Tax by Liberty Currency,* was a brief explanation of the ideas in *The Great Plan.*[33]

The books proposed, in essence, that the war debts be paid by inflation, by issuing international bonds to replace gold and silver as the basis for foreign trade. It would be impossible for most nations to pay their war debts, he contended, and relations between debtor and creditor would undoubtedly deteriorate. An international monetary fund controlled by a world congress would issue these bonds, and a sinking fund to pay for the securities would come from the money each nation saved through arms limitations. Money previously used for war expenditures and defense costs would be used for peace. Stilwell tied his hope for peace to a device that would enable the world to pay for the cost of the Great War through a form of currency inflation. It is interesting to note how Stilwell's point of view had shifted since his involvement in the McKinley campaign of 1896 and his defense of the gold standard. But he did not fear this charge:

---

rection, Number 2 (December 1915), 1. This publication was a device to raise funds for war orphans and was published by The League of Hope. The patrons of the League included distinguished Americans and Europeans including Senora Porfirio Diaz.

32. Arthur E. Stilwell, *The Great Plan: How To Pay for the War* (London: Hodder & Stoughton, Publishers, 1918); and *Le Grand Plan: La Viaie Societe des Nations* (Paris: Troduit de l'Americain, 1919).

33. Arthur E. Stilwell, *How To Reduce Your Income Tax by Liberty Currency* (London: Hodder & Stoughton, Publishers, 1918).

Call Liberty Currency inflation if you will; but what are the appalling war debts but inflation?—and inflation so great that conscription of capital is considered by a great many thinking people to be the only remedy.[34]

The London *Times* reviewer of *The Great Plan* simply noted the scheme without comment, but the New York *Times* greeted the idea with condescension and sarcasm. Labeling "Liberty Currency" fiat money, the *Times* stated that most solvent nations would reject the whole concept; the article failed to note the long list of less-than-solvent nations in Europe. The inflation produced by Stilwell's plan would be ruinous the article concluded. It is questionable whether "Liberty Currency" would have been worse than the inflation that came after 1918 in Germany, England, and even the United States, but the scheme was doomed more because of its involvement with arms reduction than because of its inflationary aspect.[35]

Again there was a two-year hiatus before Stilwell re-emerged to public notice, this time as a novelist. In 1921, he published *The Light That Never Failed: A Tale of Australia, America and England.*[36] The novel concerned one Harry Waterall, a young Australian who, determined to become rich and famous, left his home to seek his fortune in the United States and England. He leaves a girl who loves him and all that has had significance in his life pursuing fame and adventure. He makes a fortune, loses it, and returns to rural Australia where he finds a light in the window of his true love's home. Throughout the book a mysterious "light" guides the destinies of the characters. With a typical Victorian conclusion, the hero marries the heroine, and a torrential rain erodes the land around her home, revealing an enormous deposit of gold. It may be that Stilwell had read Rudyard Kipling's *The Light That Failed* wherein the adventurer goes blind, is filled with self-pity, and the "light" fails, or perhaps he simply desired to parade before readers once more the shopworn theme of home and hearth.[37] Although some reviewers endorsed the book with faint

34. *Ibid.,* 17.
35. *The Times Literary Supplement,* June 27, 1918; New York *Times,* June 29, 1918.
36. Arthur E. Stilwell, *The Light That Never Failed: A Tale of Australia, America and England* (London: Jarrolds, Ltd., 1920).
37. Rudyard Kipling, *The Light That Failed* (London: Standard Book Company, 1930).

praise, the London *Times* panned the novel saying, "there is little strength or art in this tale."[38] Nothing is known of the sales of this novel, but the publicity generated by its "Foreword" and Stilwell's subsequent revelations may have increased purchases.[39] The foreword declared,

All of Mr. Stilwell's books are dictated to him by those in the spirit world. They come to him in his dreams, as they did in the case of Robert Louis Stevenson. The remarkable part of Mr. Stilwell's vision is that, not alone books come this way, but plans for great industrial development.

By these visions and plans from the spirit world, he has built 2500 miles of railroad in the United States and Mexico—more miles of railroad than any living man. He was told in this way of the Great War in 1910, and published a book entitled "Universal Peace—War is Mesmerism."

For years he called these messengers his Brownies, not aware until 1920 that Robert Louis Stevenson used the same title for his "Spirit Counsellors."[40]

This startling revelation that not only his books, but also his railroads and the location of Port Arthur were products of "Brownies" or "Spirits" was enlarged upon in a second volume published in 1921, *Live and Grow Young.*[41] (Stilwell was then residing in New York and had become his own publisher.) *Live and Grow Young* revealed that Stilwell's "Brownies" had told him in 1910 that the "Great War" would "deplete" the world, so he appealed for *Universal Peace.* Further, the "Brownies" had presented him with twenty novels, books, songs, poems and photoplays. The books were dictated a chapter a night until completion. He heard voices while asleep, and when he awoke the memory was so vivid that he could reproduce the stories verbatim. How did he explain these phenomena?

There is no doubt in my mind that these messages come from the spirit world, and that this circle of spirits that communicates with me by this rare method is comprised of engineers, poets and authors. . . . This book is no brief for spiritualism. . . . "Is the Author a spiritualist?" In the common acceptance of the term he is not a spiritualist and he has read very little on the subject. . . . He is a spiritual-list. He lists for spiritual messages.[42]

38. *The Times Literary Supplement*, March 10, 1921.
39. Gerald Austin, director, Jarrold's Ltd., to the author, January 13, 1970.
40. Stilwell, *The Light That Never Failed*, "Preface." n.p.
41. Arthur E. Stilwell, *Live and Grow Young* (New York: Youth Publishing Company, 1921); The address of Youth Publishing Company, 576 Fifth Avenue, was also the address of Stilwell's office.
42. *Ibid.*, 4–5.

He simply tried to follow the Bible, which implored, "Test the Spirits," therefore he accepted what they told him. He cited the experiences of Stevenson and Sir Arthur Conan Doyle as evidence that other authors received their stories via "spirits."

Spiritualism was a power in the world, and men should use that power, he contended. Death was but the passing on to a new plane of consciousness, and men achieved an immortality they did not comprehend. He opposed the gloom of Calvinistic Christianity and urged men to be free to express themselves and their ideas; what men needed was not fear of death but zest for life. In a passage which sounds like Norman Vincent Peale's "power of positive thinking," Stilwell urged his reader to "stand before the window each morning and for five minutes think of the sun kissing and gladdening the earth," and "say a dozen times—I am strength, I am power."[43] Acceptance of the spirits and living every moment to the fullest would let men live and grow young, not old.

Stilwell's revelations are a strange mixture of spiritualism and Christian theology. While living in Chicago in the 1880s he had been ill and, through the efforts of a Christian Science practitioner, was cured and became an active member of that faith. Throughout his years in Kansas City he belonged to the First Church of Christ, Scientist, and helped to build its edifice.[44] He remained a Christian Scientist, and yet he would later say, "no creeds bind me."[45] Certainly Mary Baker Eddy, founder of Christian Science, opposed popular spiritualism, and mystical experiences were not characteristic of the religion. On the other hand, Christian Science did urge the mobilization of the "infinite light" of the "divine mind" to combat errors of health and morality. The church taught that since Spirit was the sole reality, all human institutions were relative and temporal, powerless of themselves.[46] The curious mixture of idealism and mysticism of Christian Science appears in Stilwell's writings including *The Light That Never Failed* and *Live and Grow Young*. Undoubtedly

---

43. *Ibid.*, 29–30.

44. The Kansas City *Journal*, February 11, 1900; Kansas City *Post*, July 7, 1915.

45. Arthur E. Stilwell and James R. Crowell, "I Had a Hunch," *The Saturday Evening Post*, CC (December 17, 1927), 102.

46. Robert Peel, *Christian Science: Its Encounter with American Culture* (Garden City: Doubleday & Company, 1965), 66, 159; Stow Persons, *American Minds: A History Of Ideas* (New York: Henry Holt and Company, 1958), 427–429.

his religious beliefs were highly influential in shaping his books, and apparently his "Brownies."

During his sojourn in England, he may also have come in contact with the writings of Robert Louis Stevenson and Sir Arthur Conan Doyle and perhaps even met Doyle. Stevenson claimed that *The Strange Case of Doctor Jekyll and Mr. Hyde* came to him in a dream, as did "Olalla," published in *Court and Society Review.* In sleep, part of the mind continued to function, wrote Stevenson, and, aided by "little people" or "sleepless Brownies," he dreamed tales and stories in sequence.[47] The similarity with Stilwell's revelations are so close as to suggest that perhaps Stilwell "borrowed" from Stevenson's "Brownies." Several reports indicate that Sir Arthur Conan Doyle also had spiritualistic experiences and became acquainted with Stilwell through the latter's books. Doyle reviewed *The Great Plan* for the London *Evening Telegram,* and he later declared that Stilwell had enjoyed the greatest psychic experiences of any man alive at that time. When Sir Arthur lectured in New York City in 1924, he introduced Stilwell from the stage at Carnegie Hall, and the former railroad builder spoke of his experiences.[48] Certainly Sir Arthur's praise encouraged Stilwell to further revelations of his knowledge of the "Spirits," as did the enormous publicity he received from the daily press.

Not since he began the Kansas City, Mexico and Orient Railway had Stilwell been so widely quoted in newspapers. Out of the country for several years, removed from the business world he loved so much, Stilwell seized this new opportunity for fame, and he used it for every ounce of value. At an exhibit of "spirit pictures" in New York City in 1922, he spoke of his "Brownies," whom he had kept secret all of his life, fearing that people would think him a "nut." "Today," he said, "I am telling everything." His "corps of spirits" never misled him or gave him false information. While he resided in England the "Brownies" had dictated twenty novels, of which only *The Light That Never Failed* had been published. "I never read fiction," he declared, "I take no interest in it." He

47. Graham Balfour, *The Life of Robert Louis Stevenson* (New York: Charles Scribner's Sons, 1901), II, 15, 18; Robert Louis Stevenson, "A Chapter On Dreams," in *Across the Plains with Other Memories and Essays* (London: T. Nelson & Sons, Ltd., 1892), 217–223.
48. The Kansas City *Star,* September 26 and October 12, 1920; New York *World,* April 6, 1924.

used literary secretaries who took down the stories as he quoted from his dreams of the previous night. He announced several new publications and also that the "spirits" were dictating poetry too.[49]

By 1924 numerous accounts of his spiritual encounters were published, usually with a portion of one of Stilwell's literary efforts. One poem will illustrate the quality of the works of the Brownies.

Slumberland
Do you wish to know where the Brownies stay.
Who romp all night and in moonlight play.
A merry happy little band?
They live on the shores of Slumberland.
They live on the shores of Slumberland.[50]

The Brownies were as lacking in talent when writing poems as when writing novels. Nevertheless, Stilwell announced a series of photoplays to be published by the Brownie Comedies, Inc., and another new book, *The Empire of the Soul*. Unfortunately, no copies of these are extant in either published or manuscript form.[51]

Reporters flocked to his luxurious apartment at 305 West End Avenue, and he described for each his various psychic adventures. The number of brownies in the corps often varied as did their total literary output, but he assured each interviewer that the experiences were genuine. He did not understand it himself; he simply accepted the facts. Although he suffered a five-month illness in 1924, he planned to move ahead with his publishing efforts. Sometimes a reporter would be received at Stilwell's office in the "lofty eyrie" of a New York skyscraper. Pictures taken at these interviews show that his physical appearance had changed little in twenty years; his hair was gray, he wore rimless glasses, he was heavier, but his eyes remained keen, and his demeanor and dress were distinguished.[52] The news articles reported his comments only slightly tongue-

49. New York *Times*, June 15, 1922.
50. New York *World*, April 6, 1924.
51. Stilwell, *Live and Grow Young*, advertisement for "The Brownie Comedies"; The only citation to *The Empire of the Soul* appears in the 1922–1923 edition of *Who's Who*.
52. New York *World*, April 6, 1924; New York *Times*, April 20, 1924; Kansas City *Journal-Post*, November 16, 1924; Advertisement for *Live and Grow Young*, H. P. Wright Scrapbooks (University of Missouri–Kansas City Library, Kansas City, Missouri).

in-cheek, but one wonders why reporters did not ask Stilwell why the Brownies failed to warn him of the loss of his two railroads, of the coming of revolution in Mexico, of the hurricane at Port Arthur, or of other disappointing events in his life.

These disappointments in his career were enumerated in a memoir published in 1926 or 1927. Marked on the cover, "For Private Circulation Only," *Forty Years of Business Life* told of Stilwell's dreams, ambitions, frustrations, and eternal optimism.[53] In the memoir Stilwell repeated earlier accounts of his "heroic" efforts to build his railways, of the duplicity which led to their going into receivership, and of his epic vision for the economic development of the south central states. His companies were always profitable, investors never took losses, and only the opposition of "Wall Street" prevented his enterprises from achieving absolute success. Because of derogatory reports about his business life, he decided to publish his memoirs, in which he also praised capitalism, most business leaders, and "free enterprise." He pleaded guilty to being a "visionary" and an "optimist" and felt confident that he would eventually be honored for his contributions to the economic development of the region. It is interesting to note that virtually no mention is made of Brownies or spirits in this volume, only hard-headed business tactics.

Stilwell achieved his greatest national attention between December 3, 1927, and February 4, 1928, when *The Saturday Evening Post* published his autobiography, "I Had a Hunch," in six lengthy installments. Aided by James R. Crowell, Stilwell told the story of his life in a rapid, shotgun style, with illustrations by Raeburn Van Buren to depict high points in the promoter's career. Like all memoirs or autobiographies, this one must be used with caution, as Stilwell failed to remember much that was unpleasant and his "facts" were sometimes in error. It was, however, a remarkably well-told tale, with a good sense of the dramatic, and offering some insight into his childhood and adolescence. He constantly cited his faith in himself and God as his two sources of strength, and the entire memoir is filled with the cult of the self-made man and the rags-to-riches theme. In this version of his life story the Brownies became hunches, the

53. Arthur E. Stilwell, *Forty Years of Business Life* (New York: n.p. 1926 [?]); The volume in the Gates Memorial Library is marked on the cover "For Private Circulation Only," as were other copies according to the Houston *Post*, April 16, 1943.

mystical aspect undoubtedly toned down by Crowell. Considering the price being paid by the *Post* for material, the series was probably quite lucrative for Stilwell.

Only a few months after the publication of "I Had a Hunch," and a year before the financial world collapsed in panic, Stilwell died. On September 26, 1928, after an illness of sixteen days, he succumbed to pulmonary edema, cerebral embolism, and respiratory failure, at his home on West End Avenue. Survived only by Jennie, he left instructions that there would be no funeral, and the body was cremated at the Fresh Pond Crematory. Ironically, obituaries throughout the country emphasized not his economic contributions, but his psychic experiences. The *Democrat and Chronicle* of Rochester did say that he was "probably . . . the greatest figure Rochester has ever produced."[54]

Just thirteen days after Arthur's death, the body of Jennie Stilwell was found on the roof of a structure next to their apartment building; she had leaped to her death. A note to her sister-in-law said simply, "I must go to Arthur." After forty-nine years together, she was unable to accept separation. She had tried to communicate with him through spirits, but failing in this attempt, she became despondent and committed suicide, believing that they would be united in the "spirit world." Her body, too, was cremated, but in both cases the remains have disappeared. A lengthy search by officials of Port Arthur, Texas, has failed to locate the ashes of the founder of the city. Although newspapers at the time of Jennie's death said that her sister-in-law would dispose of the Stilwells' property, no will has been found, so the size of the estate is unknown.[55] Some reports said that Stilwell died leaving only $1,000, but journalists in 1924 reported that he was a millionaire. The extent of his estate remains another of the unanswered questions about Stilwell.

Arthur Stilwell's contributions to the economy and urbanization of the south central states were significant. He committed errors of judgment, to be sure, but he brought to the area millions of dollars in capital improvements, created new towns, and linked them together with almost 2,300

54. Kansas City *Journal*, September 27, 1928; New York *Times*, September 27, 1928; Copy of Stilwell's death certificate, Arthur Stilwell Collection (Port of Port Arthur, Port Arthur, Texas); *Democrat and Chronicle* (Rochester), September 28, 1928.

55. The Kansas City *Star*, October 9, 1928; New York *Times*, October 10, 1928.

miles of railway. Fired by ambition and dreams of empire, he acknowledged that "my whole business life was molded from an inspiration of youth."[56] The memory of his grandfather always provided Stilwell with a desire to build permanent monuments to himself and to glorify the family name. That his "monuments" were sometimes built on sand is true, and the Kansas City, Mexico and Orient Railway is the best example of Stilwell's dreams at their worst. A man able to sell securities in the most speculative of ventures, he possessed a talent not unlike that of other western promoters, but as a manager, his talents were severely limited. Gifted with an appealing personality, he made his way into the business community of Kansas City and the financial offices of Philadelphia, New York, Boston, and Amsterdam. Confident, energetic, magnetic, and highly verbal, he believed himself to be an empire builder and a humanitarian, and to a degree he was. In his war on the "Cannibals of Finance" he predates the efforts of a mid-century railroad man, Robert R. Young, who also tried to save capitalism from the capitalists. Neither a James J. Hill nor a John W. Gates, Arthur Stilwell was neither a financier nor a Wall Street plunger. He was, as he said, "a promoter with a hunch."

56. Stilwell, "I Had a Hunch," December 3, 1927, 3–4.

A NOTE ON SOURCES

The traditional formal bibliography has been dispensed with because of the limited usefulness of many of the sources cited in the footnotes. A bibliography would prove to be of considerable length without noting the relative value of the items. Therefore, this note will mention only those sources which proved to be more extensive or which were deemed of particular value.

There is extant, as far as the author could ascertain, no substantial body of Stilwell papers. Such materials apparently existed in the late 1940s or early 1950s in an office building in Kansas City but were inadvertently burned by a janitor. No trace could be found of the effects of Arthur and Jennie Stilwell, so that those letters and private documents that exist are in the public collections of others or in the archives of the companies he formed or their successors. In the absence of personal papers, one is forced to turn to Stilwell's publications. The two memoirs, the "I Had a Hunch" series in *The Saturday Evening Post* and *Forty Years of Business Life,* reveal Stilwell's view of events but must be used with caution for factual information. His memory for the general was usually quite good, but errors in the particular abound. The memoirs are important for what they contain as well as for that which they omit. The absence of any mention of brothers and sisters is interesting, as is the almost completely negative picture of his father. Other publications such as *Universal Peace—War Is Mesmerism* or *To All The World (Except Germany)* are helpful but fail to reveal much about Stilwell. On the other hand, *Cannibals of Finance* and *Confidence or National Suicide?* are more significant in terms of Stilwell's views of himself, certain business practices, and governmental regulation of industry. Several of his publications have been lost completely, including the "Brownie Comedies" and *The Empire of the Soul*. Despite these limitations, the use of Stilwell's writings and the few extant manuscripts provides some insight into the man and his evaluation of his life's work.

Somewhat balancing the absence of personal manuscripts is the extensive coverage of Stilwell and his activities in newspapers. Stilwell always proved to be good copy, and press reports abounded with articles about his projects and with interviews which he delighted in granting. These too must be used very cautiously, not only because of Stilwell's tendencies to exaggregation and hyperbole, but also because many journalists failed to exercise restraint in writing their stories. To gain an over-all view of the man and his environment, the Kansas City *Star* was read daily from 1886 until 1901, and other Kansas City papers were read for particular stories or during crucial developments. The Port Arthur *News* and Port Arthur *Herald* from 1897 to 1910 were read, augmented by clipping files at the Gates Memorial Library in Port Arthur, and the large scrapbooks of clippings compiled by Mrs. James T. Carr of that city. The early years of the Stilwell family were revealed in the various newspapers of Rochester, and of great aid was the detailed index prepared by the National Youth Administration. Clipping files in the Missouri Valley Room of the Kansas City Public Library were also helpful.

Archival material of Stilwell's corporations proved accessible and highly beneficial. The offices of the Kansas City Southern Railway Company in Kansas City contain many records of the early Stilwell railway companies, and the officers of the KCS generously made these archives available. Minute books of the railroads, construction companies, and their subsidiaries were used, but large gaps exist in terms of stockholder lists and information about internal transactions. The Burlington Northern offices in Chicago have the basic records of three of the lines Stilwell controlled north of Kansas City, and the remainder of these records are in the Chicago, Burlington and Quincy archives at the Newberry Library in Chicago. Additional business materials are to be found in the Corporate Records Division of the Baker Library, Harvard Graduate School of Business Administration, and the Bureau of Railway Economics Library, Association of American Railroads, in Washington.

Manuscript materials of both a corporate and personal nature are widely scattered. The Benjamin Newton Duke Collection at Duke University and the Edward F. Goltra Papers at the Missouri Historical Society in Saint Louis contain business correspondence concerning the Kansas City, Mexico and Orient Railway. Correspondence relating to real estate schemes and the early days of Port Arthur is to be found in the George M. Craig Papers at the San Jacinto Museum, San Jacinto, Texas, and a lengthy memoir by Craig is located in the Historical Files of the Port Arthur Chamber of Commerce. The Missouri Valley Room of the Kansas City Public Library holds the John A. Prescott and James A. Anderson scrapbooks, and these volumes contain newspaper clippings, brochures on stock issues, maps, and other materials not available elsewhere. Dow Wynn has gathered at the offices of the Port of Port Arthur a variety of Stilwell memorabilia, most of which is in the form of copies, such as his marriage license and death certificate. Here too will be found copies of Stilwell's correspondence with George M. Pullman. These valuable letters were copied by the Pullman-Standard Company from their files which are now deposited with the Newberry Library, but which are not open to scholarly use at present. The Manuscript Division of the Baker Library has several collections of significance: the Samuel Morse Felton report on the Kansas City, Pittsburg and Gulf; the reports of Edward Dickinson on the Kansas City, Mexico and Orient; and the Dun and Bradstreet Collection which consists of detailed information on the financial status of individuals and companies gathered by Dun and Bradstreet agents. The latter collection proved very helpful for ascertaining the financial position occupied by the Stilwells in Rochester.

Financial evaluations of the Stilwell railroad projects as well as construction reports and articles on locomotives, bridges, and other facilities were found in various financial and railway journals. The annual reports by Henry V. Poor and John Moody were helpful, but journals such as *The Railroad Gazette, Railway Age* and the *Commercial and Financial Chronicle* provided much more detailed information on daily progress. Of immense value were the clippings found in the Pliny Fisk Collection at Princeton University. This archive of a leading New York brokerage house contains a massive collection of clippings from the *Wall Street Journal, Journal of Commerce,* other newspapers, and foreign publications. Two of the "puff pieces" published by the "Orient," *The New Empire* and *The Kansas City Gateway,* were helpful and are located at the Kansas City Public Library.

Public documents were of little value, with one exception. While some use was made of publications of the Interstate Commerce Commission and the Department of Commerce and Labor, House Document 549, "Ship Canal at Sabine Pass, Texas," proved to be a major source. Published in House Documents Volume 68 as Serial 3696 by the Second Session of the Fifty-fifth Congress in 1897–1898, this report contains copies of letters, engineering reports, maps, blueprints, and legal briefs on the development of the Port Arthur canal, harbor, and urban scheme.

Several secondary works were quite beneficial. Blake McKelvey's history of Rochester enabled the author to gain some insight into the community in which Stilwell achieved maturity. The first volume of A. T. Brown's history of Kansas City and the manuscript of the second volume, which Professor Brown generously lent the author, provided a wealth of material about the booming city on the bluffs of the Missouri. Charles N. Glaab's analysis of earlier Kansas City railroad promoters and the city's ardent courtship of the "iron horse" proved helpful, but Glaab's numerous and discerning studies of the promoter genré were of even greater benefit. The analysis of Stilwell contained in David Pletcher's award-winning *Rails, Mines, and Progress* was not only helpful in its general view but also provided references to a variety of fugitive sources. John Leeds Kerr's history of the Kansas City, Mexico and Orient Railway, *Destination Topolobampo,* is aimed primarily at the railway buff and is most important on the history of the Chihuahua Pacific Railroad since 1940. The articles by W. R. Draper in *Railroad Magizine* are a mixture of secondary materials and memoirs and are valuable in the latter instance because of Draper's work as a townsite salesman on both of Stilwell's major schemes.

Historians are often indebted to the pioneering inquiries of graduate students, and in this case the master's essays of four scholars proved most helpful. Rose McMasters's history of the Kansas City Southern written while a student at the University of Missouri provided suggestions on the location of sources, as did the biography of Stilwell written by Francis Leverett at the University of Texas. John R. Rochelle's study of the port of Port Arthur, completed at Lamar State College of Technology, details the oftimes discouraging history of the port and has much to say about the process of urban growth at Port Arthur. Clarence O. Senior's scholarly and well-written history of the "Orient" to be found at the University of Missouri–Kansas City proved very helpful. The lengthy manuscript history of the Kansas City Southern by H. F. Haag is a compilation from company records and may be found at the KCS office.

No attempt has been made to indicate all of the sources, which would duplicate the footnotes, but only to suggest the more significant materials used. The conceptualization of Stilwell's career, for example, draws from several published accounts, particularly John E. Sawyer's "Entrepreneurial Error And Economic Growth," published in *Explorations in Entrepreneurial History*. Studies by Thomas C. Cochran, Fritz L. Redlich, Arthur H. Cole, Arthur M. Johnson, Barry E. Supple, Richard C. Overton, and Edward C. Kirkland were also used to place Arthur Stilwell's career in a broader spectrum of business careers and experiences.

INDEX

251